6-17-75

FISH
COOKERY
OF
NORTH
AMERICA

FISH COOKERY OF NORTH AMERICA

Frances MacIlquham

Drawings by E. B. Sanders

Winchester Press

Library of Congress Catalog Card Number: 73-88880
ISBN: 0–87691–140–8

Published by Winchester Press
460 Park Avenue, New York 10022

Printed in the United States of America

For my family

". . . who is more welcome to my dish,

than was my angle to my fish" *(The Compleat Angler).*

Acknowledgments

Many people, knowledgeable in the ways of fish, by their generous assistance and encouragement, have made the writing of this book not only possible, but a gratifying experience.

Their interests in fish of North America range from its origin in the sea to its service on the table. They are the fishermen, those who derive their livings from the deeps and the sportsmen who angle for recreation; the various service and governmental agencies devoted to the conservation and management of fish and their environment; the individual scientists; the chefs of professional standing and those who cook because they love to; and my fellow outdoor writers, whose interests encompass it all.

I am particularly indebted to Dr. J. Frances (Jaydee) Allen of the U.S. Environmental Protection Agency in Crystal City, Maryland. Dr. Allen's assistance has been invaluable to me.

Others in giving of their resources have furnished data, contributed material, helped authenticate research, read manuscript, and helped in other ways. They are experts in their various and often highly specialized fields; therefore I must assume sole responsibility for any error, misinterpretation, or faulty presentation that appears in this book.

Frances Asam of Poplar Dale, Ontario
Capt. Don Ashley, Florida Game and Freshwater Fish Commission, Tallahassee, Florida
Tiny Bennett, author and outdoor editor of the Toronto *Sun,* Bolton, Ontario
Berndt and Clare Berglund, authors, National Wilderness Survival Inc., Campbellford, Ontario
A. H. Berst, research scientist, Ontario Ministry of Natural Resources, Maple, Ontario
Emil J. Bourque, commercial fisherman, Cap Pele Bas, New Brunswick
T. B. (Burt) Collins, Booth Fisheries Canadian Co. Ltd., Winnipeg, Manitoba

David Corney, Freshwater Fish Marketing Corporation, Winnipeg, Manitoba

Dr. Ed J. Crossman, Associate Curator of Ichthyology, Royal Ontario Museum, Toronto, Ontario

Charles Daigle, Co-operative Canning Plant, Cap Lumière, New Brunswick

Dr. A. R. Emery, Associate Curator of Ichthyology, Royal Ontario Museum, Toronto, Ontario

Leon Kossar, Ontario Folk Arts Council, Toronto, Ontario

Clorice Landry, Fisheries Inspection Branch, Environment Canada, Shediac, New Brunswick

Norm Lee, sportsman and chef, The Pas, Manitoba

Carl Lees, Fisheries Service, Inspection Branch, Environment Canada, Toronto, Ontario

Gwen Leslie, Consumer Consultant, Fisheries Service, Environment Canada, Winnipeg, Manitoba

W. A. MacDonald, Dept. of Tourism, Province of New Brunswick, Moncton, New Brunswick

Hugh MacMillan, research historian, Ontario Archives, Toronto, Ontario

Ronald S. McGavin, Booth Fisheries Canadian Co. Ltd., Winnipeg, Manitoba

R. J. Mooney, Acadian Fisheries, Toronto, Ontario

Barry Penhale, outdoor writer, Scarborough, Ontario

John Power, outdoor editor of Toronto *Star,* Canadian field editor of *Field & Stream,* and author, Mississauga, Ontario

Elizabeth Purser, angler and artist, San José, California

Graydon Reipert, Toronto, Ontario

Harry Shorten, Government of Canada "Project Newstart," Richibucto, New Brunswick

Shirlee Smith, librarian, Hudson Bay House, Winnipeg, Manitoba

Harry Souci, commercial fisherman (retired), Sault Ste. Marie, Ontario

Dr. J. S. Tait, York University, Toronto, Ontario

Wilf Taylor, outdoor writer, Lewisville, New Brunswick

United Maritime Fishermen, Richibucto, New Brunswick

Joe Van Haagen, chef and sportsman, Rexdale, Ontario

W. T. (Bill) Ward, editor, *British Columbia Wildlife Review,* Victoria, British Columbia

My special thanks are expressed to McClelland and Stewart Limited, Canadian publishers of *Canadian Game Cookery* by Frances MacIlquham, for permission to draw upon pertinent material from that book.

To Abby Allan, writer and editor, for editorial assistance.

And to my staunch friends, Doreen Fawcett of Weston, outdoor writer and editor, and Jean Power of Mississauga for countless hours of critical editorial assistance and typing.

The many generous contributors of recipes are acknowledged throughout the book.

Encouragement is essential. In this respect I am indebted to the editors of the Toronto *Globe and Mail,* which over the past years has published my articles on the cookery of fish and game.

—*Frances MacIlquham*

Contents

7 *Curing Fish*   244

Introduction

An objective introduction to this book could better be written by another.

What *does* an author say in an introduction? Not what's in the book. The table of contents in the front tells it all in sequential order; the index at the back, alphabetically. How the book came into being, perhaps?

Writing this book I found to be something like rearing a child. You nurture the baby through infancy, make plans for its growth and well-being, only to find the years slipping along and the offspring growing up on its own terms.

So what started in infancy several years ago as an anglers' booklet on "how to cook the catch" simply took its own course and grew up to become *Fish Cookery of North America.*

As with the growing child, certain boundaries had to be set for practical purposes. This book confines itself to fishes and shellfishes of the temperate and cold waters of the United States and Canada.

The years that the book has been "growing" have seen changes invalidating much of the early research. Plans to include certain amphibians such as snapping turtles and frogs were abandoned because of the recent exploitation of these species in parts of Canada. Until they all enjoy protection such as that given the alligator snapper and other turtles by the state of Florida, it would be irresponsible to contribute to their demise. Treatment in the book of saltwater big-game fishes has been affected by the discovery of the hazards of mercury contamination.

But the positive side outweighs the negative. Through research and development, inland fish management agencies are looking to a future where fish will help alleviate the world demand for protein. Through fish culture and farming, and water quality control, what were formerly considered nonproductive waters are now supporting fish populations. Even the relationship between water quality and flavor impairment is under study in the United States. The success of introductions of exotic species to inland waters is illustrated in the story of the family Salmonidae—trouts.

Another positive aspect has been the phasing out of the term "coarse fish" from marine and market terminology, largely because of the preferences of ethnic customers—who know their fish. This may seem of little import until one considers the countless edible, palatable fishes that have been overlooked by consumer and sportsman alike, and the prospect of a hungry world.

The growth of the book has taken me into the lore of our native Indians and the lives of the explorers and settlers of North America, and into the romantic history of the fishing industry on this continent. It has provided glimpses of the workings of the fishing industry, and of the army of scientists and sportsmen dedicated to the study, conservation and management of our fish populations.

In its wake I have slipped by a side door into the great brotherhood of anglers and outdoor writers (not on my record—I am an enthusiastic but unlucky and unskilled fisherman).

One of the most rewarding experiences has been meeting the many culinary artists from abroad who have made their homes here and brought with them the traditional and festive fish dishes that make up the final chapter of the book.

If the pleasure in the use of this book equals the joy in its writing, then it's a success.

F.M.
Toronto, 1974

FISH
COOKERY
OF
NORTH
AMERICA

ex 1 xo

Campfire Fish Cookery

North American campfire cookery is a legacy of the North American Indians, dating back thousands of years, and from it have derived our various methods of outdoor cookery. There were clambakes and pressure-cooker pits of coastal tribes five thousand miles apart, and, in between, method was a matter of expediency. Cooking was done by means best suited to the circumstances. The open hearth was used extensively by the eastern Iroquois farmers; the feasting pits of the rough-and-ready Algonquin warriors ranged in capacity from fish to moose. On the plains the stone-boiling Assiniboine coped with sparsity of fuels by their ingenious methods of immersion boiling.

All the while the barbecue was moving up from the south, and in the Arctic the Eskimos were part cooking, part curing their meat and fish on the barren tundra, as they did for centuries and still do.

Actually, a method was not confined to any one tribe, and across the continent natives cooked by whatever means was suitable to materials at hand. They baked fish in clay or mud; cooked in pits, on racks, on spits; and boiled in beautiful pots and baskets, in birchbark boxes, bags of hide, and in hollows of tree stumps.

Everywhere they cured in sun and smoke. In 1593 Richard Fisher wrote home from Cape Breton Island: "They also lay them on raftes and hurdles and make a smoke under them of a softe fire and so drie them as the Sauages used to do in Virginia."

This is not to say that campfire cookery has not undergone change. The Indians themselves were as quick to see the advantages of the iron and copper kettles of the *coureurs des bois* over clay and tree stumps as the Frenchmen were to appreciate a good method of cooking when they saw it, and with their native culinary talents, they added refinements to the pot. Methods remain the same; the modern food industry has changed the bill of fare.

The instant food products may be convenience foods in the urban kitchen, but they are wonder workers in the woods. Provisions that were limited in

variety by their weight and bulk now travel in pocket packets, carrying a wide variety of high-quality foods, and seasonings and spices that have come from around the world to enrich the woodsman's kettle.

WOODFIRES

Woodfire cookery involves the use of fires. Before entering the bush, check with the local forestry authorities on the fire-making situation. It can change from day to day. Obtain a permit if necessary, and information on building safe fires and how to put them out. (At the same time get instructions on garbage disposal.)

In very dry weather, or where there is a forest-fire hazard, campfires may be forbidden. Even if you hope to live by an open fire in North American bushland, be sure to take along a camp stove, no matter how small. Under severe conditions it may be the only type of heat source permitted. Sometimes a properly controlled charcoal barbecue grill may be permitted where an open woodfire is not.

Anyone planning a fishing trip into unfamiliar or sparsely inhabited woodlands of North America, and especially into Canada's vast wilds, is well advised to learn the basics of water safety and wilderness survival, and to travel with a qualified guide. The latter may even be mandatory. It is not improbable that in the future water safety and wilderness survival training may be a qualification for a nonresident fishing license as hunter safety training now is for a hunting license.

Choose a campsite with a safe fireplace in mind. Never build a fire on rocks with crevices (fire can travel unseen along the dry, rotted vegetable matter

to erupt weeks later and miles away); don't build a fire near a rotten or fallen
log or tree, or under overhanging branches, or on or near dry muskeg.

The best spot for a campfire is close to water. The sandy mineral soil or
smooth, clean rock of stream or lake shore is best. Clear the area of all debris.

If making a midday luncheon stop, there is no need for an elaborate fireplace.
A very small fire will boil a pail of water and fry a few fish; build it between
a couple of rocks or pieces of green hardwood logs to provide draft and support

the frying pan. Two forked poles, driven upright into the ground with a cross-pole, will support a tea pail.

Fire-building equipment is fundamental to outdoor cookery, whether your life actually depends on it, or you're just going down to the beach for a clambake.

While Indians of old may have unceremoniously tossed live fish into a fire started by rubbing sticks together, and then feasted with satisfaction, over the centuries certain refinements have crept into our outdoor life style. We like to clean the fish and use matches. As for rubbing sticks together, even the Indians occasionally were seen running through the woods from a neighboring camp with a borrowed pan of live coals.

A hatchet or small axe, a small spade, hunting knife or jackknife (not your prized filleting knife), a hone, a pail or bucket, and wooden matches in two or three separate waterproof safes will take care of the clambake. In the woods, additional items that may pay their way around a campfire and take up little space are a few nails, steel S-hooks, a few feet of coiled baling or other light wire, and a roll of heavy-duty aluminum foil. The foil may be bought in sheets or taken off the roll and folded for packing.

If you don't trust your talents in starting fires, take along a box of commercial barbecue fire starters. *Never* use gasoline or camp-stove fuels on an outdoor woodfire.

Use kerosene with extreme caution. Don't throw it on the fire; dip small twigs or branches in it and bury them in the kindling *before* lighting.

CAMP UTENSILS

Cooking utensils for camp are just what you want to carry.

A large frying pan. Most woodsmen, if backpacking, prefer to carry a sheet-steel pan, as it is considerably lighter in weight than cast iron. If packing is no problem, take the cast-iron pan, and, for an extended stay, a Dutch oven as well.

A deep saucepan or two nested. These should have bail handles.

A kitchen spatula, basting spoon or fork. The short-handled utensils are much easier to pack for a camping trip than the long-handled barbecue tools. Handles may be extended if necessary, simply by wiring a green pole to the handle.

A kitchen tongs and an asbestos or even a garden glove are most useful around a campfire. A burned hand can hamper one's fishing.

Tea kettle. The traditional tea kettle is a billy can—that is, a lard or honey pail or such with a bail handle. It may be small, medium, or large. A bail-

handled pot may be made from a clean can by punching two holes just under the lip and looping doubled wire through the holes.

An old oven grate of any size that can be packed in. Be wary of refrigerator racks for broiling purposes, as plating or finish may become toxic when heated.

Plastic garbage bags. Uses are myriad—from ground sheet, to raincoat, to protecting food and clothing. Also for garbage disposal.

Other useful specialized camping utensils are available. The four-way basket fish grill and the long-handled hinged grill are two. The hinged omelette pan is a very practical item on a campfire—two separate pans take the space of one.

Forked pole. Beyond the above, utensils for just about any campfire need may be fashioned or improvised from forked poles, baling wire, and aluminum foil.

Camp-stove fuel. For the camp stove, carry the appropriate fuel in a metal container manufactured for the purpose, or buy it in the convenient and safer one-quart cans. A hand spark starter is reliable for use with camp stove fuels.

THE LARDER

A speculative look at the camp larder should reveal the ingredients to produce a fine fisherman's meal, from a fish fry to a hearty chowder. Regardless of how lightly you travel, you should find what you need among the following. This is a guide, not a checklist or shopping list.

Staples
Salt
Pepper
Mustard (dried, prepared)
Sugar (white, brown)
Lemon (in plastic container)
Eggs (freeze-dried, dry-egg powder)
Fat: margarine (it travels better than butter)
    salt pork (it has good camp life)
    slab-side bacon (slab has a better camp life than sliced bacon)
    bacon drippings
    cooking oil
Dusters: flour or crumbs. These are essential to fried fish. Bread crumbs may be prepared at home for the purpose: Dry out bread trimmings in warm oven, crumble fine with rolling pin or in blender; pack and seal in tough plastic bag. Other dusters are pancake mix, instant mashed potatoes, cornmeal, oatmeal, cream of wheat—we have even used the baby's pabulum. Prepared cereals like cornflakes are good, but too bulky to pack on most camping trips.
Milk: dry milk powder
    canned evaporated milk (the 4-ounce can is a convenient size)
Beans, lentils (dry)

Rice: instant-cooking for stuffings. Available is an instant rice curry, good with
    mushroom soup-and-fish casserole.
Convenience foods:
    freeze-dried vegetables
    biscuits and pancake mix
    soups and sauces (Dry instant mixes—chicken, mushroom, celery, tomato,
        green-pea purée soups. Various well-seasoned sauce mixes.)
    dried vegetable flakes (onion, green and sweet red peppers, celery, mixed
        vegetables)
Canned vegetables (corn, creamed or niblets)
Canned fish for the luckless day (salmon, solid-pack tuna, clams or other
    shellfish)
Seasonings: varying from a fine prepared seafood-seasoning mix to hamburger
    and meat-loaf improvers and salad dressing mixes. A small packet of
    favorite herbs and a small cheesecloth bag of pickling spices add a fine
    touch. Used with a light hand, a very small packet can last through a
    lot of cooking; it takes up no room to speak of and adds zest to the
    fish. Garlic salt or powder and hickory smoke salt.
Larder of the wilds: wild herbs, such as watercress, chervil, mint, sage and
    so on as they occur in your camp locale. Consult a good book on edible
    wild plants.
Fish cures: coarse pickling (noniodized) salt, black pepper, saltpeter—you may
    not find unless planned.
Paper or plastic bags·
Garbage bags (Burn or bury garbage or take it out of the bush. Don't throw
    refuse in lakes or streams; it contaminates water to detriment of future
    fishing.)

CAMP CARE OF FISH

    Fish is extremely perishable and, if not properly cared for, can deteriorate
in quality in a matter of hours. (Ice fishing doesn't pose such problems and
is not included in this chapter.)

    To say that fish to be at its best should be cleaned on its way out of the
water and flipped into the pan might be something of an exaggeration, but
not by much. Fish must be fresh. A fish that has not been properly cared
for is enough to put an initiate angler off fish flesh forever and deprive him
of one of the finest aspects of a fishing trip, if not of life.

    Gut the fish as soon as possible after catching. In hot weather do it immediately. Keep the fish cool, out of the sun, clean and protected from insects, and out of the reach of animals.

The following methods are for camp care of your catch, to keep it at its freshest for the hours from catch to cooking. This also applies to fish cured by the crude smoking and salting methods given in this chapter; these are not preservative measures. To "pack out," see Chapter 2, in which care of fish is discussed in great detail and ice fishing also is discussed.

There are various in-camp methods which will provide a measure of refrigeration by evaporation and keep the dressed fish dry and in good condition. Essential to all is a shady, breezy spot.

Pail in a stream. Put a stone or two in the bottom of a pail, line it with fresh green foliage, lay the dressed fish on it, and cover with more foliage. In a shaded, shallow spot in a fast running stream or cold lake, arrange a circle of stones to hold the pail upright. Place the pail in the circle, the lip of the pail above water level, and cover with a piece of wet canvas. Place a board or branch heavy enough to support a stone on top to frustrate animals.

Splash the canvas occasionally with water and generally keep an eye on the pail.

Canvas and water. First method, duffle bag in the trees: Put the fish, surrounded by fresh foliage, in a canvas bag, and hang from a rope or pole between two trees in a shady, breezy spot, out of reach of animals. Throw water on the canvas, repeating as it evaporates. Second method: Place the fish on an arrangement of loosely piled branches in a breezy shady spot, safe from animals; cover with canvas and sprinkle with water.

Keep an eye on it, and repeat sprinkling as the water dries.

Salting. A method of quick salting overnight is explained in the recipe for Windblown Trout in Chapter 4.

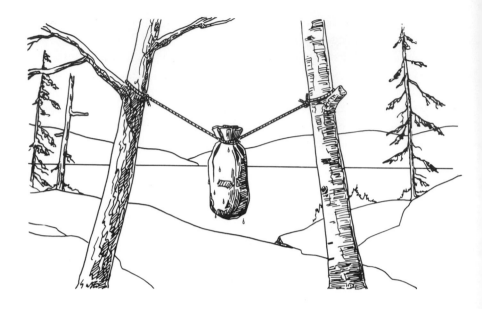

Pepper treatment. Pepper the dressed fish, coating all surfaces, and hang from a line between two trees. The pepper discourages insects, birds, and animals as the fish dries. Fish have been kept for days in dry weather by this method, and then fried to a tasty meal. In damp or wet weather, use the fish at once.

In very hot weather, or lacking any facilities to keep the fish cool, either cook them as caught or release the fish to bite another time.

Whatever you do, *don't* leave your freshly caught fish in water or lying in the bottom of a boat, exposed to dirt and sun–and *don't* leave them stuffed in a creel throughout a day's fishing. In the boat or on shore, lay the fish on fresh green foliage, or newspaper if you have it. Spread a piece of canvas or burlap over the top, and keep it dampened. During early spring fishing in mountains or Northland, and with attendant variation between day and night temperatures, there may even be ice. If so, use it to pack the fish. Otherwise carry the fish back to camp on a stringer.

Cooking by Woodfire

Woodfire cookery in general, and fish cookery in particular, may be divided into three categories: open hearth, pit cooking, and curing. All three are a matter of method rather than precise recipes, and each can be subdivided into specific techniques. For example, open-hearth cookery includes frying, broiling, baking, steaming, and poaching.

Amounts of ingredients listed in this chapter are approximate, and given for guidance only. All methods and recipes, except the salt cure, require the application of heat.

Because of the fast-cooking nature of fish flesh as compared with animal meat, most methods of native origin are on a modified scale. Fires needn't be so big or long-lasting, pits are shallower, and cures are faster.

Outdoor cooking appliances, from the camp stove to the many more or less elaborate barbecue devices, are merely adaptations or modifications of the woodfire; even the fashionable covered ceramic fish brick or cooker is but an adaptation of the clay pack. The same methods or recipes may be used for the woodfire counterpart. Properly operated, the camp stove and portable charcoal barbecue are safer to use where the open fire is hazardous.

PAN-FRYING

Small dressed fish or fillets of larger fish can be pan-fried. The panfish of interest to the shore chef are the small fish weighing under a pound—a convenience for quick meals, but too perishable or unimportant to pack any distance.

Don't try to pan-fry fish in butter or margarine only—unless you want to be bothered with clarifying. Milk solids will sink to the bottom of the pan and scorch. Either product should be combined with bacon fat or cooking oil to prevent this calamity. Or fry in plain bacon fat—it lends a nice camp flavor to the fish. Fat should be hot enough to spit back to a flick of water, but not smoking.

Freshly caught, out of the water and into the frying pan, crisp-fried panfish are a breakfast food unsurpassed. Clean and cut out gills as soon as the fish is caught. Scale or scrape, but don't skin. Cut off the heads and tails if you must. A fish that is a little too thick to fry may be flat split. Wash and wipe dry. Proceed as in Chapter 3, Pan-frying.

Fillets with skin on. Fish with clean-flavored, fine skin, such as the salmons, trouts, chars, mackerel, snappers, pompanos, etc., are best cooked without skinning.

Scale and fillet the fish; don't skin. Cut large fillets into serving portions. Dust with flour, season, and cook the same as pan-fried whole fish. Cook skin side down first, turning when brown and crisp.

Fillets with skin off. Fillet the fish and skin each fillet. Wash and wipe dry.

Cut into serving portions. Mix some freeze-dried or powdered egg with water and whisk with two forks to a thin, scrambled-egg consistency. Proceed as in Chapter 3, Panfrying, *à l'Anglaise.*

DEEP-FRYING

Deep-frying is not usually considered very practical in the woods, especially in a movable camp. However, if you have a Dutch oven, or a bail-handled pot or pail, and are settled in for a few days, the pot of fat may be used repeatedly if it can be kept clean, cool, unscorched, and free of burnt particles.

It's worth the trouble to deep-fry fresh fish in a salty Beer Batter.

Put the fat on to heat, about 3 inches deep. When it reaches a temperature where a flick of batter browns instantly, it is ready. Cut the skinned fillets into half-size serving portions. If you have pancake mix on hand, whisk in beer until you have a light, medium-thick batter. Otherwise mix Beer Batter following recipe. Proceed as in Chapter 3, Deep-Frying.

Note: A styrofoam cooler keeps hot food warm as well as cold food cool. Line bottom with branches and a towel or clean newspaper and place fish on it. Keep covered. A few hot stones well wrapped in newspaper and placed on bottom of cooler will help.

BROILING

An age-honored universal method of cooking by woodfire is simply the direct application of intense, dry heat. It is a quick method ideally suited to fish flesh. Broiling may be done over, under, beside, and by any arrangement that exposes the flesh to, and within quick cooking distance of, the source of heat. Thus in primitive terms it includes barbecuing, grilling, spit-roasting, planking, or any method by any other name that fits the description. While desert nomads of the Middle East were shish-kabobbing on their swords, Indians of North America had long been expert at skewer-broiling on their forked poles.

FISH ON A FORKED POLE   A method for 1- to 2-pound fish, cleaned, scaled, and head left on.

Choose a long, slim, green hardwood pole with branches. Trim the branches, leaving four or five barbs about an inch to an inch and a half from the base, cutting them off at a sharp angle. Clean the fish, leaving head and tail on.

Slip the slim end of the pole through the fish's mouth, wrap the body around the pole, and close it with wooden skewers. Should there be any wild sorrel, mint, or seaweed around, stuff it in the cavity of the fish. Hold the fish in one hand and give the pole a backward jerk to set the barbs. Brush the fish with fat. Stick the pole in the ground, propping it securely with stones beside a good campfire or hold it over the coals. Turn it often until cooked.

FLORIDA BROIL.   Along the Florida shores the small, freshly caught whole fish, scaled, is broiled over the coals whole, or "in the round." The pole or skewer is run through the fish and it is held or supported over the coals. When done to a crispy gold, the fish is slit up the middle and viscera and pole come away, leaving the succulent fish. A favorite method for Florida pompano.

BROILING ON A SKEWER.   Scale and fillet a firm-fleshed fish, leaving the skin on. The skin helps to hold the pieces of fish together. Cut the fillets into chunks. Make a skewer from a slim, freshly peeled, green hardwood pole, leaving small barbs at the end.

Skewer a couple of chunks of fish on the pole, giving them a little push to let the barbs set in the flesh. Dust with flour, brush with fat, and hold over the coals, turning until nicely browned. Fish cooks very quickly; don't overcook it or it may fall in the fire. This arrangement, of course, may be elaborated upon until one arrives at the colorful popular patio shish kabob done on stainless steel skewers, far removed from woodfires and forked poles.

FILLETS AND STEAKS BROILED OVER THE COALS   Cut fillets into serving portions. Wipe with a damp cloth or paper towels. Brush well with oil or melted fat, or sprinkle with lemon juice or vinegar. Make a basting sauce of melted fat or oil, lemon juice, salt, pepper, and a sharp sauce, adding seasonings to taste. Mix in a few drops of rum or whiskey. Grease a hinged wire grill and put the fish in it. Baste well with the sauce and grill over the hot coals, a few minutes on each side, basting frequently.

A secure grill may be improvised from slim, green forked poles or switches, the fillets or steaks sort of woven into it.

PLANKED FISH.   An old Indian method.

Clean the fish, wash, and wipe dry. Cut through the ribs from inside the fish just to one side of the backbone, and flatten it. Select a piece of heavy bark or use a board about a foot longer than the fish. Warm the plank by the fire. Fasten the fish securely by the tail, scales next to the concave side of the bark. Season and baste the flesh with cooking oil or fat. If it's a lean fish, fasten a couple of strips of bacon from the tail end to furnish some basting. Support the bark with sticks and stones, propping it upright, tail end up, in front of a good campfire.

Baste occasionally with oil or fat as it cooks. Add salt and pepper and eat right from the bark.

An advantage of this method is that one needn't wait for a bed of coals. It's done facing the campfire and not directly exposed to the flames. The plank may be moved about to avoid smoke.

BARBECUING

Barbecue is a word from the tongue of a West Indian Carib tribe that simply means to cook on a rack.

Whether the word and method moved northward via the peculiar system of intertribal communication, or whether the exploring La Salle and the Lemoyne brothers recognized it as a superior way of open-fire cooking, is anybody's guess. In any event, the barbecue has traveled the plains and hills of North America to become a fixture at our back doors.

The term today is applied extravagantly to all sorts of elaborate preparations indoors and out, some of which don't involve any close contact with a rack.

Loosely as it is used, it would seem valid to call a stew or soup made in a pot on a hibachi "barbecued." Again, there are a myriad of more or less sophisticated patio appliances called barbecues, some of which in construction and function are more on the order of a charcoal or gas full-scale cooking range than a primitive woodfire, and they virtually convert the patio into a convenient summer kitchen. Thus "barbecued" fish recipes occur throughout the general cookery chapters, and recipes in general from those chapters may be used on most of the patio appliances. In this chapter, barbecuing means broiling on a rack over wood coals. Applied to fish it is fast and simple.

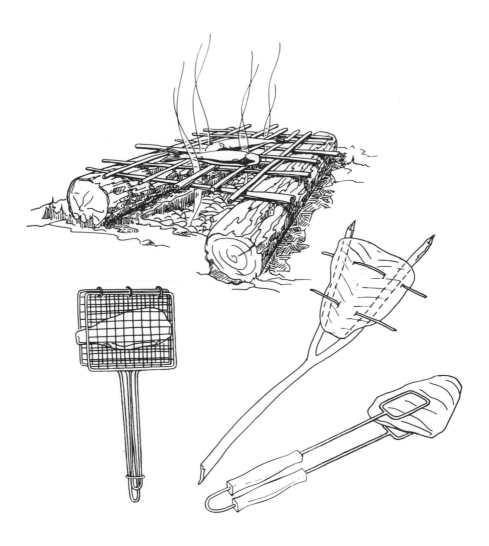

PREPARING BARBECUE RACK AND COALS   Scoop out a shallow pit in sandy ground for the fire and arrange stones or chunky logs at either side to support the rack. Lacking an iron or steel rack, fashion one from slim, green hardwood poles—maple, birch, fruitwood, willow, or aspen. Do not use evergreen. The poles may be peeled or not. The fish will cook before the green poles burn and the rack may be reused if removed from the fireplace when the fish is done. The rack should be made large enough to extend beyond the supporting stones or logs for security and ease of handling. Build a fire, preferably of hardwood, and let it burn down to a deep bed of glowing coals. The bed of coals should be big enough so that the fish is exposed to an area of even intensity of heat. There should be heat enough to last until the fish is done; there can be no refueling during cooking.

Some judgment is required to barbecue to perfection in the primitive manner. A reflector may be needed for wind control. Where the rack should be placed depends on the intensity of heat from the coals. It should be close enough to sear the fish quickly but not so close that smoke or flame from the drippings will taint the fish or set fire to it (or so close that the wooden rack catches fire). A sprinkle of water will quench small flare-ups. (A youngster's water pistol is useful here.)

Over a properly built bed of coals, a rack set about 6 to 8 inches high should be about right. The rack of steel or iron or wood should be well greased before placing it over the coals. The height of the rack may be adjusted by adding or removing supporting stones. The rack is heated before putting the fish on it.

BARBECUING THE FISH   While the fire is burning down, prepare the dressed fish. Barbecue the fish dressed whole, or in thick fillets, or, in the case of larger fish, in steaks of about one-inch thickness. Larger fish may be barbecued whole, but they should be split—that is, cut through the ribs along the backbone from the inside and flattened out.

PREPARING FILLETS OR STEAKS   Prepare as for broiling, or marinate in a basting sauce.

Any aspect of direct dry-heat cooking requires almost constant oily basting to avoid drying of the fish, although the fatty fishes are less susceptible than the lean ones. The conspicuous difference between current barbecue practice and broiling seems to be in the degree of complexity of basting preparations. Broiled fish gets a simple oil or butter treatment. Barbecued fish is subjected to a bath of oily sauces of many and diverse flavors and textures—many with little to recommend them other than pointing up the merits of simple broiling.

The variety of barbecue sauces that may be concocted in camp is limited only by the larder and the chef's imagination. Combined with melted fat or oil are pepper and other seasonings and a little sugar and vinegar (or pickle juice) or lemon. Salad dressing mixes provide a tasty seasoning. Spaghetti mix or hamburger seasoning add a savory touch to a barbecue sauce. Add a few drops from the liquor supply, mix it all well, pour it over the fish, turn the fish a few times, and let it marinate while the fire is getting underway. Turn the fish occasionally in the marinade.

When the coals are ready and the rack is heated, drain the fish from the marinade and place it on the rack. As one side cooks to a crisp brown, baste the top side and turn the fish, then baste the other side. When both sides are brown and the fish flakes with a prod from a fork, the fish is done.

PREPARING WHOLE FISH   This method is for pan-size fish, or fish one inch thick, dressed.

Sprinkle the inside of the fish with lemon juice and a little seasoning, if desired; rub the outside well with fat or dust it lightly with flour and have oil or melted margarine ready to dip or brush on the fish and for basting. Broil on rack, or on hinged grill.

Note: When broiling fish, poke the coals occasionally to dislodge any build-up of ash which forms and tends to insulate the coals. The purpose here is fast-cooking heat, not long-lasting coals.

BAKING

A reflector oven for baking can be improvised from forked poles and aluminum foil. It is simply a miniature lean-to tent or canopy of aluminum foil arranged, shiny side to the heat, over the grill or rack over the coals—or toward the edge, depending on the fire—flap-side facing the fire and back to windward. (See illustration.) A fish may be baked as in a kitchen oven.

Cooking film is a great boon to fish baking. Handled with care, it may be reused. The fish can be seen as it browns through the film, moisture is retained, and it bastes itself as it bakes and there's no need to disturb it. Cooking film has a high heat tolerance, but it should not be in direct contact with flame.

Time is no object in reflector baking. The fish is done when the flesh flakes when prodded with a fork.

BAKED STUFFED FISH   Clean a 3- to 4-pound fish, cut out the fins, and scale, wash, and dry it. Prepare a Camp Kitchen Stuffing from the larder:

CAMP KITCHEN STUFFING

2 cups cooked instant rice
½ envelope dry leek-soup mix
1 tablespoon mixed herbs (or to
    taste)

¼ cup diced cooked bacon
2 tablespoons oil and melted
    margarine or butter, mixed
1 cup warm milk, stock, or water

Mix everything except the liquid. Sprinkle liquid over top of stuffing and toss lightly until well blended.

Stuff the fish lightly and close the cavity with pins or wooden skewers. Wrap any stuffing left over in foil with a dab of margarine and bake separately. Oil the fish well and dust it very lightly with flour. Dab with butter or margarine. Wrap loosely in cooking film, closing the edges with a double fold and tucking the ends under the fish. Place on a baking pan or on a supporting rack covered with aluminum foil, and put it on the grill over a good deep bed of glowing hot coals. Arrange the reflector over the fish and let it bake. As there can be no accurate baking guide for campfire cooking, raise the flap of the oven after about 30 minutes and check the fish's progress. When it is browned all over to a deep gold, it should be done. Open carefully with gloves on, letting steam escape, and check for flakiness. If not quite done, replace the reflector and leave uncovered a little longer.

BAKED FISH WITHOUT FILM   Improvise a baking pan of doubled heavy-duty aluminum foil on a rack, dull side to the heat. Dress the fish as above, using extra fat if the fish is a lean one. Put the fish in the reflector oven. Baste frequently from the pan during baking. After it has begun to brown nicely, dust lightly with flour and continue baking until the flesh flakes and the fish is a crusty golden brown.

In the bush one makes do with what one has, like the Rocky Mountain prospectors and their "gold panners' salmon." The cleaned, well-oiled and seasoned fish is wrapped in greased brown paper, placed between two gold pans and baked in a pit of coals.

BASS ON THE ROCKS.   This is a simple cooking method that works with many fishes—bass here only because largemouth bass was our reward for dropping a line in passing, so to speak, on a Sunday outing. With no equipment other than matches, the fish was cooked as follows:

Heat a large, flat stone to sizzling in the middle of a good campfire made on sandy soil near the water's edge. Clean the fish, but do not skin or scale. Split the large fish, and flatten the small ones. Lay the fish, scales down, on the hot stone. When the flesh flakes, remove the fish. The skin and scales will stick to the stone, thus no utensils are required. (A little salt is a good thing to have.) This method, of course, uses the same principle as the ancient hearthstone where bannocks, biscuits, scones, and so forth were baked.

Flat hot stones can be used to great advantage around any campfire, making handy warming shelves among other uses.

STEAMING AND BOILING

Lean fish are best steamed; fatty fish poached (simmered, that is).

Clean a 2- to 4-pound fish. There is no need to scale it. Leave the smaller fish whole, and fillet the larger ones.

Cut off heads and tails if too big for the pan. To improvise a steamer, spread a few round stones, jar tops, or even sticks over the bottom of a large sauce pan or frying pan, and add water to not quite cover the stones. Add a few drops of vinegar or lemon juice. Tie the fish in a cheesecloth and lay it on the stones. If you have an aluminum pie pan, punch several holes in it, invert it on the stones, and lay the fish on it. Salt lightly. Cover the pan and steam gently over the fire. When the fish flakes, it is ready. Just fold back the skin and eat with salt, pepper, butter or margarine, and lemon juice.

To poach a fat fish, just leave out the stones and add more water. (See Stone Boiling, later in this chapter.)

Pan fish or small fillets may be steamed by wrapping them in aluminum foil, shiny side in, with seasoning and a bit of basting, and burying them in hot ashes (not live coals) at the edge of the fire or over the coals. This is a modern version of an ancient culinary method of universal practice—as the wrappings of grape leaves in Greece, papaya leaves in Hawaii, and corn husks in Quebec, as well as the elegant *papilotte* of French cuisine.

STEAMING FISH IN THE COALS   Lay a 2-pound or more dressed fish on large double sheets of heavy-duty aluminum foil, shiny side up. Season the cavity with lemon juice, seasonings, and if wild edible herbs are available, tuck them in along with a few dabs of bacon fat. Wrap the fish loosely but moisture-tight in the foil; bring edges together in a double fold and close the ends in the same way. Scoop out a hollow in the glowing coals near the edge of the campfire and lay the fish in the hollow. Push the coals in around the package.

Lift the package into and out of the coals with a spade. A 2-pound fish should steam in its own juices in about a half hour, depending on the coals.

Large fillets of fish may be steamed in the same manner.

Corn husks are used in much the same manner. Wet the husks before and after wrapping the fish.

SAVORY LAKESHORE CHOWDER

Amounts of ingredients are to be used only as a guide; fresh items can be used if you have them.

1 2- or 3-pound fish, or a couple of smaller fish, freshly caught
2 thick slices of bacon
Lemon juice
2 large raw potatoes, diced
Dried celery flakes
1 package dry, clear, onion soup mix
1 small can tomato soup
1 28-ounce can tomatoes

1 teaspoon prepared seafood seasoning, and/or other seasoning to taste
4 cups milk (reconstituted milk powder, or evaporated milk and water)
Margarine, or bacon fat
Handful of fresh watercress, if handy
Whiskey (optional)

Clean the fish, leaving on head and tail. Cut in half if necessary to fit the kettle. Tie it loosely in cheesecloth or clean white netting. Sear the bacon in a deep kettle. Add the fish with enough water to cover and lemon juice. Bring to a boil and let simmer until the flesh begins to flake. Remove the package of fish. Remove all flesh from the bones and break into chunks. Don't miss the succulent little cheeks. Set the fish aside. Rewrap bones and return to pot.

Bring the stock to a boil and add the potatoes, celery flakes, and onion soup mix, stirring until the soup mix has dissolved. Add the tomato soup and tomatoes. Turn the heat down to a simmer, or in the case of a wood fire, move the kettle away from the center of intense heat. Leave uncovered, letting the stock boil down.

Seasonings may be as you fancy from what is on hand. To really set this chowder up it should have, besides salt and pepper, a dash of garlic powder, a bit of oregano, a few drops of Tabasco or hot pepper sauce, and a dash of Worcestershire or steak sauce. Taste and adjust as it cooks, which should be for about 20 minutes. Remove the package of bones.

Add milk and heat at a low simmer for about 15 minutes. Don't let it boil or it will curdle. Add the shredded fish and swirl in a few dabs of fat. Add watercress. A dash of whiskey goes well at this point.

If you prefer a thicker chowder, stir in an extra ½ cup of instant mashed potato flakes, and stir until thickened. (Potato flakes may be used instead of diced raw potatoes.)

Serve hot with hot biscuits or garlic bread.

Makes about 2 quarts of chowder.

STONE BOILING

Keep several round, smooth stones without cracks, 2 to 3 inches in diameter, in the campfire. With them you can boil water, keep food warm, or (well wrapped) warm your sleeping bag.

Two or three white-hot stones dropped into a pot or pail of water will bring it to a boil quickly and replacement of the stones will keep it boiling. They will also keep a kettle of soup or stew boiling. The immersion boiling of the North American Indians of old, used where hardwood fuels were scarce (it was commonly used by the Plains tribes—Assiniboine means "stone boiler"), is the principle behind the modern electric kettle. In camp it releases precious space in the fireplace.

Kettles may be improvised. The Indians used carved wooden boxes, beautiful, finely woven baskets, earthenware, bags of hide in pits or above the ground, or hollowed tree stumps. A simple camp arrangement is a pit dug in sandy soil and lined with heavy aluminum foil or even wet canvas. Or fashion a kettle by lining a box with foil for a small-scale operation.

Pit Cooking

The clambake of the Eastern seaboard and the underground ovens of the West Coast are similar in principle, and of Indian origin.

By the primitive method, a deep hole is dug in the sandy beach and in it the clams are steamed between layers of wet dulse or kelp, or other seaweed, over hot stones. The stones, fired to a crackling white heat, may be fired in the pit or outside it. The latter-day large-scale clambake is often done in a clean metal drum or in a barrel lined with protective pieces of sheet iron and sunk into the pit.

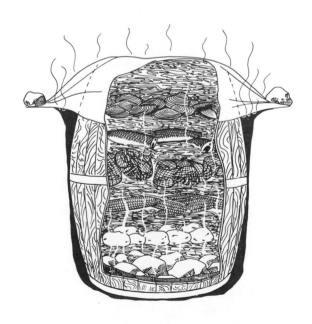

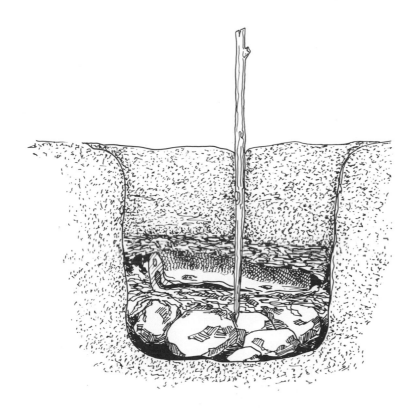

Into the modern clambake might go, in layers along with a couple dozen well-scrubbed live clams per serving, potatoes in their scrubbed skins, ears of husked corn, lively lobsters individually tied in cheesecloth (1 per person), and a few fresh fish. Each layer is separated by wet seaweed. The whole assembly is covered with another deep layer of seaweed, then with a sheet of clean, wet canvas. Gaps are plugged with seaweed, letting only whiffs of tantalizing fragrance escape.

Clambakes may be done over an open fire. A large clam steamer designed for the purpose is available; a tin-lined copper wash boiler serves the same purpose with more rustic class if less efficiency. On a family scale, the clams may be steamed in any large covered kettle over a woodfire or on your camp stove.

(See more about clams and clambakes in Chapter 6.)

PACIFIC UNDERGROUND OVEN   The primitive underground oven of the Pacific coast was more like a pressure cooker than the steaming process of the Eastern clambake. A hole was dug in sandy ground and into it white-hot

stones were loaded. The stones were covered with wet seaweed, leaves, and grass matting. On them were laid the roots of the camas, cleaned and oiled fish, clams, and perhaps a dressed waterfowl or two, and all covered with more seaweed and matting. A long pole was then pushed down through the middle to the stones before the pit was filled with earth. When the pole was withdrawn, water was poured into the opening, which was immediately plugged with more earth. A good head of steam formed and the cooking was done in short order.

DEEP-PIT OR SAND-HOLE COOKING   A favorite of the French Canadian *coureurs des bois,* sand-hole cooking involves the use of a bail-handled Dutch oven or heavy covered iron kettle. Sand-hole cooking is convenient for meats and long-cooking dishes. (Sand-hole beans are famous in the Quebec woods.)

For fish the method is practical more for large quantity stews or chowders where there is considerable amount of liquid to bring to and maintain at a low simmer.

KING-SIZE CHOWDER

Dig a pit in sandy ground two feet deep and just big enough to accommodate the Dutch oven. Cover the floor of the pit with small stones. During the evening, fire the pit with green hardwood until the walls of sand are hot enough to spit back at a flick of water. This may take all evening. Meanwhile prepare the chowder.

2 5-pound fish, or equivalent in smaller fish
½ pound salt pork, diced
2 packages dry, clear, onion soup mix
12 cups water
1 cup assorted dry vegetable flakes (onion, mixed vegetable, mixed pepper, celery and/or others)
2 cups freeze-dried potato cubes, or instant mashed potatoes,* or 2 cups rice or lentils
1 large can lima beans, if handy
2 28-ounce cans tomatoes
1 large can tomato juice, vegetable cocktail juice, V-8, or 1 small can tomato paste and an extra quart of water
Salt
Seasonings as they take your fancy
Rum

Clean the fish and wash well. Fillet and skin the fish, trimming all excessive fat. Set aside the heads, tails, bones, and, if desired, the skin. Cut the fillets into chunks and tie the heads, tails, and bones in cheesecloth. Put the pork into the Dutch oven, put over the fire and sear the pork. Remove from heat.

Mix the soup mix in a little hot water and add it along with everything but the fish to the pot. Mix well and test for salt. It may need about 2 teaspoons. Add the fish and bag of trimmings.

Cover the Dutch oven and seal the lid with a thick flour-and-water paste or with clay, and cover it with a wet towel or cloth.

Scoop out burning wood with a spade, leaving the coals in the bottom of the pit. Using a strong forked pole, lower the Dutch oven into the pit. Cover completely with hot sand from the sides of the pit. Rake the remaining

---

* The instant mashed potatoes will thicken the chowder.

fire back over the pit, build up the fire and let it burn out. Don't leave it unattended until it is *out*.

Build the next morning's fire over the pit. (Be sure it is out before leaving.) A hearty chowder will be ready at noon, and still hot by late afternoon.

Dig sand out around the pot and carefully lift it out of pit.

Remove the lid from the pot, fish out the bag of trimmings and discard. Blend in a little rum. Let the heady aroma tantalize 20 hungry anglers for a few minutes, and then feed them. Hot biscuits or bannock complete the meal.

This large-scale recipe requires a large kettle, of 2- to 4-gallon capacity, to allow head room in the kettle, which should be one-third of its capacity. The recipe may be reduced to accommodate a smaller kettle, but a small, or regular size, chowder is relatively quickly made; there's no need for the pit.

Sand-Hole Beans. These are cooked exactly the same way. Use your favorite recipe for Boston baked beans, letting the beans soak for several hours before assembling the recipe. A pinch of baking soda from the first-aid kit will hasten the softening of the beans. Sand-hole beans and pan-fried fresh fish by a campfire at dusk is a memorable meal.

CLAY BAKING

Clay baking is an ancient method used by North Americans coast to coast wherever fish, wood, and clay or mud occur. Hardwood and its long-lasting coals is best. Where soft-wood fuels and their short-lived coals are used, stones are heated in the fire and used to boost the heat in the pit. Where clay is lacking, a heavy malleable mud substitutes. One accustomed to clay considers mud second best. The best clay is considered to be the slick blue-gray clay from riverbeds or from under the sand at water's edge of lake or bay. The ceramic fish brick is an adaptation of the clay pack.

To bake a freshly caught game fish in clay, dig a hole in sandy soil big enough to hold a 3- to 4-pound fish with several inches to spare. Scatter a few stones in the bottom. Fire the pit with hardwood until the coals are deep enough to bury the fish completely. Whether to clean the fish or not is a matter of debate, but either way the method is a favorite of woodsmen.

Uncleaned: Encase the fish just as it comes from the water in a thick coat of clay. The 3- to 4-pounder should have about an inch. (Smaller fish require less.) Bury it in the coals. Scoop the coals over the fish and cover the coals with more clay. Build a fire over everything and let it burn until it is out.

The fish may be left for several hours in the pit, still hot and ready to eat. Remove from the pit, crack away the clay, and skin and scales will come with it. Lift out the flesh, moist, sweet, and succulent, cooked in its own juices. The viscera, which roll out like pebbles, are discarded.

Cleaned: Clean and dress the fish. Cut off the head or leave it on, bearing in mind that the more protection the better. Sprinkle the cavity with lemon juice, and add a few local wild edible herbs or seasonings. Coat in clay and bake as for uncleaned fish.

SMALL FISH BAKED IN CLAY   Small fish in the 2-pound-and-under range, encased in about a half inch of clay or mud, may be baked by simply burying the package in live coals in the campfire. They bake in about an hour and hold the heat for another hour or so. It's all relative. The bigger the fish, the thicker the clay will be, the bigger the pit of coals required to hold it all, and thus the greater and longer-lasting the heat required to cook it.

Smoke Curing

In this chapter curing is treated superficially. It includes heat-smoking, with or without salting, by methods practical on a fishing trip of limited facilities and duration. Curing fish by more sophisticated methods is discussed in Chapter 7.

Curing is not offered as a preservative measure. Fish smoked by the following methods require the same care as fresh fish. However, fish packed in a salt cure withstand travel with less fuss and risk than fresh fish.

Heat-smoking cooks the fish to a golden succulence for immediate consumption. It is a treatment especially good for fatty fish.

Heat-smoking does not substitute for refrigeration other than for the time the fish is in the smokehouse; even in the salt cure it's best kept cool.

Fish may be heat-smoked with no preliminary treatment. However, they smoke much more quickly and are more flavorsome and less prone to spoilage when first given a salt cure. And, of course, they may be salt-cured without smoking.

THE SMOKEHOUSE

To improvise a smokehouse is a simple matter. Any number of arrangements can be made in the bush whereby smoke may be directed to the surfaces of the fish to be smoked.

A rough-and-ready smokehouse may be constructed from a hollow log. The smokehouse at the top of the inclined log may be a large tin pail with the bottom knocked out, or a cylinder arrangement made from birch bark. Small fish are suspended from sticks or wire laid across the top of the drum. Smoke is generated from a smudge at the base of the log. The whole arrangement

is the same in principle as the sophisticated smokehouse barrel described in Chapter 7.

Another arrangement is a simple tepee of fresh green boughs or tarpaulin over a tripod of forked green poles supporting a shelf or a rack woven from trimmed branches, over a smudge. The tepee need be only big enough to hang the fish inside and allow for a good circulation of smoke. A smudge pot is prepared *outside* the smokehouse and inserted onto the floor.

THE SALT-SMOKE CURE

Clean and scale the small fish (pan size) and fillet or steak the larger ones. Leave skin on the fillets and steaks; the skin helps to hold the fish together. Prepare a mixture in proportions of 1 cup brown sugar, 1 cup coarse pickling salt, 1 tablespoon black pepper (coarse or cracked), a pinch of saltpeter, and mix it well. Rub the mixture into all exposed parts of the fish. Lay the fish in an earthenware or plastic platter. Fashion a pan to fit the fish from aluminum foil *lined with plastic.* (Don't let a salt cure contact metal.) Or simply line a cardboard box with plastic.

The cure will draw fluid from the fish, forming its own pickle. Cover lightly but securely. Take home to smoke there.

To smoke in camp, leave the fish in the cure a few hours or overnight. Remove from the cure, and let it drain while you get the smudge going. Put the fish in the smokehouse and heat-smoke for up to a couple of hours, depending on the thickness and degree of salt-curing of the fish. Small, delicate fish like smelts salt-cured will smoke in a few minutes. Small salted fish should be supported by a rack arrangement in the smokehouse; they tend to fall apart from their weight. Large pieces, fillets and steaks should be bound with gauze bandage, with a loop left. When the flesh takes on a gold-tinged shiny glaze, and the aroma is more than one can resist, eat it.

Camp Dishes for the Luckless Angler

Total dependence on freshwater fishing for one's meals can be unreliable. Sometimes because of the time of day, the weather, the season, the vagaries of the fish, or the overfishing of accessible waters, the fish are either not biting or not there.

Oddly enough, according to Berndt Berglund, northern wilderness survival expert of Campbellford, Ontario, in a survival situation the most dependable source of food is fish, as the lake or pond where you've set up camp will be far off the beaten track and not as heavily fished as the favorite fishing holes. (If it is, presumably you are not lost.) And, of course, in such a desperate situation, the mode of capture is not restricted to sporting methods.

The following recipes look to the larder for quick meals. (See Chapter 3 for other camp-easy recipes for cooked or canned fish meals.)

CLAM SUNDOWN

1 10-ounce can green pea soup
1 10-ounce can cream of mushroom
   soup

1 10-ounce can baby clams
2 cups evaporated milk
1 tablespoon whiskey

Using a deep saucepan, blend the soups together until smooth. (Instant soup mixes may be used. Reconstitute using half required water.) Drain the juice from the clams into the soups, mix well, then add the milk and mix until all is smooth. Heat slowly until quite hot but don't let it boil. Add clams, mix and heat through. Just before serving, stir in the whiskey.

Serves 4.

Variation: Substitute light cream and freshly steamed clams with juice for the canned milk and clams, and use sherry instead of whiskey.

LEFTOVER FISH CASSEROLE

Leftover cooked fish, or 1 7-ounce
   can tuna or salmon
1 package cream of tomato soup mix
1–2 tablespoons each assorted dry
   vegetable flakes

2 tablespoons onion flakes
½ teaspoon prepared seafood
   seasoning
Salt and pepper to taste

Prepare cream of tomato soup mix, reducing water requirement by one-third.

Add mixed vegetable flakes, onion flakes, and other flakes to taste or at hand. Add prepared seafood seasoning and salt and pepper. Stir until the soup begins to thicken.

Add the fish to the soup and continue to simmer until thickened. Serve with hot biscuits.

Variation: Combine cooked fish with instant onion soup or sauce mixes. (Reduce water content of soup mix as above; use sauce mixes as directed on package.)

INSTANT FISH CAKES

1 cup shredded, leftover cooked fish,
    or 2 small cans tuna or salmon
2 tablespoons melted margarine,
    butter, or oil
1 cup instant mashed potatoes,
    prepared
1 package dry instant onion soup
    mix

1 teaspoon prepared seafood
    seasoning
Pepper to taste
2 eggs, beaten (or equivalent in
    freeze-dried or powdered eggs)
Fine, dry bread crumbs

Shred the fish, removing all bones. Mix margarine into prepared mashed potatoes and add the fish, soup mix, and seasoning. Blend. Add beaten eggs and mix well. Form into patties. Dust with bread crumbs. Fry in hot fat, turning once, until both sides are crisply browned. Serve with a sharp tomato sauce.

Note: Many soup mixes are rather salty. Omit salt when using them. Salting may be done to individual taste.

ᘓ 2 ᖇ

Catch to Kitchen

"...we brought home our limit—80 speckled trout—in perfect condition. It was a five-hour climb into the mountains. At that elevation there was still ice around the shores. As we caught the fish, we cleaned them, all 80 of them, put them in poly-bags and packed them in ice in our packsacks.... The fish were perfect, still in rigor, and ice still left when we checked out our week's catch at the park gates."

—Clorice Landry, Shediac, N.B.,
describing spring trout fishing in Laurentide Park

Fish, or one should say fishing, whether sport or commercial, falls generally into one of two categories: saltwater and freshwater.

The principles of general care of the fish from catch to table are essentially the same for both. It's the circumstances in which they are applied that differ considerably. Inland freshwater fishing by its nature can present the sportsman with a diversity of physical problems not usually encountered in modern saltwater fishing.

Fish flesh is extremely perishable, some more so than others. Fatty fishes, both saltwater and freshwater, are more quickly perishable than the medium-fat and lean species. For example, given equal expert attention, walleye will keep twice as long as mackerel (and this applies in the freezer as well). On the other hand, the fatty fishes take to salting and smoking better, the time in the cure extending the margin of safe storage for immediate use or longer, depending on the nature of the cure. (See Chapter 7.)

Inland or at sea, any fish exposed to atmosphere and hot sun can spoil in less than an hour. Whether the fish is to be fresh-cooked, frozen, canned or cured, the field care and dressing of fish involves attention from the time it's caught until it reaches the cook. Methods of successfully performing this feat vary as greatly as do the locales and circumstances in which the fish is caught. Essentially, the achievement hinges on cleanliness and a low temperature.

Competent anglers have devised their own procedures for getting the catch to the kitchen. The following methods and tips are a composite offering from

guides, outfitters, fisheries biologists and officers, sportsmen and commercial fishermen from across the continent, all knowledgeable and skilled in the care of fish, to aid the angler in keeping his catch at its peak of quality until it reaches the cook.

To preserve the flavor, texture, and general quality, the fish should be killed and cooled upon catching and cleaned immediately, or within hours, provided it can be kept cold and clean, and then off to refrigeration.

The reason is that bacteria are not found in the flesh of live, healthy fish;

they are present on the skin, over the gills, and in the intestinal tract. Exposed to warm atmosphere, these bacteria, accustomed to a cold environment, multiply rapidly and invade the flesh. It's only reasonable to remove them before they can go to work.

In the northern and mountain areas of the continent, spring and fall freshwater fishing is usually favored by cool, if not chilly, weather, though this can mean cold nights and warm, sunny days. Winter ice-fishing poses no problems with refrigeration. In warm weather, some planning is required but the job can usually be done.

In hot weather, with no immediate refrigeration available, the fish should be cleaned on the spot, protected from heat, dirt, and insects, and cooked and eaten within hours, or else it should be returned to the water alive and well.

To be acceptable in the kitchen a fish must be firm or rigid, and fresh-smelling or odorless. And this means keeping it clean and cold. If is shows signs of softening, it's beyond repair.

These two qualifications are the basis of the six-point system given at the end of this chapter for judging fresh fish at the market.

When a fish is killed, like a mammal it begins to stiffen; rigor mortis sets in. Rigor mortis lasts for hours up to days, depending on temperature conditions, then the fish softens again. Fish properly refrigerated will stay rigid for a matter of days.

Fresh fish should still be in rigor when delivered to the cook or at the market.

Many people think a fish without odor is at its freshest. Not so, say fisheries experts. A fish straight from the water has a characteristically fresh, mild odor of the water from which it came; from the sea it suggests iodine or kelp, dulse or other seaweed. This lasts for a day in iced fish. After two or three days on ice, the odor is absent, the flesh still firm; this is called the neutral stage, which may last a couple more days and the fish is still fresh. Then the flesh begins to soften, it starts to smell, the odor increases in intensity and offensiveness as rigor leaves, and the fish is a loss.

Field Care

Kill the fish as soon as caught. Not only is it more humane, but the flesh deteriorates more rapidly in fish left to die slowly. Don't put live fish in pails of water, or on stringers to struggle and drag after the boat. Don't put the dead ones there either. Water impedes the natural drainage of the fish. The water at the surface is warmer—it interferes with rigor mortis, aids bacterial action, and altogether speeds up spoilage of the fish.

TROPHY FISH, JAPANESE STYLE

The Japanese, enthusiastic anglers, take a print from the fish as it comes from the water, then clean and wash the fish and cook it.

A fine-quality rice paper of the kind used by artists and Japanese *sumi* ink used in brush writing, or a water-soluble ink, and a brush are all that is required by way of kit, and it all fits easily into the tackle box. The operation is accomplished in three easy steps.

Wash the slime from the fish and wipe it dry. Lay it on a flat surface and brush the ink over one entire side, covering head, eye, gill, fins, and tail. With both hands, grasp the paper, precut larger than the fish, stretching it gently, and bring it straight down on the fish. Smooth it lightly over the entire fish, end to end, using the flat of the hands, and pressing lightly with fingers around mouth, eyes, and gills. Extend the fins with one hand and press the paper over them with the other. (As the ink shows through the paper, the process can be checked to see that all parts are printed.) Peel off the paper and the print remains.

If the first attempt is less than successful, wash the fish, reink it, and take off another print. Take as many as you want.

Inscribe the statistics of the catch, and frame the print for your den or recreation room.

Wash the ink off the fish, clean it, and cook it.

COOLING

Wash the fish well and put it in a roomy cooler, pan, or bucket of crushed ice. A portable food cooler or ice chest filled with ice, with arrangement for drainage, pays its way on a fishing trip, inland or on the sea.

Ice. Ice is best crushed. To crush blocks of ice, put them in a burlap sack and crush with the side of an axe, or anything handy that will do the job. Outside the freezer, natural ice is the preferred cooling agent for fish, as it furnishes the right degree of moisture.

Freezer pads. Freezer pads are useful to have on a fishing trip, provided there are facilities to freeze them. A couple of the large, handy pads, frozen hard, should see a day's limit safely back to camp or home. The pads should be separated from the fish with damp, not wet, paper, moss, or foliage.

Lacking ice or freezer pads, sandwich the fish between layers of cool, fresh, damp moss or other green foliage. Place in a box or pan in the boat, or on shore simply lay them on the ground in a shady, breezy spot until ready to go back to camp.

Whatever the packing, cover loosely with canvas or burlap, and sprinkle with water over the top now and then. Evaporation of the water will keep things cool.

Creels. A creel is a convenient device, indispensable to anglers up to their waists in water, for collecting a string of fish. It is not an all-weather, all-purpose storage container for fish. Fish in a creel require the same care as other fish. Get them out of the creel, cool them and clean them as soon as possible. Then repack in ice or leaves. Don't pile them; if you have a number of fish and not far to go, carry them on a stringer. Do not carry ungutted, unwashed fish stuffed in a creel through the heat of the day; don't carry them in your pockets; and don't carry them in plastic bags.

CLEANING

For anything bigger than small panfish, the conventional cut for gutting or dressing fish is through the abdomen. A back cut, or split, is used in boning finnan haddie (kippers). Fillets may be cut directly from the undressed fish.

Use a sharp-pointed knife. Push the point of the knife through the skin at the base of the throat. With a light, easy stroke, slit the skin as far as the vent, using the point, or just about an inch of edge of the blade, taking care not to cut into the viscera. Separate the edges, feel for the throat, and with the point of the knife, cut across the throat, freeing the gut. Gently work fingers under the viscera and push them out. With the point of the knife, cut the skin around the vent, being careful not to sever the intestine, and everything will come away clean, all parts intact.

Cut out the gills. Separate the liver, roe, and sound if present (in many fishes a delicacy), and dispose of the remaining entrails. Bury them, burn them, but don't throw them back in the water.

Wash the fish and flush out the cavity with plenty of clean water, wiping out any blood or matter clinging to the backbone, until the inside of the fish is glistening clean. The fish is now dressed.

Immediately chill the fish. If you can't, cook it or salt it.

Under adequate refrigeration all the way (32°F–ice), or frozen immediately as in ice fishing, freshly caught fish may be shipped in the round, i.e., as they come from the water.

Cleaning panfish. Very small fish are usually cleaned through the gills, a procedure called "gibbing." Spread open the gill cover, slip forefinger in around the inner gill, and with a gentle pinch, draw it out, bringing viscera along with it.

FREEZING

If the fish are destined for freezer storage, or home is a long way off, have the cleaned, chilled fish frozen as soon as possible after catching.

If it can't be done at the fishing camp or on board, take the chilled fish to a frozen-food locker plant where they will be filleted (see note following) if desired, packaged and fast frozen, and held for pick-up or shipped directly home.

Or do it yourself. Wrap the fish in plastic film, chill and fast-freeze, wrap in newspaper, pack in dry ice, and ship or take home to the freezer at once.

The fish should be well protected from direct contact with the dry ice to avoid freezer burn. Crumpled newspaper will do; inch-thick slabs of styrofoam are excellent.

DRY ICE   Dry ice, which is carbon dioxide in the solid state, has a temperature of −109°F, at which it remains until dissipated or, in chemical terms, sublimated. That is, it goes directly from the solid state to the gaseous state, with no liquid state in between. Thus its value in freezing foods is obvious. Dry ice is very heavy; a 10-inch-cube block weighs 54 pounds.

Dry ice freezes food an estimated five times as quickly as the deep freezer, and as a fish-packing material is without compare. It is gradually replacing deep freezing and natural-ice packing in commercial packing of fish and fowl. Dry ice in powdered form is blown on the meats and they freeze instantly.

Dry ice is available in the 10-inch block or sliced into 1-inch slabs. (The blocks may be cut with a saw.) Well-operated marinas and fishing camps, as well as guides, are usually in touch with a source of supply; a well-distributed source is ice-cream packers.

A 5-pound fish, wrapped in newspaper and placed between two 1-inch slabs of dry ice in a cooler, will freeze hard in eight to ten minutes.

Whatever the container, it should be well insulated and allowance must be made for the escape of the gas. (Don't roll up the dry ice in your sleeping bag or mattress.) The fish should be wrapped to protect it from direct contact with the dry ice. Generally speaking, under such conditions the estimated loss of dry ice through sublimation is 15% to 20% over 24 hours. However, the many variables involved in handling fish in the wilds or on the seas—the packing, the amount, the shape and temperature of the fish, the weather—all make it risky to predict any exact performance. The need for dry ice should be anticipated and an adequate supply prearranged.

Information on quantity requirements and procedure for the use of dry ice may usually be obtained at the source of supply or from guides and outfitters. Use it generously. And don't handle dry ice with bare hands; use dry gloves and a wooden-handled tool.

Freeze only freshly caught fish.

PACKING

A large fish, or a number of small fish in individual plastic bags wrapped together and frozen hard, will stand a six- or seven-hour trip if well wrapped with lots of newspaper and/or corrugated paper. The packages can be rolled up in a sleeping bag, or, better still, in a crimped foam-rubber camp mattress. The foam mattress offers excellent insulation for frozen or chilled fish. (Put chilled fish in a plastic bag, tie securely, and roll it up.)

When the fish arrive at home, they may be glazed before they go into the freezer. The process is explained later in this chapter.

Note: There is no doubt that the most convenient way to pack frozen fish for shipment is in fillets or steaks. But before doing any cutting, check the fishing regulations of state or province regarding such practice. It is generally required that the skin, or a piece of skin, be left on fillets and steaks for identification purposes. Fish frozen bundled together should be done in such a way that they can be inspected for number and identification.

Dressing Fish

Whether the fish are going into the pan, into the freezer, or to market, a set of generally recognized terms describe their form:

In the round:	The fish as it comes from the water.
Dressed:	Gutted only and gills cut out (sportfishing); or gills left in (commercial).
Head-dressed:	Dressed and head cut off.
Pan-dressed:	Dressed, with head, tail, gills, fins, and scales removed.
Steaked:	Cross-sliced.
Filleted:	Flesh cut from sides of fish.
Split:	Cut down through back to clean; front intact (finnan haddie, kippers).
Boned:	Bones cut out.

In the round and dressed. Fish in the round are gutted in the conventional manner as described earlier, and thus they become dressed fish. If the fish is to be skinned, it is done now. Fish in the round are also filleted, split, or boned, with the cleaning taken care of in the process.

Skinning a fish. Cut through skin around neck below gills of dressed fish. Slip knife between skin and flesh at neck, draw skin back, easing it away from the flesh of one side with blunt side of knife, working toward the tail. Skin other side. If tail is to remain, cut through skin around caudal peduncle.

Head-dressed. To cut the head from a dressed fish, simply make a clean cut across the throat just under the gills. (Don't throw away the head—there's good fish flesh there.)

Pan-dressed. Remove fins, scales, and tail from head-dressed fish. With the point of the knife, cut through flesh close to and around the fins. With a firm grip, using pliers if necessary, give the fin a sharp backward jerk. Fin and root bones will come with it. Don't cut fins off with scissors or knife, or the roots will be left in the flesh.

When dressing a large whole fish, we sometimes like to leave the dorsal fin for appearance's sake. It can be rough handling, especially in a fish like walleye.

Scaling. Lay the fish on a solid surface. Grip it firmly by the tail and, using the blunt edge of a knife, holding it at about a 45° angle, scrape away the scales, working from tail to head. We have found it much easier to scale a semithawed frozen fish, but the scales do fly.

All fish have scales, although some are scarcely discernible, like the salmons, trouts, and mackerels. Scrape these with the blunt side of knife when preparing to cook in the skins.

Plank split. Head-dressed and pan-dressed fish too thick to fry whole may be plank or flat split by cutting through ribs to one side of backbone. Flatten the fish or cut into two halves.

Steaked. Steaks are cut from pan-dressed fish. Fish above, say, 8 pounds are cut into meal-size portions or steaks by cutting in slices through the backbone to desired thickness. Portions can be recut for chowders, deep frying, casseroles, etc.

FISH FILLETS

Fish from 2 to 3 pounds up are filleted.

Scale the fish before filleting, if keeping the skin on. If it's to be skinned, there's no need to scale. Whether you skin the fillets depends on the fish. Practically all the fine game, or sport fishes, have inherently good-flavored skins, tending to thicken as the fish grows toward trophy size. Flavors good and not so good settle in the skin and in the fat under the skin.

In the general run of fine sport fishes with excellent skin, whether you skin or not depends on how you plan to cook it. It's best to leave at least some of the fillets unskinned until time to cook. It's all added protection against drying in refrigerator or freezer, and the skin is easily removed from a semi-thawed fish.

Leave the skin on fillets to be smoked, as it holds them together in the smokehouse.

The cleaning step may be bypassed by simply cutting the fillets from the "round" fish, but care should be taken not to cut into the viscera.

The filleting knife is important. It should be razor sharp and have a very sharp point. It should be of strong thin flexible steel (not stainless) that hones to a good edge and keeps it.

The blade should be slim and about eight inches long. However, a filleting knife is a very personal matter to an angler or cook, and the knife he or she does the best job with is the best for the job.

Extra-large fillets are cut to meal-size portions.

Filleting flatfishes. The smaller flatfishes, such as the soles and summer and winter flounders, are usually skinned before filleting.

Lay the fish on a cutting board, eyes up. Slit the skin along the fin lines, close to the fins. Cut the skin across the tail, and with the knife loosen enough

1. Lay fish on side. Cut around neck, below gills, almost to backbone.

2. Holding head down with one hand, with other hand cut meat from sides. With blade of knife flat, cut meat away from bones in a sweeping slice downward and toward tail, bypassing dorsal fin.

3. Cut through flesh at caudal peduncle.

4. Trim last remaining bones away.

5. To remove skin, separate flesh and skin at tail end, grasp skin, and with knife flat and edge slightly inclined toward skin, cut between skin and flesh.

skin to get a grip on it. Hold the tail end down firmly with one hand, and with the other grasp the skin and pull it off toward the head. The skin is slippery; wrap a towel around it. The operation reveals a pair of fleshy fillets with a well-defined separation. Working from this separation outward, cut the fillets away from the bone. Turn the fish over and fillet the other side.

A flatfish may also be filleted before skinning. Cut across the neck, just behind the gill cover, to the backbone. Starting at the tail end, cutting at a bit of an angle, make an incision alongside the dorsal fin, then deepen the cut. Starting from the head end, work the flesh from the ribs, easing the knife between flesh and ribs, folding the fillet back until it is off. Turn the fish over and fillet the other side. Skin the fillets as usual.

The gelatinous nature of the trimmings, especially the skin and fins, of the flatfishes make them eminently suitable for fumets, stocks and soups.

Larger flatfishes, like halibut and turbot, are usually cut into thick steaks or cuts.

Wash and scale or scrape the fish. Carefully cut out gills and clean. On the dark side of the fish, under the head and just above the pectoral fin, make a cross cut. Draw out the entrails. Cut the fish in half up the middle (along the spine), wipe clean, cut off fins, and cut each half into thick steaks.

BONING FISH

Boning fish is a simple operation requiring only the skill that comes of faithful practice.

Boning fish in the round. Scale and cut out fins. Cut along back through flesh to the bone, from just above the gill covers to the tail. Starting midway at the back with knife, slip the point of the blade broadside between flesh and bone, and cut, easing the flesh from the backbone and ribs and gently drawing back the flesh as you work. Take care not to puncture the skin or abdomen. Continue working either way toward head and tail.

Turn the fish over and repeat on other side.

With point of knife, cut through skin around vent. Cut through backbone at neck and sever cords in throat; cut through backbone at tail. Be careful not to cut through skin; carefully lift backbone and ribs from the fish, bringing entrails with them. Cut away any flesh adhering to bones and use it to pad thin spots of the fish.

Large fish around five pounds and up are more easily boned than small fish.

Boning head-dressed fish (head off and tail on). Scale and cut out fins. Before cutting off the tail, continue the slit from vent to tail. Cut across to backbone.

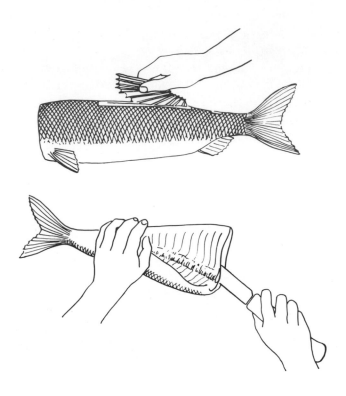

Put the fish on its side on a cutting board, and pressing the tail end down in one hand, bone the lower side first. Slip the tip of the boning knife broadside in between flesh and ribs. Ease the knife along toward the head, cutting the flesh away from the ribs. Now work back toward tail end until flesh is separated from bones on one side. Turn the fish over and repeat. Cut off the tail, and lift out the bones and any flesh adhering to them. Use this flesh to pad thin spots in the fish.

Freezing Fish

Clarence Birdseye, an American chemist working in Labrador in 1912, discovered what the natives had always known, and that was that freshly caught fish left outside in subzero weather froze instantly and retained freshness for as long as the low temperature held. That was the beginning of a complex multimillion-dollar industry from commercial processing plants to home-freezing appliances, leading up to the appearance of high-quality fresh fish year round on tables of consumer and sportsman alike.

Though winter ice-fishing, as in Birdseye's Labrador, offers conditions most favorable to the sportsman for freezing fish fresh and fast, the problems of fair-weather fishing for the freezer are considerably lessened by modern facilities, as may be seen in the foregoing pages on the care and packing of fish.

Only freshly caught, chilled, and dressed fish should be frozen, and once frozen they should remain so until thawed for cooking.

A constant temperature of $-10\,°F$ to $-15\,°F$ in the freezer assures best results.

Fresh fish are frozen dressed whole or cut into steaks, fillets, or meal-size portions. The fish is packed for the freezer in a glaze or ice blocks, or it is wrapped.

Before packing soak *lean* fish for a few minutes in a cold brine (about 1 cup coarse salt to 1 gallon water) to firm up the flesh, and *fatty* fish in a solution of ascorbic acid (1 teaspoon ascorbic acid to 1 cup water) to help delay rancidity.

If not dressed, clean the fish and wash it in cold running water. Cut off head and tail if desired. Cut out the gills, but do not scale. The more natural the covering, the better the protection from drying in the freezer.

Soak the fish as instructed above and glaze and/or wrap.

GLAZING

Glazing is a superior method of home-freezing fish; the term also covers freezing the fish in a block of ice, referred to as "blocked."

Glazing a whole fish. Freeze the fish hard. Simply dip the frozen fish in ice water (a bucket of water kept on the floor of the freezer, and used before it freezes, is a handy and quick way to do it) until a good coat of ice is formed over the entire fish, letting it freeze between dips. Wrap well in butcher's paper, food wrap or aluminum foil, pressing out all air possible. Store in the lower regions of the freezer. Check and reinforce glaze from time to time, giving thin spots special attention. No part of the fish should be exposed.

A fairly large fish, that is up to six or seven pounds, may also be frozen in a block of ice. Bigger than that can become rather cumbersome to handle in the freezer, though of course it can be done.

Block freezing. The block method, as the term suggests, means freezing the fish in a block of ice. Process baking-size whole fish individually and smaller-size fish, fillets, and steaks in meal-size quantities. Use any size or shape of container that will accommodate the fish without distorting it. Baking pans, loaf pans, lard pails—any may be used (and reused). But the container need not be of a permanent nature. A waxed cardboard milk carton is a favorite container. A cardboard box lined with plastic does an admirable job. A shoe-box, for example, accommodates a good number of small fish, fillets, or steaks. Panfish and smelts are simply frozen *en masse.*

For the big fish, a long florist's box will take it, including head and tail. A pre-paste-wallpaper-wetter serves the purpose well.

Line the bottom of the container with ice slush, or chipped ice. Lay the frozen fish on the ice. If freezing a number of head-dressed fish or fillets, arrange them neatly and without crowding to avoid distortion. Pour in chilled water until the fish is well submerged, and place the container in the bottom of the freezer, at least at −10°F. When frozen, pour more cold water over the frozen fish to be sure it is well covered with ice. If you want to retrieve the container, just remove the block of ice and wrap it well in paper or aluminum foil. Label the packages with contents and date frozen, and return to the freezer. Store at −5° to −10°F.

Examine the blocks from time to time and reinforce any thin-looking spots by pouring a little ice water on them.

Properly dressed and cared for, freshly caught lean fish have been kept moist, fresh, and sweet for more than a year by each of the above methods. Fatty fish are best used within a few months.

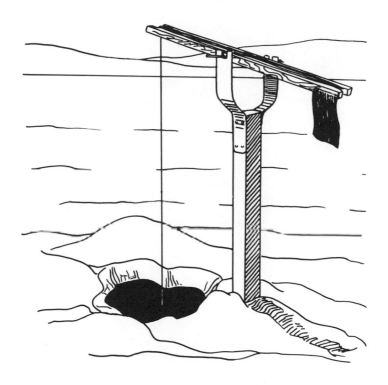

WINTER ICE FISHING

Glazing is a simple matter for the ice fisherman in freezing weather. His fish freezes instantly and he can just dip it in and out of the fishing hole. In such weather the fish often freezes hard before it can be cleaned. It should be glazed and frozen as is. Do not refreeze a frozen fish which has thawed.

If the weather permits, it's advisable to clean the fish as soon as possible. To forestall freezing, it may help to pack the fish in clean, deep snow.

In any event, refrigeration poses no problem for the ice fisherman. He has a choice of glazing his catch on the spot or taking his frozen or well-chilled fish home and doing it there.

FREEZER-WRAPPING

Package small fish, fillets, or steaks in meal-size packages. Small packages of fish tend to dry out more quickly than larger ones. A close airtight wrap, free of air pockets, is necessary to ensure a fine quality and freshness of frozen fish. Use only tough, moisture-vaporproof wrap manufactured for freezing purposes.

Use heavy duty aluminum foil. Bring edges together with a close double fold, and press out air pockets. Fold and tuck the ends under. Wrap a second time.

Use a plastic freezerproof wrap. Wrap the fish well, pressing out air pockets, and seal with freezer tape. If using plastic bags, press out air and twist-tie securely. Don't heat seal as the seal may break on freezing.

Label contents and date of freezing.

Place in lower part of freezer to freeze quickly; maintain at at least −10°F. Properly wrapped lean fish should keep for from four to six months; fatty fish are best used within three.

THAWING

For ease of handling, and generally best results, thaw frozen fish before cooking. It should be kept as cold as possible until cooking time. If you can plan ahead, let it thaw in the refrigerator; for immediate use thaw at room temperature, but do use the fish immediately while it is still cold.

Thawed fish requires the same care as fresh fish; it is even more perishable due to "drip" or loss of fluid in thawing.

Don't leave the fish uncovered while thawing, keep it well chilled, and don't keep it long before cooking.

If the fish has been glazed, wash the ice off the fish with cold water. Cover with aluminum foil or food wrap and let thaw at room temperature for immediate use, or thaw in the refrigerator.

Ice-blocked fish may be thawed quite quickly by running cold or tepid water over the block. When the fish is freed of ice, let it stand in clean, cold water until just thawed, drain and wipe dry, and cook at once; or cover with aluminum foil or food wrap, and refrigerate until thawed; drain, wipe dry, and cook at once.

If the fish is wrapped, leave wrapping on until thawed. Thaw at room temperature for immediate use, and in refrigerator for later use.

Thawing times vary with size and shape of package, and with ambient temperature. A flexible rule of thumb for each packaged or solid pound is approximately 6 to 8 hours in the refrigerator, and 2 to 3 hours at room temperature. (If packages are stacked, thawing time is increased.)

Buying Fish at the Market

The amount of fish you need to buy per serving varies a great deal, depending on appetite, the rest of the menu, and budget. However, the following amounts are reasonable: fish in the round, 1 pound; dressed fish, ¾ pound; pan-dressed fish, ½ pound; fillets and boned pan-dressed fish, ¼ pound.

The quality of fish flesh is determined chiefly by its freshness. Fresh fish have certain recognizable characteristics valuable to know when buying at the market—or accepting gifts.

The fish should pass the following tests 100%.

WHOLE FISH, ROUND OR DRESSED

1. Flesh should be firm, springing back to finger pressure.
2. Scales should be firmly attached and glisten like sequins.
3. Eyes should be well rounded and protruding, not sunken.
4. Look inside the cavity (dressed fish); there should be no bones sticking through the flesh.
5. The gills should be bright red. (Sportsmen usually cut out the gills when cleaning their fish. In commercially caught fish, the gills remain. Examination of gills indicates to fishery inspectors how long the captured fish has remained at sea.)
6. The fish should have a mild, light, fresh odor, especially noticeable in the gills. In saltwater fish, there is a trace of iodine.

FILLETS AND STEAKS

1. The flesh should be fresh-cut in appearance, the color resembling that of freshly dressed fish.
2. The flesh should be firm.
3. Odor should be mild and fresh.
4. Wrapping, if any, should be of moistureproof material with no air space between wrapping and fish.

FROZEN FISH

To be first quality, frozen fish is held at a *constant* temperature of −15°F all along the line. Otherwise it deteriorates.

As a guide offered the consumer by Canada Fisheries the following characteristics indicate that frozen fish has been properly handled:
1. The flesh is solidly frozen when purchased.
2. Appearance is firm and glossy, with no evidence of drying out, i.e., no
   white spots or parched, paperlike corners or edges. No dark spots or discoloration in the flesh and no fading of pink flesh.
3. Wrapping should be of moisture-vaporproof material, with no air space
   between wrapping and fish. (A layer of frost or snow inside a transparent
   wrapper is evidence of long storage or poor condition or both.)
4. The majority of frozen fillets on the market are packaged in cardboard boxes
   and wrapped with wax paper. The consumer must rely on established brand
   names and the reputation of the retail outlet as an assurance of quality.
5. Whole fish, frozen in the round or dressed, are frequently not wrapped.
   In this case they should be coated with a thick glaze of ice.

HOME CARE OF MARKET FISH

Care of the fish doesn't end at the market. The following precautions will
help maintain the quality even when holding it for short periods.

Fresh fish. Rush it home from the market, remove the wrapper, and wipe
the fish with a clean, damp cloth. Wrap in waxed paper, place in a tightly
covered container, and store in refrigerator. Use it within a day. If the fish
is in the round, clean it (eviscerate) and store in the same way.

Frozen fish. Keep solidly frozen in the unopened package. A *constant* temperature of −10°F to −15°F is required to maintain the quality of frozen fish.
This may be difficult to maintain in household freezer compartments, and thus
it is recommended that packaged frozen fish be kept for short periods of time.

Once thawed, use the fish immediately. Don't refreeze fish that has been
thawed; the result has little flavor and is dry, tough, and/or rubbery. Frozen
fish once thawed will not reabsorb the juices lost in thawing. In the industry
this loss is called "drip" and the drip varies with length and temperature of
frozen storage and the rate of freezing. Under ideal conditions, drip formation
is small.

Smoke and salt-cured fish. Whether frozen or unfrozen, these should be given
the same home care as other frozen or fresh fish.

Canned fish. This is graded according to quality, and stored like other canned
goods. (Avoid freezing.)

Regardless of their origin, all fishery products conform to U.S. and Canadian
specifications and are inspected on entry.

ॐ 3 ॐ

Fish and How to Cook It

Third fisherman. Master, I marvel how fishes live in the sea.
First fisherman. Why as men do aland; the great ones eat up the little ones.

—Shakespeare, Pericles

While fishes can vary enormously from one species to another, and even within a species, there are basic consistencies in fish flesh in its value as food and in its response to the application of heat. For example, a characteristic common to all fish flesh is that it has little connective tissue and it cooks quickly. Fish must not be overcooked. Fresh fish flesh may be coarse in grain, but it is never tough. It toughens or hardens, or becomes mushy with over-cooking, depending chiefly on the type of fish and the method of cooking.

The food value of fish generally is rated high, as is its digestibility; its dietary importance may be seen charted in reliable food guides. And, as explained in Chapter 2, fish flesh is very perishable.

Fish is not hung or aged in the sense that beef is. It is impossible for a fresh fish to be too fresh. Even various cures start with fresh fish.

There are consistencies in size, form, and texture in a number of different species or families that make a recipe for one species applicable to another. Then in others there are variables that must be considered, such as covering, boniness, and even appearance, that have segregated many species of edible, good flesh into another category unfortunately labeled "coarse."

Inherent texture and flavor, size, and physical characteristics all have a bearing on fish cookery. As in other animal flesh, texture and flavor are closely related; combined, the result is palatability. Inherent fattiness, the size and age of a fish, its general health and vitality, and the quality and nature of the fish's life in the water affect the texture of the flesh and in turn its flavor.

FATTINESS AND LEANNESS   Inherent fattiness is a basic factor in segregating fish for cooking purposes. Some fishes are inherently fat, some lean, and some in between. Like other animals, all healthy fish have some fat. Unlike mammals, the fat in fish is not deposited in between the muscle tissues but is distributed throughout the flesh, with the fat content higher in some parts of the fish than in others, such as under the skin, along the backbone and belly. In fishes from extremely cold northern waters it is heavy along the abdomen and around the vent.

Since flavor is in the fat, the lean fishes are generally more delicately flavored than the fatty fishes. Some lean fishes may have as much fat as the fatty ones, but the fat is concentrated in the liver. A familiar fat-and-flavor example is cod and halibut. (It's difficult to reconcile the good flavor of the fresh flesh of either with early memories of cod or halibut liver oil.)

The division can be only general, as fattiness is variable. It may depend on locale. A species may live in comfortable fattiness in a cold northern habitat, and be quite lean in warmer waters to the south.

The fat content of a fish also varies with the spawning season, and lean or fatty, the texture of the flesh is least agreeable after spawning, improving as the fish recovers its vitality.

Spring-spawning fish are at their best from fall into winter, though some of the very fatty ones like mackerel are preferred in summer when they are not fully fattened up—a matter of taste. Likewise, the fall-spawning lake whitefish is best during winter months, becoming fat and sluggish in summer.

The fatty fishes bake or broil well, as the oils provide a built-in basting and help keep the flesh moist. They take to moisture-drawing salt-curing and smoke-curing better than the lean for the same reason. However, in moist-heat cooking, the fat fish are poached rather than steamed, and even parboiled to remove excessive oils.

Lean fish, generally more delicate in both flavor and texture, cook well in dry heat with plenty of supplementary larding. By moist heat methods, lean fish are gently steamed or poached quickly, thereby retaining their natural moisture and oils and, incidentally, flavor. Properly done, deep frying in batter captures the delicate beauty of fine, lean fish flesh.

FEEDING HABITS   Both texture and flavor are affected by the feeding habits of the fish.

Basically predatory fishes—that is, those that feed on smaller fishes—have firmer, richer flesh due to their active life as hunters than do those that live lower on the marine food chain, some settling for anything edible that might come their way. Not only are the less discriminating fishes not in such trim form, but the nature of their diet is such that it requires more digestive energies, and it all shows up in the texture of the flesh.

FLAVOR   The predators at the head of the marine food chain are generally rated superior in flavor as well as texture, especially those from cold, clear, northern waters, such as the salmons, trouts, and swordfishes.

Lower on the chain are the flatfishes—the flounder family of soles, etc. Not as active as the predators, their flesh is softer and delicate in both texture and flavor, usually described as bland, a quality desirable to many, and this is a commercially valuable group of fishes. A deviant from the group is the more predaceous halibut, with firmer flesh and more flavor, one of the most valuable—and expensive—of the marine fishes.

Bottom feeders like the cod and sturgeon have rather vulgar tastes and consume anything handy that is edible.

Suckers, carp, and other so-called "coarse" fish which feed on low levels of life have not been held in high regard on the North American table. However, all can provide excellent fish flesh when caught at their best from clean, cold waters, and handled with proper field care.

SIZE   Fishes vary greatly in size and there are obvious variations within a species. A brook trout may weigh ten ounces or four, even five pounds. For practical reasons both can't be pan-fried, nor are both stuffed and baked in the whole form. But the five-pounder can be filleted and fried, or prepared in other ways.

Coarseness of grain is relative to the size and age of the fish. That is, a small fish like smelt is finer grained than a big-game game fish like tuna, and within a species the grain coarsens as the fish grows.

As mentioned above, the unprepossessing appearance or other physical characteristics of a fish of suitable size may disqualify it for baking whole or for other, so to speak, full-dress presentation on the table. This includes so-called "coarse" fish, which will be discussed presently.

HABITAT   Water quality itself has a bearing on fish flesh, and contaminants, man-made and natural, will affect flavor. Wild freshwater fish from cold, clear waters have a purity of flavor lacking in those from warm, muddy waters. Bottom feeders carry traces of their haunts, and if the bottom is muddy, a muddy flavor shows up in the fish. (Fish markets serving an ethnic trade keep carp swimming about in huge tanks. The carp are taken home and kept alive in tubs of water to rid them of their muddy flavor.) Hatchery or stock fish are generally considered inferior in flavor to their cousins in the clear-water wilds. Polluted waters are another matter.

Industrial and domestic pollutants of fresh waters and their effects on the flavor of fish have been under the scrutiny of the U.S. Environmental Protection

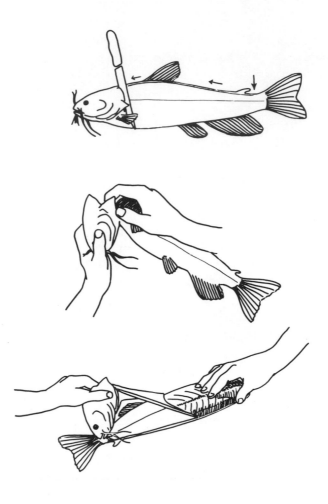

Catfish and other bottom-feeding fishes are much improved by skinning. Here is how to do it:

1. Starting at tail end, cut through skin along one side of adipose and dorsal fins. Cut through neck below gill cover under pectoral fin to backbone.

2. Snap head down to break backbone, holding the body firmly with one hand, forefinger over end of backbone.

3. Firmly but gently, pull head toward tail, bringing skin and entrails with it. Cut off at tail end.

Agency. A report prepared for that body, "Impairment of the Flavor of Fish by Water Pollutants" by Dean L. Shumway and John R. Palensky of Oregon State University, states that a wide variety of organic compounds are capable of imparting objectionable tastes and odors to the flesh of fish and in many cases at concentrations far below levels otherwise considered detrimental. "To adequately protect our freshwater fisheries, both commercial and sport," it goes on, "we must not only ensure that reproduction, growth, migration, and other essential activities of fish will be protected, but also ensure that the flavor of the flesh of fish will not be impaired beyond acceptable limits. Without this protection, otherwise productive fish populations may become largely unutilized by man."

Flavors, strong and mild, good and bad, are more evident in the skin and in the fat under the skin. An interesting example of this is the lake trout, which generally has skin of excellent flavor. The lake trout from Lake Superior and from the large, very cold lakes of northern Canada and Alaska has a strip of strong, oily fat under the skin on the backbone. Removal of this fat greatly enhances the flavor of the trout. This fat has also been found in winter-caught lake trout.

Undesirable or off-flavors may be greatly improved by filleting and skinning the fish and trimming excess fatty flesh. The court bouillon acts as a corrective flavor aid, especially in fatty fishes where there is often just too much of the flavor. (It does nothing to correct the effects of inadequate preliminary care of the fish—no treatment does.) If fish with normally good-tasting skins from a certain body of water consistently taste off-flavor, the odds are the problem is in the water, and filleting and skinning will improve the flavor.

COARSE FISH

The term "coarse" as applied to fish is an unfortunate label that sticks with some freshwater fishes in Canada. In marine fishery circles, where it simply means unmarketable fishes, it is no longer valid.

Thus in the marine sense the term reflects a culinary point of view. The coarse fish is lacking the refinements and general attributes that the consumer seeks in a good table fish, and hence it is of little or no market value. Few fish today qualify for the label.

The years of great immigration since World War II have seen much cultural enrichment in North American life, notably in the area of fish cuisine. Ethnic fish markets serving a clientele knowledgeable in fish flesh and its cookery have burgeoned over the continent, creating an unprecedented inland demand for fishes generally considered worthless, or considered not at all. Herring and cusk are no longer unmarketable; red snapper and Florida pompano no longer unheard of.

Over the past decade marine fisheries agencies of both the United States and Canada, in accommodating this interesting trend, proceeded to explore and exploit the dietary values of fish flesh in general and to wipe out the word "coarse" and its prejudicial inference. Whether attracted by the table merits of unfamiliar fishes when cooked with skill and understanding, or viewing with respect the high prices they are now inevitably commanding, the general consumer is tasting and coming back for more.

The term "coarse" in reference to freshwater fishes in Canada can be as misleading as it is confusing. It has little or nothing to do with table merits, referring simply to those freshwater species left over after game and commercial fishes have been so designated for regulation purposes.

The smelt, a "coarse" fish, has fine texture and flavor and is a very popular table fish.

The carp is a "coarse" fish in increasing demand at the fish market.

The northern pike and muskie, however, have the coarse-grained flesh that goes with their size, not to mention a superabundance of bones, but far from being coarse fish, these are among the great game fishes of Canada. They have the firm and flavorsome flesh of the predator, but are more famed for fight than for food among anglers, who have been observed to leave pike to rot on a Northern river bank in favor of the more desirable walleye.

The very qualities that segregate the coarse fish from the firm and fine of flesh make many of them particularly receptive to a flavor-enhancing smoke cure (see Chapter 7). An impressive example is the smoked Winnipeg goldeye, a gourmet viand. (See Chapter 4, Goldeye.) Before its destiny in the smokehouse was discovered, the coarse Winnipeg goldeye was described as tasting like putty. Suckers, exposed to the same treatment, provide tasty fare.

Fatty Fishes and Lean Fishes

The following list is merely representative of the edible fishes of the temperate and cold waters of North America. Fishes are listed into two major divisions: those considered characteristically "Fatty" and those considered "Lean."

Each division is grouped according to habitat: Saltwater; Saltwater and Freshwater; Freshwater Only. Fishes appear by their common names under family or genus as deemed appropriate for the purpose: *cooking*.

FATTY FISHES

H: High in fat
M: Moderately fatty

SALTWATER
Anchovies (H)
Billfishes
    Marlins (M–H)
    Sailfish (M–H)
    Spearfish (M–H)
Bluefish (H)
Butterfishes (H)
    Pacific pompano (H)
Drums
    Corvinas (M)
    Kingfishes (M–H)
    Weakfish (M)
    White sea bass (M)
Herrings
    Atlantic herring (H)
    Pacific herring (H)
    Pacific sardine (pilchard) (H)
    Spanish sardine (H)
Jacks and Pompanos
    Florida pompano (H)
    Jacks (H)
    Lookdown (H)
    Permit (H)
Mackerels
    Atlantic mackerel (H)
    Bonitos (H)
    King mackerel (H)
    Little tunny (H)
    Pacific (chub mackerel) (H)
    Skipjack (H)
    Spanish mackerel (H)
    Wahoo (H)
Porgies
    Sea bream (M)

Rays (H)
Rockfishes
    Pacific ocean perch (H)
    Redfish (ocean perch) (H)
Sablefish (M)
Smelts
    Capelin (H)
    Whitebait smelt (H)
Surfperches (H)
Swordfish (H)
Tunas
    Albacore (H)
    Yellowfin (H)

SALTWATER AND FRESHWATER
Drums
    Croakers (H)
    Red drum (H)
    Spotted seatrout (H)
Eel, freshwater
    American eel (H)
Lake whitefish (M–H)
Lamprey, sea (H)
Mullets
    Striped (M)
Porgies (M)
    Pinfish (M)
    Sheepshead (M)
Salmons: see Trouts-Salmonidae
Shads
    American shad (H)
    Hickory shad (H)
Smelts
    Capelin (H)
    Eulachon (H)
    Rainbow smelt (H)
    Surf smelt (H)
Striped bass (M)

Trouts—Salmonidae
  genus *Oncorhynchus*
    Chinook salmon (H)
    Chum salmon (H)
    Coho salmon (H)
    Pink salmon (H)
    Sockeye salmon (H)
  genus *Salmo*
    Atlantic salmon (H)
    Brown trout (H)
    Cutthroat trout (H)
    Rainbow trout (H)
  genus *Salvelinus*
    Arctic char (H)
    Brook trout (H)
    Dolly Varden (H)

FRESHWATER ONLY
Ciscos
    Bloater (M)
    Lake herring (M)
Drum, freshwater (H)
Mooneye
    Goldeye (H)
Paddlefish (roe-caviar) (H)
Sturgeon, lake (H)
Temperate basses
    White perch (M)
    Yellow bass (M)
Trouts—Salmonidae
    Arctic grayling (H)
    Golden trout (H)
    Inconnu (H)
    Lake trout (H)
    Mountain whitefish (H)
    Splake (hybrid) (H)

LEAN FISHES

SALTWATER
Codfishes
    Atlantic cod
    Cusk
    Haddock
    Hake
    Pacific (gray) cod
    Pollock
    Tomcods
Dolphins
    Dolphin
    Pompano dolphin
Flounders—flatfishes
  left-eyed and right-eyed
    Dabs
    Summer flounder (summer fluke)
    Winter flounder (winter fluke)
    Witch flounder
    Atlantic halibut
    Pacific halibut
    California halibut
    Plaice
    Butter sole
    Dover sole
    English sole (lemon sole)
    Petrale sole (brill)
    Rex sole
    Rock sole
    Diamond turbot
Puffer, Atlantic
Silversides
    California grunion
Sea basses
    Black sea bass
    Nassau grouper
    Red grouper
Searobin, northern

Snappers
   Mutton
   Red
Triggerfish

SALTWATER AND FRESHWATER
Atlantic tomcod
Snooks
Southern flounder

FRESHWATER ONLY
Carp
Catfishes
   Bullheads
   Madtoms
Burbot (ling)
Perches
   Sauger

   Walleye
   Yellow perch
Pikes
   Chain pickerel
   Grass pickerel
   Muskellunge
   Northern pike
   Redfin pickerel
Suckers
   Carpsuckers
   Quillback
   Redhorse
Sunfishes
   Crappies
   Largemouth bass
   Pumpkinseed
   Rock bass
   Smallmouth bass

Basic Cooking Methods

The most imposing of fish dishes are cooked by one of five simple, basic methods which are classic and universal. Their elegance is a matter of presentation rather than of complex recipe, and the finer the fish, the simpler the production. Nothing must be allowed to upstage the fine flavor and beautiful appearance of perfectly cooked fine fish flesh.

These five methods are frying, broiling (and barbecuing), baking, poaching, and steaming. With these five should be mentioned curing, which includes salting and heat-smoking and is the subject of Chapter 7.

The methods are applied primarily according to the size of the fish and the inherent texture of its flesh—that is, whether the fish is fatty or lean.

SIZE GUIDE

The frame of reference is the kitchen, not the trophy room. A 10-pound fish in any kitchen is a *big* fish.

The following table should be useful as a general guide. (Note: "Broil" means all the direct dry-heat methods, including barbecuing, spit-roasting, etc.)

Cut	Weight (lbs.)	Method of cooking
Whole fish		
Pan-size	1, or less	Fry, broil
Small	1–4	Split, fry, broil, bake
Medium	5–9	Bake, steam, poach
Big	9–12	Bake, steam, poach
King-size	Over 12	Cut in sections (not practical to cook whole)
	Thickness	
Fillets	Under 1 inch	Fry, broil, bake, steam, poach
	Over 1 inch	Bake, steam, poach
		Cut in chunks and deep-fry or broil, or chowder
Steaks		Pan-fry, broil, bake
Cross-sections of big fish		Bake, poach, steam whole, cut up for chowder, or deep fry

COOKING TIMES

Fish cooks very quickly and must not be overdone. It is cooked when it loses its translucence and becomes opaque in appearance, and the flesh flakes readily when prodded with a fork. This happens at 140°F to 145°F; over that it begins to break down, lose its juices, and the fish is on its way to overcooking and disaster.

Pan-baked fish: Preheat oven to 400°F. Allow 10 minutes plus 10 minutes per inch thickness at thickest part.

Fish baked in cooking film: Preheat oven to 400°F. Allow 8 minutes per inch of thickness at thickest part.

Poached fish: Allow 10 minutes per inch thickness at thickest part.

Steamed fish: Allow 12 to 15 minutes per inch at thickest part.

A meat thermometer is the surest guide to doneness for medium-size and big fish and thick cuts. Insert the thermometer in the thickest part of the fish; in a whole fish this is in the shoulder area just behind the gills.

Frying

For best results in all types of frying, the fish should be at room temperature. Frying includes pan-frying, sautéing, and deep frying.

PAN-FRYING

Small dressed fish, fillets, and steaks are pan-fried.

The fish is dusted with flour *(à la meunière),* or rolled in crumbs with a sticking agent *(à l'Anglaise),* and fried. The flour or crumb coating is desirable because it absorbs moisture on the fish and crusts on contact with the hot fat, sealing off the flesh from the fat.

The frying pan should be of cast iron or heavy-gauge aluminum, and large enough to hold the fish without distorting or crowding. A large pan also holds heat more evenly.

Bacon fat, cooking oil, vegetable oil, a mixture of oil and butter, or *clarified* butter are used for pan-frying.

PREPARATION FOR PAN-FRYING   Whole fish may be dressed whole, or head-and tail-dressed (pan-dressed) if necessary to fit the pan. Fish over an inch in thickness should be split. Fillets may be skinned or scaled; steaks retain their skins during cooking. Fish should be wiped with a damp cloth, and patted dry between paper towels to remove any surface moisture.

Next, prepare seasoned flour or crumbs.

Seasonings: Salt and pepper; if desired, add thyme, summer savory, sweet basil, or any savory seasoning you like (see list), and fresh or dry grated lemon rind. Use about ⅛ teaspoon to each ½ cup flour or fine crumbs, and up to a cup of coarser crumbs.

Crumbs: Fine, dry bread crumbs, cornmeal, crushed cornflakes, cracker crumbs, crushed potato chips, instant dry mashed-potato flakes. Avoid the instant add-water-and-stir type of cooked cereals.

à la meunière: Combine flour and seasonings and mix well in a large soup plate. Dredge the fish in the flour, covering all surfaces, and shake off excess flour. Fry. (If desired, season fish first and then dredge in flour.)

à l'Anglaise: Combine crumbs with seasonings; put them in a paper bag or on a plate. Crumbs require a sticking agent. This may be ½ cup milk or a slightly beaten egg, or both combined in a soup plate. Dredge the fish in flour, shake, then dip each piece in the liquid, put it in the bag and shake, or roll it in the crumbs. Shake off excess crumbs by tossing the fish lightly from hand to hand. This serves to press the crumbs that have stuck, and shake off those that haven't. Fry.

To FRY   Heat fat in frying pan to about ¼ inch depth. The fat should be sizzling—that is, it spits back to a flick of water, and is just short of smoking.

Fry the fish uncovered on each side until crusty brown and the flesh flakes to a prod with a fork. Turn once only.

Do not crowd the fish in the pan. Fry a few at a time if necessary. Keep cooked fish hot on a paper-lined platter in a warm oven until all fish are cooked. Do not cover, and do not overcook.

SAUTÉING

The word "sauté" comes from the French *sauter,* "to jump about." Fillets and steaks of fish are usually sautéed in preparation for serving with a sauce. The fish is browned quickly in very little fat over a brisk heat, while the pan is shaken to prevent sticking, until the fish is barely cooked. Sauté in reference to onions or *mirepoix* is extended to include light frying with constant stirring in butter or oil.

A sautéing pan is a cast-aluminum or copper skillet with a heavy, flat bottom and low sides.

PREPARATION FOR SAUTÉING   The fish should be at room temperature, at least 70°F. Fillets or steaks should be no more than an inch thick and of uniform size and shape for even cooking. Fillets should be trimmed to conform. (Set aside trimmings for a fish stock.)

The fish should be wiped dry of surface moisture, lightly dusted with seasoning (see Pan-frying), and otherwise be all ready to cook before heating the pan. Lean fish should be well oiled or buttered.

TO SAUTÉ   The pan is greased with clarified butter or cooking fat, about ⅛ inch deep, heated over a brisk heat to just short of smoking, and the fish is added immediately. The pieces should be well spaced in the bottom of the pan and the heat maintained throughout cooking. Sauté in repeated lots if necessary to avoid crowding the pan. Shake or move the fish gently to avoid sticking, and the instant the fillets are golden brown on one side, turn and brown on the other side. It should take no more than a few minutes on each side. Turn only once, and don't be afraid of undercooking.

Just as soon as the flesh loses its translucence and barely flakes to a fork, remove the fillets or steaks to a warm platter lined with paper towels and keep warm in a *low* oven.

In between lots, regrease the pan and let it return to the proper heat.

When all fillets have been sautéed, immediately deglaze the hot pan with ¼ cup red or white wine (swish the wine around in the pan) and either pour it over the fish, or incorporate the chosen sauce into it, heat thoroughly, and pour over the fish.

DEEP-FRYING

The whole virtue of good *friture* lies in the element of surprise. – *Brillat-Savarin,*
Physiologie du Gout, *Paris, 1843.*

Deep-frying is the immersion of food in boiling fat, which instantly forms a shell around the food, locking the moisture in and the fat out. The term in French cookery is *friture* (hence fritters), which covers both the method and the fat.

Small chunks of fish, fish cakes, and whole tiny fish such as smelts and whitebait are deep-fried.

The fat must be deep. Regardless of the amount of fish to be fried, good results cannot be obtained by skimping. This in turn means a large, deep pot.

A 3- to 4-quart kettle takes about 3 pounds of fat. The kettle should be big and roomy, of cast iron (Dutch oven) or cast aluminum or hammered copper. The bigger and heavier the kettle and the more fat in it, the easier to maintain the necessarily constant high temperature as food is added. The electric deep-fry appliance, used as directed, of course is excellent.

The choice of fat is important, as it must be able to attain and hold a heat of 365°F to 375°F without burning. Of the animal fats, rendered beef suet is considered best for this purpose. Vegetable shortening and cooking oils on the market are designed for the purpose and are excellent. Butter is *not* used in deep frying.

A frying thermometer is handy for gauging the temperature of the fat. A time-honored test for deep-frying temperature is by bread cube. The fat is ready if it browns a bread cube in 60 seconds.

Handy accessories are a frying basket, a slotted spoon or a skimmer, and kitchen tongs.

The action when the food is dropped into the fat must be sudden—"invasion," Brillat-Savarin calls it—a surprise attack, instantaneously forming a crusty shell around the food.

PREPARATION FOR DEEP-FRYING   The fish should be at room temperature and wiped dry of surface moisture. Cut the fillets or steaks into small pieces of uniform size. If more than one-half inch thick, score (cut a small slit along the edge).

Before deep-frying the pieces are dipped in a batter or coated with crumbs.

Crumbs: See Pan-frying, *à l'Anglaise.* Use the beaten egg dip, and follow the crumbing procedures. Arrange the pieces well-spaced in the frying basket, and lower it quickly into the fat, so that the fish is submerged and instantly seared.

Batter: There are various batters for deep-frying fish. Batters should be deep-fried only, not pan-fried, for the entire outside surface of the batter covering must be seared instantly on contact with the hot fat, otherwise it will absorb grease.

When using batter, put the basket into the pot first. Spear a piece of fish on the end of a fork, dip it in the batter, and holding it well up over the fat, ease it off the fork, letting it drop into the hot fat so that it sinks and the batter is sealed off instantly. Drop only one piece at a time so as not to reduce the heat of the fat. Cook a few pieces at a time, and do not crowd them in the pot.

Poke the pieces about gently until all are an even golden, crusty brown, raising the basket to check the progress. Lift basket and fish out of the fat and lay the pieces out on brown paper, newspaper, or paper towels in a warm oven until the remainder are cooked.

BASIC BATTERS FOR DEEP-FRYING

Proportions for 2 pounds of fish.

SOFT BATTER

1½ cups all-purpose flour	2 eggs
1 tablespoon baking powder	1 cup milk
1 teaspoon salt	

Measure, mix, and sift dry ingredients into a mixing bowl. Beat eggs, and mix in milk. Make a well in the flour, pour in the liquid, and mix, working from the middle, until all the flour is blended in and the mixture is smooth.

Variations

Onion Batter: To Soft Batter, add 2 tablespoons grated onion.

Herb Batter: To Soft Batter, add ½ teaspoon (more to taste) minced parsley, sweet basil, or a pinch of powdered savory. A touch of grated lemon rind adds a nice note.

CRISP BATTER

1 cup all-purpose flour	1 teaspoon sugar
2 teaspoons baking powder	1 tablespoon salad oil, or melted fat
1½ teaspoons salt	1 cup water

Measure, mix, and sift dry ingredients into bowl, and make a well in the middle of the mixture. Mix oil into water and pour into the well. Mix, working from the middle, until all flour is blended in and mixture is smooth.

Variations: See Soft Batter, preceding.

LEMON BATTER

1 egg
¾ cup water
Juice of 1 lemon

1 cup flour
1 teaspoon baking powder

Beat egg until light. Add water and lemon juice. Sift the flour and baking powder into a bowl, make a well in the flour, and stir in egg mixture lightly, until just smooth.

This batter has no salt in it. Salt the fish before dipping in the batter.

BEER BATTER

1 12-ounce bottle (or 1 can) light
    beer
1 cup all-purpose flour

1 tablespoon salt
1 tablespoon pepper

Pour beer into a bowl. Mix and sift dry ingredients into the beer, stirring with a whisk until batter is light and frothy. If not using at once, whisk from time to time to keep it mixed.

Broiling

Broiling, which includes barbecuing, is done by exposing the fish to be cooked directly to a source of high, dry heat. Hardwood coals or charcoal are the traditional sources of heat, and reasonable facsimiles are found in modern cooking appliances. Broiling is done over the heat (outdoor barbecue), under the heat (kitchen broiler), and sandwiched in heat, as in the vertical charcoal grills used in many institutional kitchens.

Consult the manufacturer's manual for any special instructions when using broiling appliances.

Broiling requires a very high heat. Most kitchen ovens set at "broil" deliver 500°F to 550°F. Higher heat can be attained within broiling distance in a properly operated outdoor barbecue.

In general broiling requires no more than a long-handled fork or wide spatula by way of utensils. However, fish being of the delicate nature that it is, it's handier and safer to use a hinged grill designed for the purpose on barbecue or oven rack.

PREPARATION FOR BROILING   Fish high in fat content, such as trout, salmon, shad, black Alaska cod, and mackerel, broil especially well. However, dressed fish in all forms may be broiled, provided the cuts are not too thick. Over two inches is getting a little thick for good broiling, as the fish is getting too far from the source of the heat.

Scale the fish and cut out the fins. Bring it to room temperature. Then wipe with a damp cloth and pat between two paper towels to remove surface moisture.

Broiled fish require plenty of basting, especially the lean ones. The best basting liquid is melted butter.

Lean fish. Dust lightly with flour to hold the basting and crust the surface, and dab or rub with butter. Baste during cooking with melted butter. When broiling under the heat, turn and baste again generously. When broiling over the heat, baste before turning.

Fatty fish. Trim fatty flesh from edge of cavity and around vent. Rub with melted or soft butter, plain or seasoned, on both sides of the fish.

THE BROILER METHOD

Preheat broiler to highest heat. Warm up the rack or grill and grease it before putting fish on it to prevent sticking. Space the fish on the warm, greased rack and place under the element or flame, allowing a good margin of heat exposure around the edges.

Leave the oven door ajar while broiling.

The distance of the rack from the element or flame depends on the thickness of the fish; the thinner the fish the closer to the source of heat. Timing depends on too many variables to give an exact guide. The intensity of heat, the temperature of the fish, and its thickness all affect the cooking time. The following is a rough guide. Expertise comes with practice.

Thickness	Inches from heat	Approximate total time
Thin (1 inch) Panfish, pan-dressed and split fish, fillets, and steaks. Fillets and steaks cut too thin don't broil well—they tend to dry out.	2 inches	4–6 min.
Thick (2 inches) Fillets, steaks, split fish.	6 inches	10–12 min.

Fillets with skin on or split fish should be done skin side first, then turned. They are served flesh side up. Only the flesh side need be broiled if you don't plan to eat the skin. Skinned fillets and steaks are broiled on one side, then turned and finished.

Salt, pepper, and a wedge of lemon are adequate seasoning for broiled fish, especially the delicately flavored ones, with tartar sauce or relish on the side.

Fish more robust in flavor may have a sharp Tomato Sauce or Mustard Sauce.

The four-way fish basket is a handy barbecue utensil for broiling whole fish up to 2 or 3 or more pounds. Oil the fish's cavity, stuff with *fresh* parsley, dill, and green onions, and tuck in three or four small, *hot* stones (heated on barbecue). Close with skewers.

THE BARBECUE METHOD

The patio barbecue with canopy or hood provides excellent protection against wind and efficient broiling over charcoal coals. (More elaborate charcoal and gas-fueled patio appliances come with instructions for their use which should be consulted.)

Fire the charcoal to a good bed of evenly glowing coals. Poke the coals occasionally to knock off any build-up of ash. Ash tends to insulate the coals, and while desirable for the longer-lasting fire required to cook many meats, fish cooks quickly and needs intense heat for a shorter period.

Leave the hood open, back to the wind, during broiling.

Prepare and cook the fish as for oven broiling and place it in the hinged grill or on the barbecue rack, warmed and greased, over the coals. Timing may be shorter than in the oven.

See *Broiling* and *Barbecuing* in Chapter 1.

Steaks and fillets are enhanced by marinating for a while in seasoned barbecue sauce.

THE SPIT METHOD—FISHKABOBS

Apart from spit-broiling over woodfire as discussed in Chapter 1, skewer or shish kabob is the most generally favored style of home spit cooking for fish. Its recent popularity is a revival rather than a novelty in North American cookery. The shish kabob was described in *Rational Cookery or The Cook Not*

Mad in the mid-nineteenth century as the "cububs" brought to New England by a sea-roving Captain Riley.

Kabobs are small pieces of meat broiled over hot coals. In the Middle East where the word originated, the kabobs, traditionally lamb, were skewered on the nomads' swords and broiled with no more ceremony than a fish on a North American native's forked pole. The ancient method is applied with flourish to a variety of viands and trimmings. Firm fleshed fish and shellfish adapt to the style admirably.

Fillets of fish, with skin on, are cut into pieces, and along with large shrimps and/or scallops, are marinated in a barbecue sauce. They may be marinated each in an individual sauce by varying the seasonings. The pieces of different fish are then alternated on a long skewer, spaced with squares of green and pimiento peppers, pickling onions, mushrooms, sweet cucumber pickle, etc. The whole thing is then basted and broiled over the coals.

BARBECUE BASTING SAUCES

Barbecue sauces are used for the constant basting required during dry heat broiling or barbecuing. Applied during cooking, they should be heated first. They are also used for various oven dishes.

The sauces may be used to marinate the fish first, and then heated for basting purposes.

BARBECUE SAUCE NO. 1 (OILY)
(makes 1 cup)

½ cup red table wine
1 tablespoon vinegar
¼ cup olive oil (may be part
   vegetable oil)
Dash sugar

1 small onion, grated
1 clove garlic, bruised
½ teaspoon pepper
Pinch cayenne
Bouquet garni

BARBECUE SAUCE NO. 2 (LESS OILY)
(makes ½ cup)

4 tablespoons lemon juice
½ teaspoon finely grated lemon rind
2 tablespoons honey (liquid)
2 tablespoons soy sauce

2 tablespoons salad oil, or olive oil
1 tablespoon sherry
1 clove garlic, bruised

Prepare either formula several hours or a day in advance. Blend all ingredients in a glass jar with a screw top, in the order given. Shake well until honey is dissolved. Cover and let stand, shaking from time to time. Remove bouquet garni and/or garlic. Heat in saucepan when ready to use.

May be kept for several days, but best remove the garlic after 24 hours.

SAVORY BARBECUE MARINADE OR BASTING SAUCE

¼ cup olive oil
¼ teaspoon summer savory
¼ teaspoon tarragon
¼ teaspoon finely chopped fresh
   parsley

¼ teaspoon dill seed, or branch dill,
   crushed
¼ teaspoon freshly ground black
   pepper
½ lemon, grated rind and juice

Heat the oil in a small saucepan. Add the herbs, pepper, and lemon rind, and let it brew over a very low heat for a few minutes. (Do not cook.) Stir in the lemon juice. Use hot as a basting sauce, or cool as a marinade for fish steaks.

Vary the seasonings according to preferences. Melted butter may be used instead of olive oil, or a mixture of oils.

Baking

Fish of 3 to 4 pounds and up are baked whole, with or without heads and tails, or, with a very large fish, in cross-sections of meal-size quantity. They may be boned or not boned, and baked with or without stuffing.

A fish bakes better with head and tail intact, especially a lean one, as the less exposed flesh the less moisture loss, and it has a more imposing presence on the platter.

Baked fish when done should be succulently moist inside, and crusty golden brown on the outside.

The fish is baked on its side (best profile up), without bending or distorting. (Big fish, 8–10 pounds up, are usually trussed.) A proper oval oven dish lined with oiled paper or parchment is desirable, *if* it fits the fish. The bottom of a large oval roasting pan is the next choice. That failing, improvise a pan to fit the fish.

1. A low-sided baking pan can be extended enough to catch drippings from head and tail by lining it with a double thickness of heavy-duty aluminum foil, shiny side up. Tear off the pieces of foil a good 8 inches longer than the fish. After the fish is in the pan, pinch up both ends of the foil and box ein the head and the tail.

2. An entire pan may be fashioned from doubled foil, supported on the bottom by a large biscuit or cookie sheet. The biscuit sheet with its raised sides is preferable. Measure the two pieces of foil a good 8 inches longer than the fish. Spread the foil over the sheet, shiny side up, bend up the sides, and bring the ends up, folding the corners box fashion. Sides and ends of foil should be at least 2 inches high.

3. Better still, find the perfect shape and size of light, firm, cardboard box to fit the fish. Tear off a piece of heavy-duty aluminum foil, large enough to line the inside of the box without seams. Line the inside, shiny side up, folding and pressing the foil neatly into the corners. Cover the outside of the box, dull side out, and crimp both edges of foil over the outside edge of the box. For safety, place the box on a cookie sheet or removable oven rack. Bake the fish in the box. The foil will insulate and protect the box, which will not scorch or burn as long as the fish and its juices are in it. (This is somewhat on the principle of the Indians' birchbark kettle.) When done, the box can be cut away from the fish, and it needn't be lifted. Draw off juices with a basting syringe.

If using an anodized (blue-black) bread pan for baking fish, line it with foil, oiled cooking parchment, or cooking film.

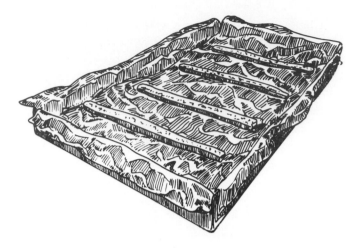

Baking pan improvised from cardboard box and aluminum foil. Pork strips across the bottom serve as a trivet.

Using any one of the above three rather precarious arrangements, take the rack out of the oven, settle the pan and fish on it, and slide it back into the hot oven. Remove the same way.

BASIC PREPARATION FOR BAKING   Frozen fish should be thawed to an easy handling point. Scale the dressed fish, cut out fins, and trim fat as required. Cut off head and tail if you must, but remember the fish bakes better with them on. The whole fish, baked to a crusty gold, garnished with cherry eyes and with a lemon wedge in its mouth is a most spectacular production of fish cookery.

Wash the fish well in cold water and pat dry inside and out with paper towels.

Stuff the fish and sew it, or bake it unstuffed. Continue according to whether fish is fatty or lean (see following).

Unstuffed fish. Rub the cavity of the dressed fish with lemon. Tuck in a few sprigs of fresh herbs (dill, fennel, thyme, savory, etc.), onion slices, and in fatty fish include a quartered apple and a few strips of green peppers. These are all discarded before serving.

Stuffed fish. Rub the cavity of the dressed fish with lemon. Stuff the fish lightly, about two-thirds to three-quarters full, leaving room for the stuffing to swell. Close the cavity with fine metal or wooden skewers or lacing pins and lace with heavy white thread, or sew it up with a darning needle and thread.

Place the fully dressed fish on a greased trivet in the pan, or on two or three slices of pork fat, or on a layer of sturdy sliced vegetables, such as carrots, onions, or thick celery sticks, in the bottom of the pan.

Preheat oven to moderately hot, 400°F. Estimate baking time at about 10 minutes plus 10 minutes for each inch thickness at thickest part.

A meat thermometer may be used. Insert it in the thickest part of the flesh—the shoulder just behind the gills. Cook to 140°F–145°F.

BAKING FATTY FISH

The fat fish bake well and retain moisture with just enough basting to help them brown. Excessive fat along abdomen and vent should be trimmed. If stuffing, choose a dry one. Rub the fish well all over with butter and put in the pan. Lightly score or gash the skin of very fat, firm-fleshed fish. Cover loosely with a piece of aluminum foil. During the cooking baste once or twice with a mixture of melted butter and white wine. Remove cover for last half estimated baking time, dust very lightly with flour, baste from the pan, and bake until the skin takes on a crispy gold and the flesh flakes to a fork.

Planked fish. Fatty fish of around 3 to 5 pounds may be baked unstuffed on a plank. A thick, unvarnished, hardwood "treed" plank is required. That is, branched grooves are cut in the surface of the plank, leading to a scooped-out dripping bowl at one end. The plank is oiled and thoroughly heated in the oven before the fish is placed on it. The plank should be longer than the fish.

The fish is served on the plank, garnished.

BAKING LEAN FISH

Lean fish tend toward dryness and require extra larding and moisture in baking. Lard them with butter or bacon fat in cavity, or use a moist stuffing. Then run a sharp knife along the backbone, making a slash in the flesh about an inch deep. Insert strips of pork fat or bacon rind with fat and hold in place with toothpicks. (Remove fat before serving.) Or score with three or four diagonal gashes; tuck in fat bacon strips.

Rub the fish with butter, dust lightly with flour, and dab it well with small pats of butter. Mix ½ cup melted butter with ½ cup white wine and pour some of the mixture over the fish, letting it run into the pan. Cover lightly with aluminum foil, pinching it to edges of pan, and put into preheated oven. Baste frequently with butter-wine mixture; when mixture is used up, baste from the pan. Remove cover for last quarter of baking time. Dust lightly with flour and baste well from the pan, letting the fish brown until gold, and until flesh flakes to a fork.

Fish baked in cooking film. Lean fish bake especially well in transparent cooking film, which allows the fish to brown through the film without loss of moisture.

Wrap the prepared fish in film. Tear off a length about 8 inches longer than the fish and spread it over the pan. The long biscuit pan or bread pan may be used, letting the wrapped fish extend over the ends if necessary.

Put the pork slices on the film. If the film is not wide enough to wrap the fish, use a second sheet for the top. Dust the fish lightly with flour, dab it generously with bits of butter, and baste with a little of the butter-wine mixture. (See Lean Fish above.) Bring up the sides of the film and double-fold it loosely over the fish. Gather up the ends and twister tie. Bake in a preheated 400°F oven, about 8 minutes per inch of thickness, until well browned. Carefully open the top fold and let steam escape. (Be careful—the steam can give a nasty burn.) Test with a fork, and if it doesn't flake, leave the fish uncovered a little longer until done. Unwrap and remove the fish carefully to a warm platter.

Remove trussing, pins, and threads before garnishing and serving. Save drippings for sauce or stock, collecting them with a basting syringe if necessary.

Garnish before or after baking, depending on the style of recipe.

A TRUSSED FISH: A PRODUCTION

Fish 10 to 12 pounds may be stuffed and trussed for baking. The stuffing, which swells, should fill no more than two-thirds of the cavity. Sew the cavity closely with needle and heavy cotton or linen thread, and truss. The fish can be made to take on the appearance of fine fighting form by lacing it as shown, manipulating the string, and settling the fish in the baking pan. It may need a little scaffolding. A secure support for the tail can be made with an open-ended coffee can dented to fit under the tail, or make one of wooden tinker toys. The head may be raised on a jar ring.

Scale and cut out all but the dorsal fins, and otherwise prepare as for baked fish.

The trussed, baked fish will not be covered during baking, and requires constant basting attention. Prepare an ample basting mixture of melted butter

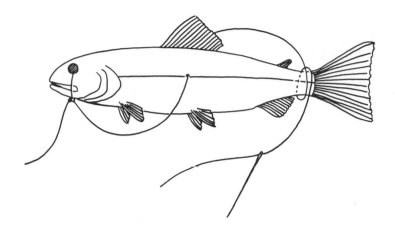

and white wine. The method is most successful with the fatty, handsome game fishes with their built-in moisture—the big trouts, salmons, chars, albacore and bonito tunas.

The trussed fish takes longer to bake, and bakes more slowly than untrussed. Put the fish into a preheated 375°F oven and bake, basting frequently, first with the wine mixture, then from the pan as drippings accumulate. If it is browning too quickly, lay a piece of aluminum foil lightly over the top, shiny side up, and remove after 15 or 20 minutes. Allow about 15 minutes per inch of thickness. When nearly done dust very lightly with flour, baste all over, and brown until crispy gold and the flesh in the thickest part flakes to a fork.

Remove carefully to a large china or highly polished silver platter (or suitably sized tray covered with aluminum foil). Remove trussing and thread, letting some stuffing spill out. Place a bit of truffle, halved black olives, or green cherries in the eyes. Should there be any unattractive break in the skin, stick a piece of cherry or truffle over it and a few more here and there for balance.

Surround with a few black olives, small pink shrimps, sprigs of fresh parsley or fennel—or an attractive garnish with an eye to the color of the fish. It should be only enhanced, not overwhelmed.

Serve one of the velouté or béchamel sauces on the side, again with color in mind. If using Wild Rice and Partridge Stuffing, simply serve extra stuffing along with lemon wedges.

Serves a dinner party of about 10 to 12.

TRUSSING A BIG FISH Big fish, in the 5- to 10-pound class, may be trussed in the shape of an "S." This way the fish not only can be made to fit into a large, round kettle or conventional roasting pan, but when done artistically, presents a most impressive appearance on the table.

To truss the fish, thread a trussing needle or large, long darning needle with butcher twine. Cut a piece of twine about four times the length of the fish. Pass the twine through the eye sockets and under the jaws, tying firmly, and leaving one long, loose end of twine. Continue, running the needle through the midsection of the fish. Draw the twine tight, and run the needle through or around the narrow part (caudal peduncle) in front of the tail. Draw the twine tightly and tie to loose end at head. This can be done so that the tail takes a pert upward flip. The fish, wrapped in cheesecloth, is then steamed or cooked in court bouillon.

CARVING A BAKED FISH

Lean fish, small to medium size. Run carving knife along the back, tip of knife between flesh and backbone, from head to tail, skipping over the dorsal fin to avoid loosening the small root bones. With fish server, lift portions of fillet from ribs, leaving the skeleton intact. The entire fillet may be lifted to a serving platter if desired. Turn the fish over and serve the other side. If stuffed, spoon out stuffing with each portion.

Fatty fish; lean big fish. Carve along back as above, skipping the dorsal fin. Skin if desired. Lift portions from the fillet only. This is the choice part of the fish. Turn the fish over and serve the other side in the same manner.

STUFFINGS

The stuffing is a savory preparation for filling the cavity of a fish. Stuffings when cooked should be light, moist, and fragrant. Like all accessories they should complement rather than overpower the feature attraction—the fish.

Lean fish which tend toward dryness require a stuffing which is moist and which serves to help keep the fish moist during cooking. Thus fats and liquids are included in its making. The naturally fat fishes require a drier stuffing which draws its moisture from the fish. Thus a variation of the basic moist recipe may be adjusted to the fatty fishes by omitting or reducing the fat or liquid content.

Bread is the traditional base for stuffing. However, when it comes to stuffing fish, bread must take second place to wild rice when available. Bread should be dry enough that it crumbles between the fingers; wild rice should be precooked to dry fluffiness, its kernels separated in little curls. Brown or white rice, which incidentally is *no* relation of wild rice, is often used as a substitute for bread; it, too, should be dry and fluffy.

The guide to seasonings given with the recipe for Basic Stuffing is applicable to any of its variations. Seasonings should not be overdone. Herbs and spices should be identifiable by bouquet rather than obvious taste.

Prepare stuffings in advance and let stand an hour or so to blend.

As a guide to quantity requirements, the basic recipe makes 2 cups, about average to stuff a 5- to 6-pound fish. Amounts may be adjusted according to need.

BASIC STUFFING
Moist Bread, or Wild Rice

1½ cups stale bread crumbs, or cooked wild rice	2 tablespoons chopped celery (optional)
1½ teaspoons thyme, or other herb	1 tablespoon minced onion
⅛ teaspoon salt	2 tablespoons butter, clarified
Pinch pepper	¼ cup warm stock, or milk

Toss seasonings and bread crumbs or rice together. Sauté celery and onion in clarified butter until translucent, and add to crumbs, or rice, and toss lightly and well.

Sprinkle stock, or milk, over dressing and toss again to blend.

For dry stuffing, omit stock from Basic Stuffing. Toss other ingredients together.

A delicate cooking oil may be substituted for clarified butter; this is a matter of taste.

In the above recipe, thyme, a medium savory, is used as an example. Herbs may be varied or mixed according to taste or supplies. The stuffing may be more or less highly seasoned by switching or blending herbs, or by using more or less of them.

HERBS

Pungent	*Medium*		*Mild*
Oregano	Basil	Rosemary	Chervil
Sage	Caraway	Summer savory	Parsley
Tarragon	Marjoram	Thyme	
Winter savory			

FRUIT STUFFING
(dry/medium seasoning)

¼ cup slivered almonds
1 ring candied pineapple, finely
    sliced
½ cup candied cherries, red and
    green, sliced
1½ cups stale bread crumbs, or
    cooked wild rice
1 small onion, chopped fine

2 tablespoons clarified butter, or
    cooking oil
½ teaspoon summer savory or thyme
1 teaspoon celery salt
½ teaspoon sweet basil
½ teaspoon salt
Dash white pepper

Combine fruit and nuts with dry ingredients and proceed as in Basic Stuffing.

For moist stuffing, add ¼ cup warm meat stock.

BROWN BREAD STUFFING
(moist/well-seasoned)

1 teaspoon crushed savory
1 teaspoon crushed sage
½ teaspoon salt
⅛ teaspoon white pepper
¼ cup raisins, washed

1½ cups stale brown bread, or
    oatmeal bread crumbs
1 small onion, chopped
2 tablespoons clarified butter
1 egg, beaten
¼ cup warm milk

Add seasonings and raisins to bread crumbs and toss well to blend.
Sauté onion in butter until translucent, and pour over crumbs. Blend well.
Stir beaten egg into milk, and pour over stuffing. Blend well, tossing lightly.
Stuff very lightly.

Variation: Add ¼ cup oysters, drained and coarsely cut.

WILD RICE MUSHROOM STUFFING
(dry/medium seasoning)

1 tablespoon grated onion
½ cup finely diced celery
¼ cup diced mushrooms

2 tablespoons clarified butter
1½ cups cooked wild rice
Salt and pepper to taste

Sauté onion, celery, and mushrooms in butter until light gold, and blend into rice. Add salt and pepper and toss lightly to blend.

BLENDER STUFFING
(moist, but not wet/well-seasoned/quick and easy)

2 cups fine, dry bread crumbs	½ teaspoon dry, crushed tarragon
1 egg	Salt and pepper to taste
¼ cup melted butter	1 stick celery, plus leaves
½ teaspoon dry, crushed chervil	1 medium onion, or to taste
½ teaspoon powdered sage or	1 small can clams, plus ¼ cup juice
savory, or seasoning to taste	1 tablespoon whiskey

In blender, process oven-dried bread to fine crumbs and put in mixing bowl. Put egg in blender, turn on, add melted butter and seasonings. Blend for a few seconds, and leave motor running. Then add, one at a time, celery, onion, and clam juice and blend to a homogenous mixture. Add clams and whiskey, blend a few seconds and turn off.

With a spoon, blend the mixture into the crumbs, tossing lightly with fingers until uniformly mixed. Let stand for an hour, and then lightly stuff the fish.

Ideal for the lean fish, this stuffing may be used for a fatty fish by reducing butter and omitting the clam juice.

WILD RICE AND PARTRIDGE STUFFING
(moist/lightly seasoned)

2 cups steamed wild rice	1 small onion, diced and sautéed
1 cup mushroom sauce, heavy OR	1 teaspoon mild herb seasonings,
1 10-ounce can cream of mushroom	chervil, parsley
soup	Dash mace or allspice
1 cup cubed cooked partridge, or	Salt to taste
other wildfowl	

If you have no wild rice, you will have to make plain rice do. If no wildfowl, then chicken. Mix everything together, let it rest for an hour or so, then stuff the fish very lightly, and sew it up. Extra fresh, diced and sautéed mushrooms may be added to the stuffing.

A moist stuffing, but good with both fatty fishes and lean.

VEGETABLE STUFFING
(moist/medium seasoning)

¼ cup butter

½ cup fine, soft bread crumbs

1 cup thinly sliced celery

1 medium onion, thinly sliced

1 young carrot, thinly sliced

½ green pepper, slivered

3 firm red tomatoes, chopped

½ cup coarsely chopped mushrooms

2 tablespoons chopped fresh parsley

1 teaspoon dill seed

Melt the butter, pour it over the bread crumbs, and mix well. Combine with the vegetables, add the parsley and dill seed, and toss lightly to blend.

Steaming and Poaching

Steaming and poaching are moist-heat methods of cooking fish, usually the basic cooking of the many fish dishes, plain and fancy, from a simple fillet in cream sauce to a magnificent Arctic char in galantine. These are gentle operations; the fish must not be overcooked.

Lean fish are either steamed or poached. Fatty fish are poached by gently simmering in a court bouillon to float off excessive oils. They may also be lightly poached (parboiled) and then steamed. "Boil" is an improper term in fish cookery. Fish is simmered, never boiled.

STEAMING

Fish is steamed over boiling water. A fish steamer, which is also a poacher, is a handsome oblong utensil. It has a perforated tray with handles to support the fish and is used to lift the fish in and out. Except perhaps for the panfishes, all sizes and cuts of lean fish may be steamed.

The size or amount of the fish to be cooked in the steamer is limited by the size of the steamer, for the whole fish should not be distorted by the kettle in any way, and pieces should not be piled into the steamer.

A steamer may be improvised to accommodate a few fillets by arranging sealer rings or small cans, both ends opened, in the bottom of a deep saucepan with a cover and placing a rack or a well-perforated aluminum pie pan on the rings, keeping the water level below the pan. Put the fish on a length of cheesecloth, long enough that the ends will hang over the edges of the saucepan, to facilitate lifting the fish in and out. A similar arrangement in a roasting pan with a cover will take a fairly big fish, using the rack for support. Again, use cheesecloth.

An old-fashioned way of dealing with the outsize (king-size) fish was to steam or poach it in a copper wash boiler. The fish was slung in a hammock arrangement of linen toweling or strong doubled cheesecloth over or in the water, ends of the cloth tied securely to the handles of the boiler. It still works.

PROCEDURE FOR STEAMING   Wipe the dressed fish with a damp cloth. Pour water into the steamer to below the level of the rack or pan, and bring to a boil. Aromatic spices and vegetables or herbs, along with white wine, may be added to the water. Lay the fish on the rack, cover tightly, and let steam until the fish flakes to a fork. Cooking time depends on the amount and shape of the fish. Allow about 10 minutes per inch of thickness at thickest part. A 2-pound fish takes about 20 to 25 minutes. Lift the fish out as soon as done. Steamed fish is served hot with one of the many basic sauces or variations thereof, and garnished, or is used cold or for recipes calling for cooked fish.

Oven-steamed fish. Unstuffed, lean small fish and fillets completely wrapped in aluminum foil may be cooked in the oven. They steam in their own juices rather than bake. It's an excellent method, especially when a few aromatic vegetables such as onion, green peppers and celery and a bit of wine basting are included in the package. Wrap the fish loosely in aluminum foil, shiny side in, closing the package with double folds to keep the steam in. Put into hot oven (450°F); allow 10 minutes plus 10 minutes for each inch thickness of the fish.

POACHING

Poaching is cooking in liquid at a low simmer. Two types of poaching are used here. One, for small items of lean fish, uses shallow liquid and is self-basting. The other is the deep court bouillon used for fatty and big fish. Fish may be poached in the deep court bouillon as a flavor aid. (See Chapter 3, *Habitat.*)

Fillets, steaks, and the smaller of whole lean fishes are poached in a fish fumet or a fish stock, or in the case of delicately flavored fish, salt and water (1 teaspoon per quart), enough to cover the rack.

Bring the fumet or stock to a boil. Lower the fish onto the greased rack, spread in a single layer. Cover with a poaching parchment (a circle of cooking parchment cut to the size of the pan and with a small hole in the center), or with a circle of aluminum foil or a disposable lightweight pie plate punched with a few pinholes to allow the escape of any steam build-up. Reduce the heat to a bare simmer and cook gently until the fish flakes, about 10 minutes for 1-inch thick cuts.

Small cuts of fish are also poached in the oven; lean white-fleshed fish and cold-smoked and salt-cured fish are poached in milk. Spread the fish in a single layer over the bottom of a buttered or greased baking dish with cover, season to taste with salt, pepper, minced parsley or other herb such as fennel or tarragon, and add a small amount of concentrated fumet, stock or milk, enough to completely cover the bottom of the dish. Cover with cooking parchment or oiled paper, put the lid on and cook in a pre-heated hot oven, 450°F. Allow about 10 minutes for each inch thickness of the fish and allow an extra 3 or 4 minutes for a glass or ceramic dish to heat through. In either case, use the remaining fumet or stock to make a velouté sauce for the fish.

POACHING IN COURT BOUILLON   Fatty fishes are poached immersed in a deep court bouillon. The fish is served directly, with a sauce, or it is used in one of the many preparations calling for precooked fish.

The court bouillon is a "shortly boiled" aromatic liquor in which fish and shellfish are cooked, the aroma arising from any number and combination of ingredients. The term, borrowed from classic French cookery, is applied rather loosely here. There is plenty of scope for creative cookery in our court bouillon. The court bouillon both enhances natural flavors and helps correct diet or inherent off-flavors in the fish. (It does *not* disguise or correct the results of inadequate care of the fish.) The court bouillon is especially useful in cooking fatty fishes, as excessive oils are rendered out.

The court bouillon is not a fish stock, though it may contribute to making one. It is usually discarded after it has done its job.

The court bouillon is usually made in the kettle in which the fish is to be cooked, and then allowed to cool. Small fish, fillets, and relatively small pieces of fish require only a saucepan large enough to allow them to be submerged. The fish should be tied loosely in wet cheesecloth to prevent separating and to ease lifting.

Large fish, dressed or pan-dressed, require a large kettle. Lacking a proper fish kettle, a large, deep stock pot, deep roasting pan or copper boiler, may serve the purpose. Wrap the dressed fish, washed and dried, in wet cheesecloth (dipped in the court bouillon), leaving tabs long enough to hang outside the kettle for easy handling. Lower the fish into the cool court bouillon. If necessary to curl the fish, let the tail take an upward curve, or truss the fish. The body of the fish must be entirely submerged. If necessary, add water and wine until it is covered.

Bring slowly to a boil, turn down the heat, and let simmer gently allowing 10 minutes per inch of thickness at *thickest* part of the fish. This applies to *trussed* thickness of a trussed fish.

Skim as much fat from the surface as possible and lift out the fish at once. If not serving hot, leave the fish in the wet cheesecloth until cool. It may be better for flavor and moisture to let the fish cool in the court bouillon, but the hazard of overcooking outweighs the advantages, and the fish can become waterlogged.

Parboiling. It may be desirable to "twice-boil" an extremely large (5 pounds and up), fat fish. Leave it in the initial court bouillon (or just salted water) at a bare simmer for 10 to 20 minutes. Skim off the oily surface broth, lift out the fish, empty the kettle and continue with a fresh, hot court bouillon or finish by steaming. Be careful the fish doesn't overcook.

MAKING COURT BOUILLON   The quantity of court bouillon depends upon the size or amount of fish to be cooked and the size and shape of the pot. The court bouillon must cover the fish. Court bouillons may be concocted to one's fancy by varying the seasonings (see following table), but always with a light hand. The *bouquet garni,* faggot, or spice bag is useful when experimenting, as it may be removed at any time from the pot.

SEASONINGS FOR COURT BOUILLONS, FUMETS, AND STOCKS

Aromatics and Spices	*Herbs*	*Aromatic Vegetables*
Capers	Bay leaf	Carrot
Chili peppers, whole	Dill weed	Celery
Cloves, whole	Fennel weed	Garlic
Mace	Sweet basil, thyme	Green pepper
Mixed pickling spices	(and others)	Onion
Pepper (black and		Pimiento
white), whole		Tomato

Following are three basic court bouillons.

COURT BOUILLON NO. 1
(mild)

1 slice of lemon
1 cup white wine
3 cups water
1 onion, sliced
3 or 4 slices carrot
1 small piece bay leaf

2 sprigs fresh parsley
1 branch fresh thyme
¼ teaspoon peppercorns
1 teaspoon salt
Dash garlic powder

Put all ingredients into a deep saucepan and bring to a boil. Cover. Turn down heat and let simmer gently for about 15 minutes. Cool.
Makes about 1 quart.

COURT BOUILLON NO. 2
(aromatic; for robust-flavored fish)

¼ cup vinegar, or lemon juice
6 cups water
1 large carrot, sliced
2 sticks celery, with tops, broken
2 strips green pepper

1 large onion, sliced
1 tablespoon mixed pickling spices
    tied in cheesecloth
½ teaspoon salt

Combine everything in a deep saucepan. Bring to a boil, cover and cook gently for 15 minutes. Remove pickling spices at discretion. Cool.
Makes about 1½ quarts.

COURT BOUILLON NO. 3
(medium)

3 quarts water
½ cup white vinegar
2 large onions, sliced
3 large carrots, sliced
2 or 3 sticks celery, with tops,
    broken

1 bay leaf
1 teaspoon dried parsley flakes
¼ teaspoon dried savory, thyme,
    chervil, or tarragon
½ teaspoon crushed peppercorns
2 tablespoons salt

Combine everything, cover, and cook gently for 15 to 20 minutes. Cool.
Makes about 3 quarts.

STOCK

Stock is called for in the preparation of many fish dishes and accessories—chowders, soups, sauces, and so on. It is the result of cooking the fish trimmings in salted water, with or without other liquid, vegetables, and seasonings. A fumet is a concentrated stock.

Court bouillon in itself is not a stock, though it may contribute to making one.

Whenever possible stocks or fumets should be made from the fish that they will eventually accompany. Avoid using stocks from strong-flavored fish like mackerel in preparing delicately flavored fish like sole. Stock should be made from fresh fish as soon as the fish is dressed.

The trimmings from the rich-fleshed fatty game fishes make an excellent stock for soups and aspics.

If the fish has been skinned for flavor improvement, don't use the skin in the stock.

FISH STOCK NO. 1

2–3 slices onion
½ cup mushroom stems or
    trimmings, if available
1 tablespoon chopped fresh parsley
1 teaspoon chopped thyme, or a
    pinch dried thyme and/or other
    seasonings and spices

1 bay leaf
½ teaspoon salt
2 pounds fresh fish trimmings,
    bones, heads, fins, tails, washed
2 cups cold water
⅓ cup dry white wine
1 thin slice lemon, twisted

Put vegetables and seasonings in bottom of stock pot or saucepan. Cover with fish trimmings. Add water and wine to cover; add the lemon. Cover lightly with lid, slowly bring to a boil, then reduce heat and skim. Simmer uncovered for about 30 minutes.

Cool slightly and strain through three thicknesses of cheesecloth or muslin which has been wrung out in cold water. Store in refrigerator until needed or freeze to have on hand. Use for poaching, chowders, or fish sauces.

FISH STOCK NO. 2

1 tablespoon butter, or margarine	A few peppercorns
1 clove garlic	1 teaspoon salt
1 onion, sliced	A small bouquet garni
½ cup chopped leeks	2 pounds fish trimmings, bones,
1 medium carrot, sliced	heads, fins, tails, washed
1 stick celery, broken	2 cups cold water
1 bay leaf	½ cup white wine

Melt the butter, add the garlic and vegetables, and cook gently for about 5 minutes. Add the seasonings, then lay the fish trimmings over all. Add water and wine to cover. Bring slowly to a boil, and cook gently for about 30 minutes. Cool slightly, strain, and store as instructed in preceding recipe.

ASPICS AND JELLIED STOCK

Aspics and cold jellied preparations call for crystal-clear stock.

To clarify stock: Cool the strained stock. Degrease completely by lifting the grease from the surface of the cold stock.

Use the white of 1 egg plus 1 teaspoon water for each quart of stock. Whip egg white and water until frothy.

Put the degreased stock back on to heat. Stir in the whipped egg white as the stock warms, and continue stirring until it comes to a boil and froths up. Stop stirring and allow to boil for about 3 minutes. Strain through a sieve lined with clean, doubled cheesecloth or fine muslin. The strained stock should be crystal clear.

Pour into clean jars, cover, and cool in refrigerator for use within days. Or fill clean glass jars two-thirds full, cover *loosely,* cool, and fast freeze. Tighten covers and store in freezer.

To make aspic or jelly. Reduce 1 pint clarified stock by half. Soften 1 tablespoon (envelope) plain gelatin in cold water. Stir into the stock, and stir over the heat until well mixed. Remove from heat, let thicken to pouring consistency, and use as directed in recipes. This makes 1 cup aspic.

Should the aspic become set, or too stiff to pour, it will be necessary to melt it down and start the cooling process again. The stiffened aspic may be refrigerated and melted down as needed.

FISH FUMET

Fish recipes involving poaching or the making of sauces call for a fish fumet as part or all of the liquid. A basic recipe may be made up and freezer-stored in likely recipe quantities.

FUMET

2 pounds fish trimmings, fins, bones, heads, tails. Include skins unless they have been removed for flavor improvement purposes. (Avoid strong-flavored trimmings from fish like mackerel, skate, mullet.)
2 cups water
2 cups white wine

1 large onion, stuck with a clove
1 large carrot, scraped and split
2 celery sticks, including tops, broken
2 tablespoons parsley
1 bay leaf
½ teaspoon cracked peppercorns
¼ teaspoon salt

Combine all ingredients in a large saucepan and bring to a boil. Cover lightly. Turn down heat and let simmer until liquid is reduced by half, about an hour. Strain the liquid through a sieve lined with double cheesecloth, letting it drip undisturbed into a container for about ½ hour.

A fumet may be made from residual juices from baking a fish

As the fumet is simply a concentrated fish stock, it may also be made by boiling down a fish stock.

Sauces for Fish

A fine sauce can transport a simply cooked fish to the realm of *haute cuisine,* extending the ways of serving beyond count. (Consider the sole!)

Sauces need be neither costly nor complicated; practically all ingredients may be found in the kitchen larder. Most fine fish sauces are made quickly from a simple basic white sauce that can be prepared ahead and kept on hand in refrigerator or freezer. What counts with a sauce is the few minutes of loving care and undivided attention that goes into its creation.

A sauce is not a disguise. Seasonings should be used with a light touch, their only purpose to enhance the fish.

CULINARY TERMS

It will help to familiarize yourself with a few basic terms that recur frequently in sauce and other recipes:

Fines herbes (fine herbs): A mixture of medium and/or mild herbs, used as called for in recipe.

Bouquet garni: A bundle of fresh or dried branches of herbs tied together with thread or string. Used in court bouillons, fumets, or any moist-heat cooking.

Clarified butter: Butter that has been heated in a pan, skimmed, and poured off, leaving sediment behind. The procedure is described later in this chapter under *Clear Butter Sauces.*

Faggot: Herbs and spices sandwiched between two chunks of celery and tied securely. Lay the herbs in the curve of a piece of celery 2 or 3 inches long, burying the small spices in the middle. Peppercorns, chilis, etc., are thus tucked safely inside the faggot instead of being lost in the brew until too late. Put a second piece of celery on top and tie the faggot securely. Practically the same thing is achieved by tying the seasonings in a cheesecloth bag.

Bouquet garni and faggots may be removed at any point of cooking, eliminating the possibility of overseasoning and the necessity of straining the brew.

Suggested contents of a faggot: 1 small strip lemon peel
1 branch parsley
Peppercorns
Bay leaf
Mace

Mixed pickling spices: A mixture of aromatic spices consisting of allspice, celery seed, tiny chili peppers, cloves, mustard seed, bay leaf, and others as desired such as cumin and coriander. Tied in a cheesecloth bag, the spices may be removed when desired flavor is attained. A packaged mixture of pickling spices is available in many areas.

Croutons: Small cubes of dry bread fried in clarified butter. May also be deep-fried in oil.

Mirepoix: A dice of aromatic vegetables—carrots, celery, green and red sweet peppers, onion—sautéed in oil or butter.

Roux: Equal parts of fat and flour cooked together, forming the base of a flour-thickened sauce. A light *roux* is usually used with fish sauces. Stir flour into melted fat and cook, stirring constantly, until smooth and bubbly.

Beurre manié: Kneaded butter, used to thicken soups and stews. Mix flour into medium-soft butter until texture is mealy, and butter will take up no more flour. Start with a fork and finish with fingers to get feel of the texture.

Seasoned flour: Flour seasoned with salt, pepper and other seasonings as desired. Mix in proportions of ½ teaspoon salt and ¼ teaspoon pepper to each ½ cup flour.

EQUIPMENT FOR MAKING SAUCES

Use a saucepan of even-heating, fast-conducting metal, such as cast aluminum or tin-lined copper, enamel, or ceramic-coated iron. White sauces requiring no browning may be made in the top part of a double boiler. If the sauce is to contain wine, lemon juice, or vinegar, avoid using aluminum or tin, as it may cause discoloration of the sauce.

Use a wooden spoon or a whisk to stir—it will scrape without scratching the bottom of the pan and stir without bruising the sauce.

Work with a deft, gentle touch and a constant eye.

Have equipment and measured ingredients ready within easy reach; to stop stirring in order to measure or find something can result in ruining the texture or scorching the sauce.

SEASONINGS FOR FISH SAUCES

Aromatics and Spices	*Herbs*	*Aromatic Vegetables*
Allspice	Basil	Carrot
Capers	Bay leaf	Celery
Cayenne	Chervil	Chive
Celery seed	Dill weed	Garlic
Chili	Marjoram	Green pepper
Commercial seafood seasoning	Oregano	Onion
Cumin	Parsley	Pimiento
Curry	Rosemary	Tomato
Dill seed	Sorrel	
Fennel seed	Tarragon	
Mace	Thyme	
Mustard, dry		
Mustard seed		
Paprika		
Pepper (black and white)		
Saffron		
Turmeric		

BASIC WHITE SAUCES

White sauces are made by thickening a fish fumet, white stock, or milk with a light *roux*. In a light *roux* equal parts of fat and flour are cooked together but are not allowed to brown. Clarified butter gives the best results. (See Clear Butter Sauces.) White sauce using stock is called velouté, and that using milk is generally referred to as a béchamel. These two mother sauces by their variations and applications have an endless number of offspring, and still offer scope for creative saucery in the use of seasonings.

Following are recipes for two basic white fish sauces, Velouté Sauce and Béchamel Sauce, and some of the variations of each, as well as, among others, a few brown sauces. All sauces need not be thickened—for example, the butter sauces; the side sauces are not even cooked.

VELOUTÉ SAUCE

2 tablespoons butter	Salt and white pepper to taste
2 tablespoons flour	Mushroom stems and skins, if handy
2½ cups hot fish stock	

Melt butter in saucepan or top of double boiler and stir in flour. Stir over low heat until mixture is a smooth, bubbly liquid, just about to turn a golden color. Add the hot stock and stir until smoothly thickened, stirring up from the bottom of the saucepan. Add seasonings and mushroom bits. Lower heat and simmer for 1½ hours, or cook over gently boiling water in double boiler. Stir and skim frequently. As the stock is usually seasoned, the sauce may not need any further seasoning; this is a matter of taste. Strain if necessary, and it is ready to serve.

The velouté may be made in advance and refrigerated for future use as a base for other sauces. Store in recipe-size covered containers, brushing the surface of the sauce with melted butter. Cover tightly. Sauce should keep in refrigerator up to two weeks as long as container is not opened.

BERCY SAUCE

1 tablespoon shallots, minced	1 cup Velouté Sauce
4 tablespoons butter	1 tablespoon chopped parsley
½ cup fish stock	½ cup white wine

Cook shallots gently in 1 tablespoon butter until soft, add stock and wine, and boil to reduce by half. Blend in the Velouté, bring to a boil, and cook for 2 or 3 minutes over a good heat, stirring gently with a wooden spoon. Remove from heat.

Blend in 3 tablespoons butter with a swirling motion, sprinkle the parsley over the sauce, and serve.

BEETROOT AND HORSERADISH SAUCE
(a Russian sauce)

1 cup Velouté Sauce	½ teaspoon sugar
½ cup prepared horseradish	½ teaspoon salt
½ teaspoon dry mustard	½ cup grated cooked beets
3 tablespoons vinegar	

Heat the Velouté Sauce in a double boiler.

To hot sauce add horseradish, mustard, vinegar, sugar, and salt and cook for about 10 minutes over boiling water, stirring frequently. Add the cooked beets and heat for another few minutes. Chill and serve with steamed or poached fish or aspics of white-fleshed fish.

DUXELLES

1 cup mushrooms	Nutmeg
1 small onion	Salt and pepper
2 tablespoons butter	

Dice the mushrooms, including stems, very fine. Press in a fine sieve or twist in a cloth to squeeze out moisture. Mince onion and cook in butter until translucent. Add mushrooms, a dash of nutmeg, salt and pepper to taste, and stir over a high heat to cook off moisture remaining in the mushrooms. Cool and store in refrigerator for use with various sauces.

DUXELLES SAUCE
(mushroom sauce)

2 tablespoons duxelles	½ cup hot Velouté Sauce
½ cup white wine	¼ cup tomato paste

Add wine to mushroom mixture, heat over medium heat, and reduce it by half. Blend the tomato paste into the hot velouté, and add the mushrooms to the mixture.

ALLEMANDE SAUCE

1 egg yolk   1 cup Velouté Sauce
1 cup fish fumet   1½ tablespoons butter

Combine egg yolk and fumet in a cold saucepan and stir until evenly mixed. Add the Velouté Sauce and mix with a whisk until evenly blended. Put over a medium-low heat to cook. Stir constantly with a wooden spoon to prevent sticking and boiling, and cook and stir until the sauce is thick enough to coat the spoon. Don't let it boil at any time. Immediately stir in the butter and remove from heat. Correct the seasonings. Strain through fine sieve and keep in double boiler over hot water, stirring frequently to prevent scumming, until needed.

NORMANDE SAUCE

1 cup fish fumet   ½ cup plus 4 tablespoons cream
2 tablespoons mushroom skins   3 tablespoons butter
1 cup Velouté Sauce

Combine fish fumet and mushroom skins in a saucepan and reduce by half over a medium heat. Remove from heat. Stir in the Velouté Sauce, blend well, then blend in the ½ cup cream. Return to heat. Stirring constantly with a wooden spoon, cook gently but don't let it boil, until reduced by half. Remove from heat and blend in butter and remaining cream. Strain through a fine sieve.

WHITE WINE SAUCE

2 cups Velouté Sauce   Pinch cayenne
¼ cup dry white wine   1 tablespoon lemon juice
1 cup fish stock   ½ cup butter

Combine the Velouté Sauce, wine, and fish stock; add the cayenne. Heat to a boil, turn down heat and reduce by half. Stir frequently. Remove from heat and stir in first the lemon juice and then the butter. Blend well. Stir until desired consistency is reached.

BÉCHAMEL SAUCE

2 tablespoons butter	Small piece bay leaf
2 tablespoons flour	Pinch of a savory herb such as
2 cups warm milk	parsley or thyme, or to taste
1 onion, stuck with a clove	Salt and pepper

Make a white *roux:* Melt butter over medium heat and stir in flour. Cook, stirring constantly, until mixture is smooth and bubbly, colored no more than a pale gold. Stir in the warm milk gradually; continue to stir until the sauce is thickened. Add onion, herbs, and season with salt and pepper to taste. Simmer over very low heat for ½ hour. Strain and serve.

An extra-smooth texture may be obtained by scalding and slightly cooling the milk before adding to *roux.*

BÉCHAMEL BINDING SAUCE
(for croquettes of fish and shellfish)

Prepare a béchamel, reducing the amount of warm milk by half; or just stop adding milk when the desired consistency has been reached.

CREAM SAUCE

1 tablespoon butter	Salt and pepper
1 tablespoon flour	Parsley, chopped (optional)
1 cup cream	Garlic (optional)

Make a white *roux* of butter and flour. Add cream gradually and stir until thickened. Season with salt and pepper to taste; add a bit of chopped parsley and a trace of garlic if desired.

Variations of Béchamel Sauce or Cream Sauce. Use 1 cup Béchamel Sauce or Cream Sauce as the base.

Sauce:

Caper. Blend in 2 or 3 tablespoons chopped capers.

Cheese. Heat sauce over hot water and blend in 2 or 3 tablespoons grated cheddar cheese.

Lobster. Blend in ½ cup cooked, chopped lobster meat, including coral.

Shrimp. Blend in ½ cup cooked chopped shrimp.

Parsley. Blend in 2 or 3 tablespoons chopped parsley.

Soubise. (*Onion.* Serve with salt fish.) Boil 4 or 5 large onions until mushy. Drain, mash the onions well, and combine with sauce. Return the mixture to the saucepan, sprinkle with 1 tablespoon *beurre manié,* and blend well over medium heat. Add ½ cup evaporated milk or cream and stir until it bubbles.

Egg. Blend in a finely chopped hard-boiled egg.

Asparagus. Cut asparagus tips, fresh, or frozen and thawed, into chunks about 1 inch long, enough to fill a cup. Reduce to a smooth purée in blender, adding a sprig of fresh thyme or parsley, and combine with sauce. Heat through.

MUSHROOM SAUCE

½ cup thinly sliced mushrooms	1 cup Béchamel Sauce, hot
1 tablespoon clarified butter	Salt and pepper
1 tablespoon sherry	

Lightly sauté the mushrooms in melted butter; add sherry and remove from heat. Mix in the hot sauce. Add salt and pepper to taste.

To make a heavier sauce, use Béchamel Binding Sauce.

SAUCE ESPAGNOLE
(Spanish sauce)

A modest household-scale version of the classic production.

1 tablespoon each raw ham, carrots, onions, celery, chopped fine	1 cup hot, strong stock, fish, veal or chicken
3 tablespoons clarified butter, or equal parts butter and olive oil	¼ cup tomato paste
2 tablespoons flour	1 tablespoon vinegar
	1 tablespoon granulated sugar
	Dash powdered garlic (optional)

Sauté the ham and vegetables in the butter until tender. (This is a *mirepoix*.) Spoon out the vegetables and ham and reserve. Stir flour into butter, mix and stir until bubbly and browned; stir in stock, cook and stir until thickened. Mix in tomato paste and vinegar, add sugar and garlic and return the vegetables and ham. Simmer over low heat for half an hour. Stir occasionally, thinning with stock if necessary. Keep hot over simmering water until required.

A large *Espagnole* may be made by increasing amounts of ingredients accordingly. Simmer the larger sauce at least an hour—the longer the better. Strained, it may be refrigerator-stored or fast-frozen. Serve with white-fleshed fish.

TOMATO SAUCE

Follow Sauce Espagnole, but instead of vinegar, sugar, and garlic, blend in 2 tablespoons dry red wine and 4 tablespoons diced mushrooms, cooked in butter. Just before serving, add 2 tablespoons sherry.

FINE HERBS SAUCE

2 tablespoons butter	Salt
1 tablespoon diced mushrooms	Pinch grated nutmeg
1 tablespoon chopped chives	½ cup Sauce Espagnole or Velouté
2 tablespoons finely chopped parsley	Sauce
White pepper	Lemon juice

Melt butter, mix in everything but the sauce and lemon juice, and simmer for 5 minutes. Blend in the sauce. Stir and cook until it bubbles up. Add a few drops lemon juice. Remove from heat. Keep hot in double boiler.

MUSTARD SAUCE
(a rather sharp sauce)

2 tablespoons olive oil	1 tablespoon flour
2 teaspoons granulated sugar	⅓ cup light cream, or evaporated
2 tablespoons dry mustard	milk
Pinch salt	¼ cup vinegar
¼ teaspoon turmeric (optional)	

Put oil to heat in top of double boiler over gently boiling water. Mix well the sugar, mustard, and salt. If a yellow color is desired for the otherwise pale sauce, add the turmeric to the mustard mixture. Set aside. When the oil is heated add the flour, stirring for a minute or two until blended. Remove from the heat.

Add the mustard mixture to the oil and blend well. Gradually stir in the cream or evaporated milk. Replace over boiling water, stir and cook until smooth and thick. Let cool.

Stir in vinegar and blend well. Pour into a dish, cover, and keep cool until needed. The sauce should be made several hours in advance to let it develop. It may be refrigerated for 2 or 3 days.

MUSTARD DILL SAUCE

To 1 cup Mustard Sauce add 1 tablespoon hot, Dijon-style prepared mustard. Mix well. Add 2 tablespoons minced fresh dill. Serve with smoked fish.

MAYONNAISE SAUCES

Mayonnaise, an excellent sauce in itself, is the base for many fine sauces for fish. For best results be sure that the proportion of oil used does not exceed 1 cup to 1 large grade A egg yolk, and that the oil is at a minimum temperature of 70°. If necessary, warm the oil slightly.

MAYONNAISE

2 egg yolks   3 tablespoons vinegar, or lemon juice
½ teaspoon salt   2 cups olive oil, or vegetable oil
¼ teaspoon white pepper   2 tablespoons boiling water
⅛ teaspoon dry mustard

Put egg yolks in mixing bowl and add salt, pepper, and mustard. Beat well with electric beater at medium speed. Add vinegar or lemon juice and beat for about 30 seconds. Without stopping beater, begin to add the oil, drop by drop at first, and increasing to a thin, steady stream until the mixture is thickened and smooth and creamy. At this stage add 2 tablespoons boiling water, beating until well blended into the mayonnaise, to prevent separation during storage. Store in refrigerator.

HOLLANDAISE SAUCE

2 egg yolks
2 teaspoons cold water
½ cup butter at room temperature,
    cut in chunks

¼ teaspoon salt
Pinch cayenne
1 tablespoon lemon juice

Place egg yolks and water in top of double boiler. Beat well with a wire whisk. Heat water 1 inch deep in bottom of boiler over low heat, but don't let it boil. Place top of boiler containing eggs over the simmering water and continue beating until light and frothy. Add butter, a chunk at a time, whisking well between each addition. Keep whisking until all butter has been added and sauce is thick and smooth. Whisk in the salt, cayenne, and lemon juice and blend well. Should the sauce separate, beat in 2 tablespoons boiling water, drop by drop. Serve at once, with steamed or poached fish and vegetables, especially broccoli or spinach.

SAUCE REMOULADE
(a sharp sauce)

1 cup mayonnaise
1 teaspoon hot English mustard
1 teaspoon anchovy paste
1 teaspoon sharp cucumber relish

1 teaspoon capers, chopped
1 teaspoon herbs—thyme, parsley,
    sorrel, or to taste

Add all ingredients to mayonnaise and mix well.

TARRAGON SAUCE

½ cup mayonnaise
½ teaspoon crushed fresh tarragon

2 teaspoons lemon juice
Pinch of grated lemon rind

Add tarragon and lemon juice to mayonnaise. Blend in lemon rind. Prepare in advance to let seasonings develop.

GREEN SAUCE

Handful watercress   Pinch of dry tarragon
Handful spinach   1 cup mayonnaise
1 teaspoon dry chervil

Wash watercress and spinach and put into a small, covered saucepan with only the water clinging to them. Cover tightly and simmer gently for 4 or 5 minutes; add chervil and tarragon, and simmer another minute or two. Put everything in blender and reduce to a smooth purée. Incorporate this into mayonnaise, blending well. Chill and serve.

TARTAR SAUCE

1 cup mayonnaise   1 tablespoon chopped sweet
1 tablespoon chopped capers   cucumber pickle
1 tablespoon sliced stuffed olives   1 tablespoon chopped parsley

Combine all ingredients and mix until blended.

CLEAR BUTTER SAUCES

Clear butter sauces are served very hot with fish, shellfish, or with accompanying green vegetables such as spinach, broccoli, brussels sprouts, and so on.

Butter contains solids which over heat tend to settle to the bottom of the pan and scorch before the melted butter becomes hot enough to cook anything. Clarification of the butter removes the offending solids.

To clarify butter: Cut butter into chunks and melt in a small saucepan; leave over medium heat until it bubbles up. Remove from heat. Skim off froth and pour off the clear butter, leaving behind the sediment which settles in the bottom of the saucepan.

Margarine may be clarified in the same manner.

Butter or margarine may be clarified a pound or so at a time and refrigerated for future needs.

CLEAR LEMON BUTTER SAUCE

Heat ½ cup clarified butter until melted, and pour immediately into a small heated gravy boat or sauceboat into which the juice of a lemon has been squeezed. Sprinkle with finely shredded parsley.

NOISETTE BUTTER

Heat ½ cup clarified butter to a light-brown color. Proceed immediately as for Clear Lemon Butter Sauce and serve the same way.

BROWN BUTTER

Heat ½ cup clarified butter to a nutty-dark brown. Add 1 tablespoon crushed chives or capers. Proceed as for Clear Lemon Butter Sauce and serve the same way.

HERB BUTTER

To Noisette Butter add ½ teaspoon fresh fine herbs, such as tarragon, parsley, rhyme, dill, etc., either mixed or singly. Let steep over very low heat for about 5 minutes before serving.

TABASCO BUTTER

Add a few drops Tabasco sauce to Noisette Butter, or for variety, to one of the herb butters.

DRAWN BUTTER
(a delicate sauce for fish, shellfish, and green vegetables)

⅓ cup clarified butter   2 cups boiling water
4 tablespoons flour   Salt to taste

In a saucepan, or in the top of an aluminum double boiler, quickly make a light *roux*. Melt 4 tablespoons butter, stir in the flour, cook and stir over a moderate heat until *roux* is smooth and bubbly. Place over hot water and gradually add the boiling water, stirring constantly until the sauce is a smooth, thick consistency. Remove saucepan to a burner on a low heat and simmer and stir until thick and smooth. Let rest over very low heat.

Just before serving add salt to taste and swirl in the remaining butter a bit at a time; beat well. Makes 2 cups.

MAÎTRE D'HOTEL SAUCE

1 tablespoon lemon juice   2 egg yolks, beaten
1 tablespoon chopped parsley   Salt and white pepper
2 cups Drawn Butter

Add lemon juice and parsley to the hot Drawn Butter. Blend a tablespoon of the hot mixture into the egg yolks and then blend the egg yolks into the sauce. Stir and cook over low heat for about 1 minute. Let sauce rest over hot water or over a very low heat but do not let it boil. Season to taste with salt and pepper and serve.

COLD SIDE SAUCES

HORSERADISH SAUCE NO. 1

½ cup heavy cream, whipped   1 tablespoon prepared horseradish,
1 pinch salt   drained

Into the whipped cream fold the horseradish and salt. Chill in refrigerator for an hour or two. Serve in silver or cut-glass dish.

HORSERADISH SAUCE NO. 2

1 tablespoon prepared horseradish   1 cup chili sauce

Blend together, chill, and serve.

COCKTAIL SAUCE FOR SEAFOOD
(dip or side dish)

½ cup catsup
1 tablespoon prepared horseradish
1 tablespoon lemon juice
2 tablespoons honey, liquid
½ teaspoon onion juice

½ teaspoon Worcestershire sauce
¼ teaspoon salt
Pinch of monosodium glutamate
3 or 4 drops Tabasco sauce
2 ounces sherry (optional)

Combine everything in a bowl and mix until blended well. Refrigerate for at least 2 hours before serving.

Fish Stews, Soups, and Chowders

Whatever or whenever their origin, there is a pattern of cultural exchange evident in fish stews and soups of the Western world. The pattern is reflected in the two great North American clam chowders (see Chapter 6)—the New

England chowder made with milk, and the Manhattan chowder using toma-toes—and, in turn, our many fish stews and soups.

The New England style is not unlike the Scandinavian creamy milk soups, minus the saffron that the Vikings brought home from their Mediterranean cruisings. The Mediterranean mariners, along with the fabulous fishes of the New World, took the American love apple to their hearts and hearths, and tomatoes are now fundamental to their fish soupery from simple codfish stew to the eclectic bouillabaisse.

About the only truly regional aspect of a brew apparently was the kind of fish in it, and as is usual in regional dishes, availability was the determining factor. Today such restrictions are voided by modern marketing facilities and anglers' mobility, and the fish may be of your choice or catch, and any method of stew or soup preparation followed by applying the basic principles of fish cookery charted earlier in this chapter.

Most of the coarse fishes, especially the bigger ones, often considered of little epicurean worth, make splendid soups and stews. Trimmings themselves, such as meaty heads and tails, make a fine brew.

Fatty fishes should be parboiled to remove excessive oils. Fish stock should be used wherever possible, whether stock on hand or made separately from trimmings for the purpose. There should never be a bone in the soup, of course. Leftover fumets are a great addition to the soup.

Salt- and smoke-cured fish, considered by many to be at their finest in a New England-style chowder, should be freshened, the degree a matter of taste and judgment.

Dried fish requires extensive soaking in fresh cold water, and freshening may be improved by simmering the soaked fish in three or four changes of fresh water to an edible texture. With the advance of refrigeration and packing, dried fish has practically disappeared from the general American market in favor of the more lightly cured, more perishable product.

GREAT NORTHERN CHOWDER
(New England style)

2 pounds skinned fillets of pike or
    other freshwater fish, fresh,
    frozen, or salted
½ cup finely diced salt pork
1 cup minced onion
3 cups diced raw potatoes
½ cup diced green pepper
1 tablespoon diced pimiento
1½ cups diced celery including a
    few tops

½ cup finely diced raw carrots
3 teaspoons salt
½ teaspoon fresh ground black
    pepper
½ teaspoon tarragon, or a trace mint
1 bay leaf
4 cups fish stock or water, boiling
4 cups milk
2 tablespoons *beurre manié*
Few sprigs parsley

Thaw frozen fish. Freshen salt fish by soaking overnight in cold water.

Cut the fish into chunky cubes. If using large salmon, lake trout, or other fatty fish, parboil to remove excessive oils.

Sear the pork in the bottom of a large, heavy kettle (uncovered pressure cooker or Dutch oven). Remove pork and reserve. Add onions and sauté in the pork fat. Add the other vegetables and seasonings. Cover with the boiling stock or water and let simmer until vegetables are tender.

Add the fish and simmer very gently until the fish flakes, about 15 to 20 minutes. Test for seasonings and adjust to taste. Add milk and heat until very hot, but do not let it boil. Blend in *beurre manié*. Keep at this heat for about 5 minutes. Add reserved pork. Serve in Dutch oven or in a prewarmed earthen soup tureen, with a few small sprigs of parsley sprinkled on the surface of the chowder.

Serve with hot French bread or potato chips on the side. This family-size recipe may be multiplied to any extent for an impressive party dish, limited only by the size of the kettle.

SEASHORE CHOWDER
(a variation of Great Northern Chowder)

2 pounds fresh seafoods: 3 or 4 varieties of saltwater fishes, such as snapper,
    haddock, cod, mackerel (parboiled); clams, lobster, crab, shrimp

Fillet the fish and skin. Scrub and steam or boil the shellfish. (See Chapter 6, Shellfish.)

Make stock from fish trimmings, adding juices and shells from shellfish. (See instructions for making stock earlier in this chapter.)

Follow recipe for Great Northern Chowder above, substituting crushed thyme or summer savory for tarragon.

BLUENOSE CHOWDER
(Manhattan style)

2 pounds fish fillets skinned, fresh
    or salted
2 tablespoons butter
½ cup diced onion
½ cup diced celery
¼ cup diced green pepper
2 cups fish stock
2 large potatoes, diced
1 20-ounce can tomatoes

1 cup tomato juice
1 small can cream of tomato soup
¼ cup tomato catsup
2 tablespoons tomato paste
Spice bag of 1 teaspoon pickling
    spices, parsley, thyme, or
    tarragon
½ teaspoon Tabasco sauce

Freshen salt fish by soaking in water overnight, changing the water several times. Drain and flake.

Heat the butter in a large kettle or Dutch oven and sauté the onion, celery, and pepper until onion is translucent. Add everything except the fish, spice bag and Tabasco sauce and boil for about 10 minutes. Taste for seasoning, and remove the spice bag according to taste. Add the fish and Tabasco sauce and simmer for about 15 minutes. Garnish with a dab of Horseradish Sauce.

Serves 6 to 8.

DORÉ EN CHAUDIÈRE

(*Doré* is the name for walleye [pickerel] in La Belle Province de Quebec, and the chowder is a favorite meal.)

2 2- to 3-pound doré, or 1 big one   1 bay leaf
¼ pound salt pork, diced   4 teaspoons salt
3 medium onions, sliced   ½ teaspoon white pepper
3 medium potatoes, peeled and diced   2 cups boiling water
½ teaspoon celery seed   2 20-ounce cans tomatoes
4 medium carrots, diced   2 tablespoons chopped parsley
1 green pepper, diced

Clean and fillet the fish. Skin the fillets and tie skin, bones, heads, and tails in a cheesecloth bag and reserve.

In a deep kettle or Dutch oven, sear the pork well over medium heat, turning it with a wooden spoon to brown on all sides. When golden, remove the pork and set it aside on a paper towel to drain. In the remaining fat, sauté the onions until translucent. Add remaining ingredients down to the water. Add the bag of fish trimmings and the water. Bring to a low boil and cook gently until vegetables are almost tender, about 15 or 20 minutes. Cut the fillets into chunks and add to the stew with the pork. Cook for 5 to 10 minutes until the fish flakes and the vegetables are cooked. Add tomatoes and heat. Lift and discard the bag of fish trimmings. Garnish with parsley, and serve immediately with thick slices of hot, buttered French bread. Serves 6 to 8.

Note: This chowder may be made from carp or bass. In each case discard the skin, as it can impart an undesirable flavor.

VIKING SOUP

¼ teaspoon saffron   4 tablespoons white wine
2 tablespoons butter   2 pounds skinned fish fillets, fresh or
2 tablespoons flour   salted, cut in small chunks
1 quart hot fish stock   1 egg yolk, beaten
1 quart hot beef stock   6 tablespoons heavy cream, whipped
1 onion, stuck with 2 cloves   6–8 large mushrooms
1 bay leaf   6–8 cooked shrimps, or Fish
1 ½ teaspoons minced parsley   Forcemeat Balls
Salt and pepper

Freshen salted fish by soaking in cold water overnight.

Dry saffron on a piece of paper in a warm oven for a few minutes. Rub or pound to powder; put into a little of the stock and set aside to steep. Melt butter in stock pot, blend in flour, and stir over medium heat until smooth and bubbly. Gradually stir in the stock; cook and stir until it is boiling and thickened. Turn down heat. Add onion, saffron, and seasonings and stir in. Add fish and cook gently until it flakes easily. Blend the egg yolk into the cream, and add wine and mix well. Ladle a little of the stock into the cream and stir well, then stir the mixture back into the soup. Cook and stir for about 2 minutes. Keep hot but don't let boil.

Slice the mushrooms and sauté lightly in a little butter. Put a few in bottom of each soup bowl with a shrimp or fish ball, and pour the soup over them.

Serve with dark rye bread.

Serves 6 to 8.

KALASOPPA
(Finnish-style fish soup)

This delicious, simple soup, says the contributor of this old recipe, is good even for someone who doesn't like fish. One doesn't have to eat the fish, only the sauce and potatoes, and it tastes great.

2 cups water	¼ medium onion
3 medium potatoes, cut in quarters	½ teaspoon salt
1 pound fresh fish (perch, or any white-fleshed fish)	1 teaspoon flour
	2 cups milk
7 whole peppercorns	1 tablespoon butter

Boil potatoes in water for about 10 minutes. Add the fish, peppercorns, onion, and salt and cook until the potatoes are done.

Add flour to milk and mix well. Stir the milk into the soup, stirring while it heats, then blend in the butter. Let the soup cook for about 3 minutes and it is ready to serve. Serves 4.

Mrs. Hilja Tapanainen,
Toronto, Ontario

TAILLEVENT
(a Mediterranean fisherman's stew)

Taillevent, literally, is a four-cornered mainsail. In old French idiom, when filled with the wind it connoted a well-fed person. For that reason it was a lasting nickname given to a famous fourteenth-century French chef who made a right hearty fish stew. The name clings, though, one might say, the stew may vary as the wind blows. Edibility of tomatoes, for instance, would have been unknown to the original Taillevent.

2 pounds skinned fish fillets, one of a kind or mixed
Salt and pepper
Juice of 1 lemon
¼ cup olive oil
4 large onions, sliced
1 clove garlic, crushed
1 large green pepper, cut in rings
½ cup fresh herbs, crushed
4 firm red tomatoes, sliced
2 cups hot water, or fish stock
1 cup white wine

Wipe the fillets with a damp cloth and cut into chunks. Sprinkle with salt, pepper, and lemon juice and let stand.

Heat the olive oil in a large iron skillet or kettle. Add the onion, garlic, pepper rings, and herbs. Sauté until the onion is translucent. Remove the vegetables with a slotted spoon, discarding the garlic, and reserve. Add the fish and cook lightly until it just begins to color. Return the cooked vegetables, add the tomatoes, water or stock, and wine. Test for seasoning. Cover tightly and cook over low heat until the fish is cooked and flakes easily to a fork.

Serves 4.

CLASSIC FRENCH BOUILLABAISSE

In France genuine bouillabaisse cannot be made to the gourmet's idea of perfection except close to a fishing port where all the fish required for its preparation are landed fresh each morning.

Two recipes adapted to North American fish follow, one classic, the other more simple. In either case bouillabaisse is an expensive dish which requires a rather lengthy preparation. That is why it ought to be served as a meal, followed only with a good salad, a mild cheese, and a light dessert.

3 2-pound fresh lobsters
1 pound fresh eels, skinned and
    dressed
1 ½ pounds perch, or sea perch, pan
    dressed
3 pounds mackerel, pan dressed
24 shrimp, peeled and deveined
24 mussels
24 clams
½ cup olive oil
½ cup diced carrots
3 leeks, cleaned and sliced
¾ cup onion, chopped

4 cups canned tomatoes
3 cloves garlic
2 tablespoons chopped parsley
1 teaspoon fennel seeds
¼ teaspoon saffron
1 bay leaf
½ teaspoon thyme
1 tablespoon coarse salt
Pepper, freshly ground
2 quarts hot water
½ cup melted butter
12 thick slices French bread

Split the lobsters in two lengthwise and remove the stomach and intestinal vein. Divide each half so as to have a piece for every guest. Do not remove the shell. Slice the eels, the perch, and the mackerel into 1-inch slices. Shell and clean the shrimps. Scrub the sand from the mussels and clams and rinse well.

Heat the olive oil; add the carrots, leeks, and onions. Cover and simmer over low heat for 10 minutes. Then add the tomatoes, 2 of the cloves of garlic, the parsley, fennel seeds, saffron, bay leaf, thyme, salt and pepper. Mix thoroughly.

Add the lobster meat, eels, and 2 quarts of hot water. Bring to a boil, lower heat and simmer for 15 minutes. Add the perch and mackerel and simmer for another 10 minutes. Add the cleaned shrimps, mussels and clams in their shells, and simmer for 20 minutes more or until the shells open up slightly.

Mix the butter with 1 crushed clove of garlic and brush each slice of bread with it. Brown over high heat. Turn the slices of bread, brush with garlic butter, and brown the other side. Set in a basket to serve with the bouillabaisse.

The success of a bouillabaisse depends on the way the cooking is done, and mostly on how quickly it is served when cooked, as the sauce loses its unctuousness as soon as done. It has a tendency to separate. Therefore prepare the bread slices in advance, and cook the mixture over continuous heat. Heat large soup plates. In each place pieces of the various fish and a few shellfish. A slice of garlic bread may also be placed in each plate, topped with the fish. Cover with a good helping of the bouillon. Serves 12.

Madame Jehane Benoit,
Encyclopaedia of Canadian Cuisine
By permission of the author

AMERICAN-STYLE BOUILLABAISSE

¼ cup diced carrots	1 cup shrimp, or crab meat
1 cup minced onions	1 quart whole clams
1 clove garlic	1 cup white wine
½ cup olive oil	1 tablespoon lemon juice
3 pounds frozen fish fillets	¼ cup minced parsley
2½ cups canned tomatoes	½ cup canned pimientos
1 bay leaf	¼ teaspoon saffron
2 quarts hot water	1 tablespoon salt
4 to 6 frozen lobster tails	¼ teaspoon pepper

Thaw lobster tails and fish fillets enough to cut. Cook the carrots, onions, and garlic in olive oil over low heat for 10 minutes. Cut the fish fillets in 3-inch pieces, and add with tomatoes, bay leaf, and 2 quarts hot water. Bring to a boil and simmer for 20 minutes over very low heat. Add the lobster tails, split lengthwise in their shells, the shrimps and clams.

Bring back to a boil, add the remaining ingredients, and simmer for 30 minutes. Serve immediately with or without the browned garlic bread, as indicated in the Classic French Bouillabaisse.

Madame Jehane Benoit,
Encyclopaedia of Canadian Cuisine
By permission of the author

Chopped, Ground, and Flaked Fish

FISH MOUSSE

1 pound fish fillets, cut in pieces	Allspice, cayenne, or celery salt to
2 cups heavy cream	taste
1 teaspoon salt	3 egg whites
¼ teaspoon white pepper	

Using an electric blender, reduce the fish to a fine, smooth paste. Blend a bit at a time, moistening with a little of the cream, according to the capacity of the blender. Blend in the seasonings. Put into a chilled bowl set in ice cubes. Mix in the egg whites a bit at a time, blending thoroughly, until the mixture is a smooth sticky paste. Check the seasonings and chill for an hour.

Very slowly stir in the remainder of the cream, mixing well. Pour into a buttered ring mold or individual timbales. Set the mold or timbales into a pan of water 1 inch deep and cover with aluminum foil. Put into a preheated 350°F oven for 15 to 20 minutes, or until the mousse is firm to the touch. Be sure it doesn't overcook.

Turn out of mold onto serving dish, and pour over it Normande Sauce or Lobster Sauce.

The fish mousse is an elaboration of the traditional Norwegian fish pudding.

FISH PILAF

4 strips bacon, cut in pieces
1 large onion, chopped
2 cups white rice
½ teaspoon each crushed thyme and marjoram, or herbs to taste
1 20-ounce can tomatoes
4 cups strong chicken, veal, or fish stock

Salt and pepper
2 cups leftover fish, fried or baked
¼ cup slivered almonds
¼ cup black olives, halved and pitted
Fresh parsley, crushed

In a large, heavy cook-and-serve skillet or a Dutch oven, cook the bacon until crisp and remove to drain on a paper towel. In the remaining fat sauté the onion until translucent (not brown). Add the rice; stir and brown lightly. Add the herbs, tomatoes, and stock, stir once to blend, add salt and pepper to taste, bring to a boil, cover and reduce heat to a simmer. Cook covered for 15 minutes, or until rice is tender but not soft. Blend in the fish and let it heat through. Heap in the middle of a large, hot platter and keep warm.

In a little butter lightly sauté the almonds and olives. Sprinkle over the pilaf along with the bacon bits and a little crushed fresh parsley and serve garnished around the rice with fried mushrooms and Tomato Sauce, or crayfish or shrimp in a butter sauce.

Variation: Substitute for fish, or add what is available of fresh, lightly fried fish livers.

FISH FORCEMEAT

2 egg yolks
¼ cup sifted flour
3 tablespoons soft butter
1½ teaspoons salt
¾ teaspoon freshly ground pepper
Pinch freshly grated nutmeg

1 cup boiling milk
½ pound fine fish meat, skinned and
    boned
¼ pound beef suet, crumbled
Fish liver,* or ¼ pound chicken or
    calf's liver

In a saucepan break the egg yolks and beat lightly.

Rub flour in butter and knead to a fine mealy texture. Stir into egg yolks, mixing well with a wooden spoon until smooth. Add salt, pepper, and nutmeg. Stirring constantly, pour in the boiling milk a bit at a time and stir until smooth. Whisk over a medium heat for about 5 minutes until thickened. Pour into blender.

Shred the fish with fingers and add to blender along with the liver and suet. You may have to process it in two lots, dividing the sauce, fish, and liver and suet as evenly as possible, and then mix the two together well. The forcemeat may be freezer-stored for a few weeks.

This forcemeat may be made from shellfish as well, omitting the liver. It is used to make quenelles (fish balls) to be served in a sauce, or as a garnish for fish dishes and soups. It may also be used to stuff boned fish. The forcemeat swells somewhat during cooking.

Quenelles: Poach in salted water; half beer may be used. Scoop out and shape the forcemeat with a spoon and slide it into the water. Simmer gently for about 10 minutes. Serve with Sauce Espagnole, or any other fish sauce, garnished with anchovies. The quenelles may be poached in the sauce in which they are to be served.

To serve as a garnish, the quenelles should be made smaller.

GEFILTE FISH

Gefilte fish is a delicious fish-forcemeat preparation traditional to Jewish cookery throughout the world. Recipes are many and various fishes are used, depending on local supply. More than one variety of fish often appears in gefilte fish.

It is prepared in the form of little cakes, but it may be a whole fish skin

---

* See Chapter 5, Fish Roe and Giblets.

stuffed with its own meat. It is an excellent way to transform the flesh of big fish, or the so-called coarse fish like carp, into a delicacy. A "gefiltepack" comprising various fresh-water fishes is marketed frozen.

The author of the following recipe prefers the light flesh of whitefish and pike.

5 pounds whitefish and pike fillets	½ cup water
(flesh only)	1 large carrot
1 pound onions, chopped	1 large onion
1 teaspoon salt	½ teaspoon salt
½ teaspoon fresh black pepper	Peppercorns
1 teaspoon sugar	2 cups water
5 eggs	

Put the fish through a food chopper or blender, and combine it with onion, seasonings, sugar, eggs, and ½ cup water. Mix well.

In the bottom of a deep kettle slice carrot and onion. Add ½ teaspoon salt and a few peppercorns or a dash of pepper, then add water. Add the bones from the fish. Boil gently for ½ hour.

Meanwhile, with wet hands shape the fish mixture into patties and carefully pile them into the kettle on top of vegetables. Cover and bring to a boil. Reduce the heat and simmer for 2 hours.

Serve hot with bread and strained sauce in which the fish was cooked.

Serve cold with lots of red horseradish, or with Beetroot and Horseradish Sauce.

Mrs. Anne Butovsky,
Ottawa, Ontario

KEDGEREE
(an East Indian dish by way of England, not unlike hash)

1 cup long-grain converted rice	2 egg yolks, slightly beaten
1 tablespoon sesame seeds	1 teaspoon dry parsley flakes
2 cups cooked fish, boned and flaked	½ teaspoon salt
¼ cup melted butter	Pepper

Cook rice according to directions on package, adding the sesame seeds. Combine the fish and the rice in the top of a double boiler and heat over boiling water. Add the melted butter to egg yolks; blend in the parsley, salt, and pepper to taste. Stir this into the hot fish and rice mixture, and cook and stir for 2 minutes. Let the kedgeree rest for a couple of minutes over the boiling water, then serve with a tossed salad on the side.

❧ 4 ☙
Species and Specialties

COD FISH BAKE, SHEDIAC BAY

Take: 1 good friend
       1 rowboat
       Jigging tackle
       1 cooler, half full of crushed
              ice, half full of beer
       1 midsummer afternoon on the bay

Jig contentedly, replacing beer with cod. That done, head for home. Clean the fish. Select one about 4 pounds and set it aside on ice. Freeze or distribute the remainder among your neighbors. Bake your cod.

Scale the dressed cod, cut out the gills. Wash it and pat dry between towels. Stuff it with a bread dressing [see Chapter 3, Stuffings] well seasoned with summer savory fresh from the garden, and sew it up. Rub it with lots of butter and put it in a baking pan. Put a little water, a half cup of white wine, a handful of summer savory, and a few slices of onion in the bottom of the pan. Cover it and bake in a hot oven for about 30 minutes. Take off the cover, baste it from the pan, and let it brown until the flesh flakes.

If you like, make a sauce from the drippings and serve it hot.

—Clorice Landry,
Shediac, New Brunswick

The five basic methods of cooking fish, with the many combinations of sauces, batters and so on described in the foregoing chapter, have considerable scope when adapted to the 140-odd species that appear here.

For convenience in reference and broad application of cookery methods, fishes are presented in alphabetical order under their common names. Where a number of species of a prestigious family generally have common culinary attributes, such as the codfishes, the flounder (flatfishes), and the trouts (Salmonidae), they are included under the family name and a cross-reference to family is given in the listing of the species.

Where numerous species are of little consequence individually, but have culinary significance as a group, they are referred to as a group—for example, the panfishes and whitebait. This rule is applied also to fishes considered outside the kitchen-range of this book, notably the saltwater big-game fishes.

Recipes given have been chosen as appropriate to demonstrate the many and varied applications of the basic methods of cooking to a typical fish or group of fishes. Thus many recipes may be applied to other fishes of comparable qualifications; these are entered in the index at the back of the book.

Recipes list by title, as ingredients, preparations that are described in Chapter 3. For example, "Mushroom Sauce" would be found under "Sauces for Fish" in Chapter 3. Specific cooking methods are also discussed in Chapter 3 and the recipes in this chapter refer to them.

Sauces, stuffings, batters, etc. are recommended for some recipes. A variety of each is given in Chapter 3 from which to choose according to taste and available ingredients.

Serving portions following a recipe are given as a guide only. Often the amount of fish one serves is the amount one has caught, to be divided among fish fanciers who are known to eat any given amount be it large or small. However, the amount of fish generally considered adequate as a main course for one person is: fish in the round, 1 pound; dressed fish, ¾ pound; pan-dressed fish, ½ pound; fillets and boned pan-dressed fish, ¼ pound. Various preparations extend the fish, such as chowders, casseroles, salads and so on.

Albacore   See SALTWATER BIG-GAME FISHES.

American shad   See SHADS.

Arctic char   See SALMONIDAE-TROUTS.

Arctic grayling   See SALMONIDAE-TROUTS.

Atlantic cod   See CODFISHES.

Atlantic mackerel and Pacific mackerel

The small Atlantic and Pacific mackerels belong to the prestigious family of mackerels and tunas which, besides providing a large commercial fishery, offers sport from child's play to big-game trophy hunting. Many a vacationing youngster wets his first line casting into a streaking school of little mackerel from a rowboat on a quiet coastal bay.

All the mackerels are very fat, sleek, and swift in the water. Always on the move, they run in schools, and during their inshore season are abundant on both coasts.

Every spring mackerel are taken by the hundreds by East Coast anglers. Delicious when freshly caught, the extremely oily fish does not take well to freezing, and the surplus is salted down in traditional thrifty colonial fashion. (See Chapter 7.) The large commercial catch is practically all salted for export; some is canned.

Two pounds is a good size for a mackerel. An active, muscular fish, its flesh is firm. A court bouillon which floats off some of the excessive oils is generally a superior method of cooking mackerel. It also broils and bakes nicely with its built-in basting. For baking many prefer a midsummer mackerel that is not yet fully fattened up after spawning. Pan-size mackerel are fried *à la meunière* (see *Basic Methods,* Chapter 3).

Mackerel has a finely scaled smooth skin. Scrape it with the blunt edge of a knife and wash well before cooking.

Recipes for bluefish and small trouts may be applied to mackerel.

Atlantic salmon   See SALMONIDAE-TROUTS.

Barndoor skate   See SKATES.

Basses   See SEA BASSES AND GROUPERS;
LARGEMOUTH BASS AND SMALLMOUTH
BASS; STRIPED BASS; SALTWATER
BIG-GAME FISHES; PANFISHES.

Billfishes   See SALTWATER BIG-GAME FISHES.

Black bass   See LARGEMOUTH BASS AND
SMALLMOUTH BASS.

Black crappie   See PANFISHES.

Blackfin snapper   See RED SNAPPER.

Black sea bass

The spirited little black sea bass is a popular sport fish of the northwest Atlantic. It averages a pound and a half; panfish size is called "pinfish." A big black sea bass may reach 5 pounds and is dubbed "humpback" because of its shape.

Its delicately flavored flesh is firm, lean and white. Skinned or scaled, the smaller fish are pan-fried; bigger specimens may be baked or steamed whole, or filleted and cooked by one of the various methods for lean fish. Recipes for largemouth and smallmouth bass and for walleye are applicable. (See also *Sea basses and groupers.*)

Bloater   See CISCO OR LAKE HERRING.

Bluefish

The bluefish is a family to itself, ranging along the Atlantic coast northward to Cape Cod, with a few mavericks as far north as Nova Scotia. A predatory fish and a fat one, the bluefish is a superb table fish, compatible with both strong and delicate herbs, and wine. Its most agreeable size is around 3 to 5 pounds, although it presents a handsome dish up to 8 pounds. The fatty blue bakes and broils beautifully; its fillets also make a splendid chowder and "deep fries."

Young, small bluefish are sometimes referred to as "snappers" or "baby blues."

BAKED STUFFED BLUEFISH

1 3-5 pound bluefish, dressed and scaled

See Chapter 3, Baking.

Prepare the fish and stuff it lightly with about 3 cups rather dry Fruit Stuffing made with bread. Close cavity as directed. Lay the fish on a bed of sliced onion, carrots, celery sticks, and fresh herbs—dill, parsley, or fennel.

Mix a little melted butter in a half cup of white wine and pour it over the fish. Bake uncovered in a preheated moderately hot oven at 400°F. Baste from the pan after about half an hour, and dust lightly with flour. Bake allowing 10 minutes plus 10 minutes per inch thickness at thickest part, or until the fish is brown and the flesh flakes to a fork.

Garnish with a lemon wedge in the mouth and cherry eyes, and serve with a Caper Sauce or Lemon Butter.

To prepare bluefish for baking without stuffing, see Unstuffed Fish under Baking in Chapter 3.

BAKED STUFFED FILLETS OF BLUEFISH

2 bluefish fillets, about 1 pound   2 cups Fruit Stuffing, or Wild Rice
   each, skin scaled and left on   Mushroom Stuffing

Wipe each fillet with a damp cloth and pat dry. In a well-greased baking pan make a bed of sliced onion, carrots, celery sticks, and herbs, as for Baked Bluefish. Lay a fillet skin down on the vegetables. Sprinkle the top with lemon juice and salt lightly. Heap stuffing in the middle and spread it over the fillet. Sprinkle lemon juice and salt over the other fillet and lay it skin up over the stuffing. Fasten here and there with trussing pins. Bake in a preheated moderate oven for about 30 to 35 minutes, or until flesh flakes.

Remove fillets to a hot platter. Discard the celery and herbs, and also the onion and carrots if they don't look presentable. Deglaze the pan with a little white wine and pour the pan juices over the fish.

Serves 4.

Bluefish fillets of smaller size may be pan-fried *à la meunière*. (See Chapter 3, Pan-Frying.) Baby blues are pan-fried or broiled. *Recipes for shad and mackerel may be interchanged with those for bluefish of comparable size; also recipes for medium-size salmons and trouts.*

Bluegills   See PANFISHES.

Blue tuna   See SALTWATER BIG-GAME FISHES.

Bonito   See SALMONIDAE-TROUTS (of comparable size).

Buffalo   See SUCKERS.

Burbot   See also CODFISHES.

Burbot is a freshwater cod, commonly called ling. It is not related to the lingcod. Relatively small (3 to 4 pounds) in its range through the border states northward, the burbot grows to 40 pounds or more in the high north.

The winter-caught burbot is superior to the summer catch; unfortunately, it is often overlooked by the ice-fisherman.

It should be skinned, cleaned, and cooked or frozen promptly as taken from the water, especially in mild, nonfreezing weather. Warm or cold weather, it should be skinned at once to rid it of any muddy taste.

The burbot's merits lie in the quantity of delicious lean white meat of the loin (the flesh of the back between the lateral lines) and its large, valuable liver. Burbot loins may be cooked according to recipes for fresh cod fillets. They are excellent deep-fried in crumbs or batter (see Chapter 3, Frying).

Most anglers devoted to burbot or ling cookery consider the fish at its finest in a chowder. All the flesh of the winter ling may be used, the loins reserved for solid fish content and the remainder of the fish used in making the stock. Recipes for chowders given in Chapter 3 may be used.

Carp

The cosmopolitan carp has an Old World history of table prestige and adaptability to transplant. Native to Asia, many an Oriental royal estate contained a carp pond for the emperor's amusement in the garden and his pleasure at the table. Carp were apparently introduced into European waters in the pre-Christian era, where they adapted and flourished in and out of imperial ponds.

The carp was introduced to the United States in the 1830's, and about fifty years later several lots were supplied to applicants from Ontario; from that beginning the oversize minnow established itself across the continent and southward. It is most plentiful in the eastern part of North America. Growing as large as 40 pounds, the average catch is approximately 3 pounds.

Carp has not earned the high regard as a table food here that it has enjoyed in Europe. A muddy bottom feeder, its untidy habits have been considered detrimental to the habitat for more desirable fishes; certainly they are detrimental to the flavor of the fish.

Overcome the latter condition and we have the excellent, coarse-grained fish flesh enjoyed by kings of old and North Americans of European tradition today, who keep the carp alive in fresh water for days to rid it of the muddy flavor. For this reason carp at the fish market are sold alive from tanks of water which should be kept fresh and changed frequently. These are the fish that provide the delicious stuffed carp and gefilte fish of internationally renowned Jewish cookery.

Carp angled from fresh, clear lake waters should present no problem of muddy flavor if killed, dressed, and skinned immediately, and then cooked in a court bouillon or by an aromatic moist-heat method. Though a lean fish, the large carp's coarse flesh takes a good smoke cure.

BOHEMIAN GYPSY CARP

2 pounds carp fillets, skinless	¼ teaspoon dill seed
Salt	½ teaspoon paprika
2 strips bacon, diced	1 cup sour cream
2 or 3 onions, minced	Fresh dill, or parsley (optional)

Cut the carp into serving pieces. Sprinkle the pieces well with salt, covering all sides. Let stand for half an hour.

Meanwhile, fry the diced bacon; add the onion, dill seed, and sprinkle with paprika. Brown lightly, stirring while it browns.

Butter a loaf pan lavishly. Spread fish in a layer in the bottom of the pan, shaking the salt from each piece. Add a layer of the onion-bacon mixture, another layer of fish, and top with remaining onion and bacon. Pour half the sour cream over the dish and bake in a 425°F oven until the fish flakes. Pour remaining sour cream over the top and return it to the oven for about 5 minutes. Garnish with sprigs of fresh dill, if available, or parsley. Serve with baked potatoes.

Serves 4 to 6.

Bert Jarsch
Chef, Club Edelweiss
Toronto, Ontario

CARP STEW

1 cup white wine	2-pound carp, pan-dressed and
½ cup lemon juice	skinned
½ cup fish stock, or light meat stock	2 tablespoons butter
½ teaspoon salt	2 tablespoons chopped fresh parsley
2 medium onions, chopped	1 tablespoon pine nuts

Combine wine, lemon juice, and stock; add salt and onions and cook over low heat until onions are soft. Strain through a sieve into a large, shallow saucepan. Bring to a boil. Tie the fish loosely in cheesecloth and poach it in the broth until the flesh flakes, about 20 minutes, depending on the thickness of the fish.

Remove the fish, reserving broth, unwrap, and remove bones. Place the fish in a warm, deep serving platter and keep warm. Stir the butter and parsley into the broth and pour over the fish.

Sprinkle a few lightly fried pine nuts over the fish and serve.

Serves 4.

Catfishes

The beauty of the catfish is under the skin, for its outward appearance generally does not endear it to other than dedicated fanciers of the species. Skin a catfish and you will find attractive, lean fish flesh of fine succulence, varying in color from pink to white.

Southerners understand and appreciate the flesh of this otherwise often underestimated fish, and the channel catfish supports a growing fish-farming industry in Louisiana.

The freshwater catfishes are many in species, among them bullheads and madtoms, ranging from panfish size to the big channels and blues. The average catch, and also the best table size, ranges from under 1 pound to about 8 pounds.

The catfishes are excellent when promptly dressed out and skinned fresh from the water, then cooked in moist heat, bones removed and the flesh made into stews, chowders, or casserole-type dishes. Catfish fried *à l'Anglaise* with white cornmeal is a Southern delicacy. (See Pan-frying, Chapter 3.)

Carp recipes in which the fish is skinned may be applied to catfish.

Cavalla   See SALTWATER BIG-GAME FISHES.

Channel catfish   See CATFISHES.

Char   See SALMONIDAE-TROUTS.

Chub mackerel   See ATLANTIC MACKEREL AND
                  PACIFIC MACKEREL.

Chubs See PANFISHES.

Cisco or lake herring

The cisco or lake herring is a member of the trout family and no relation to saltwater herring. Of general northern distribution, there are several subspecies of cisco (genus *Coregonus*), all similar in flesh and dress, though varying in size. (Lake whitefish belongs to this group.) They average around 1½ pounds and may go up to 8 pounds. Ciscos range from New England fresh waters through the Great Lakes into central Canada.

The lake herring is but one, though the name is used freely and loosely in reference to ciscos in general and folk names or local names help confuse things.

Early fur traders named the cisco or lake herring "tullibee" and the name persists in the northern plains and prairies in reference to lake herring in general, or more particularly to a larger cisco which in those parts grows to 7 pounds. "Cisco" is used to eastward, while on the Great Lakes the terms "chubs" and "bloaters" may take care of the entire group.

Straightening out the ciscos can be very confusing; fortunately, when it comes to cooking them it's a matter of size rather than species, and they taste their best when cooked under their charming Ojibway name "kee-we-sens."

As trouts go, the lake herring is on the lean side. Its flavor is delicate and it is best simply pan-fried *à l'Anglaise* or *à la meunière,* or broiled, with the larger fish filleted and poached in a wine fumet. (See Basic Cooking Methods in Chapter 3.)

KEE-WE-SENS

Fumet:

1 cup fish stock, or light meat stock	Few peppercorns, cracked
½ cup white wine	Pinch thyme
Liquid from 1 10-ounce can mushrooms (see below)	Salt

Poached fish:

2 pounds lake herring fillets, skinned	2 tablespoons flour
1½ cups fish fumet	1 10-ounce can mushrooms
2 tablespoons butter	2 tablespoons heavy cream
¼ cup minced chives or green onions	2 tablespoons minced fresh parsley
	Salt

Make the fumet: To fish stock or light meat stock add white wine, the liquid drained from the mushrooms, peppercorns, thyme, and a little salt. Cover and bring to a boil; simmer for about 10 minutes. Strain and cool.

Place the fillets on a greased plate in a large skillet. Add the fumet. Bring to a boil, turn down heat, cover, and let poach very gently until the flesh flakes to a fork and takes on an opaque milky color. Carefully remove the plate with the fish to a warm oven.

Melt the butter in a saucepan, cook the chives in it until soft, stir in the flour and cook until smooth and bubbly, stirring constantly. Stir in a cup of the fumet and cook and stir until thickened. Slice and stir in the mushrooms. Stir in the cream, blend, and stir in the parsley. Add salt to taste.

Carefully move the fillets to a warm serving platter and pour the sauce over them, or serve on individual plates.

Serves about 4.

FILLETS OF CISCO OR LAKE HERRING WITH SPINACH

1 pound lake herring fillets, skinned   1 bay leaf
½ pound fresh spinach   1 cup Béchamel Sauce
1 slice lemon   Parmesan cheese
Sprig of fresh dill, or parsley

Wash the fish fillets in cold water and pat dry between towels.

Wash the spinach well, shake it, and cook gently in its moisture, covered tightly. Drain well and chop fine.

Poach the fillets in salted water (see Chapter 3, Poaching), adding a slice of lemon, a sprig or two of fresh dill or parsley, and a bay leaf.

Put the spinach in the bottom of a greased, heated baking dish, lay the fish on the spinach, cover with Béchamel Sauce, and sprinkle lightly with Parmesan cheese. Brown quickly in a hot 425°F oven and serve.

Serves 2 to 4.

Mountain whitefish, also of the trout family, averages about the same size as the lake herring and may be prepared in the same manner. The winter catch is preferable for cooking; the summer catch is quite palatable when smoked.

Codfishes

The codfish family includes the cods of the Atlantic and the Pacific (but not Alaska black cod [sablefish] or lingcod), and cusk, haddock, hakes, pollocks, and tomcods. Scrod is the young codfish. The burbot or ling is a freshwater member of the cod family (see *Burbot*).

Recipes for the various species of the codfishes are applicable one to another of comparable size.

Large cod are cut into steaks and cooked like halibut steaks. Scrod are especially good split, boned, and broiled. Cod of any size go into the classic fish chowder.

Smoked cod referred to in this chapter is *cold*-smoked, i.e., dried and preserved by the cure, and is generally market fish. (Smoking methods given in Chapter 7 are *heat* smoking—actually a method of cooking—for immediate consumption.) Both salt- and smoke-cured cod are freshened and cooked similarly to fresh cod.

Atlantic and Pacific Cod

The abundance of Atlantic cod on the northwest Atlantic coast is legendary. The usual catch is up to 12 pounds, though cod does grow much larger.

Cod is unlike other fish, say the cod experts. Called the "beef of the sea," its flesh is rich and gelatinous without being fatty. The cod is a predaceous feeder, and the flesh is firm of texture and fine of flavor. It not only lends itself to all methods of cooking, but to efficient salt and smoke cures. The cod's unique propensity to rehydrating was considered a most valuable factor in the early days when shipping of fish was dependent on salting.

Nor can any other fish claim an influence of 500 years standing on the entire economic and political development of Western Europe and North America.

The abundant Pacific (gray) cod is an important fishery on the northwest coast where it grows to enormous size. Historically it has been overshadowed there by the salmon fishery.

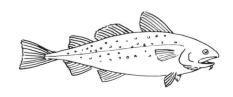

COD À LA CLARENDON

2 pounds cod, tail end (end cut after
    steaks have been cut from
    center)
Juice of 1 lemon
Salt and pepper
¼ cup butter
½ cup aspic jelly

1 cup mayonnaise
2 hard-cooked eggs, sliced
Few thin strips pimiento
1 cucumber, peeled and sliced
Capers
Pickled walnuts
Few sprigs fresh fennel or parsley

Wash the fish and pat dry. Place in well-buttered baking dish. Sprinkle lemon juice over the fish, salt and pepper lightly, and dab generously with butter. Cover with aluminum foil and bake in a 375°F oven about 20 to 30 minutes, or until flesh flakes to a fork. Remove from oven and carefully peel the skin from the fish. Let the fish get cold, and carefully move it to serving platter. Melt aspic jelly (see Chapter 3, Aspics and Jellied Stock) and stir into mayonnaise, blend well, and immediately coat the fish, covering it entirely. Chill.

Garnish the fish with egg slices, pimiento, cucumber, capers, and walnuts, with a few sprigs of fresh fennel or parsley on the platter.

Serves 4 to 6.

COD BAKED IN FILM (*en papillote*)

1 5- to 7-pound cod, head- or
    pan-dressed
¼ cup cooking oil
½ cup melted butter
½ cup dry white wine
1½ cups lobster meat, or crab or
    shrimp, preferably uncooked

2 large, firm tomatoes, sliced
1 green pepper, sliced
½ cup stuffed green olives
½ teaspoon salt
Pepper to taste

See Chapter 3, Fish Baked in Cooking Film.

Rub the fish inside and out with butter (not the melted butter) and salt lightly. Mix oil, melted butter, and wine.

Lay the fish on the cooking film in a large baking pan. Arrange the lobster meat, tomatoes, pepper rings, and olives around the fish, tucking in a few lobster claws if available. Salt lightly and pepper to taste. Pour the oil-wine-butter mixture over the fish, letting it run into the pan. Fold the edges of the film together and gather up and twister-tie the ends. Bake in a preheated 375°F oven, allowing about 10 minutes per inch thickness of the fish.

If the baking pan is presentable, serve the fish right from the film. Otherwise, open carefully, let the steam escape, and transfer the fish to a serving platter, arranging the garnish around it. Pour the pan sauce over everything. Serves about 6.

This is an excellent recipe for lean freshwater fish, such as walleye or pike.

COD AU GRATIN

1 pound fresh cod fillets	½ cup grated cheddar cheese
2 cups Cream Sauce	Dry, browned bread crumbs
Trace tarragon (optional)	

Thaw fillets if frozen, and wipe with paper towels. Poach the fillets in salted water. (See Chapter 3, Poaching.)

Prepare a medium-thick Cream Sauce, adding tarragon if desired, and into the hot sauce blend half the cheese until melted and evenly mixed. Break the cooked fillets into chunks and arrange in a casserole. Pour the sauce over the fish. Mix remaining cheese with the bread crumbs and sprinkle over top.

Put in 425° oven for about 10 minutes, until nicely browned. Don't let it overcook.

Serves 4.

Freshened salt cod may be used in the above recipe.

SMOKED COD POACHED IN MILK

2 pounds smoked cod fillets	Cayenne
Butter or bacon fat	Milk
2 onions, sliced	Salt
3 or 4 cross-slices green pepper	*Beurre manié*
Black pepper	Parsley, chopped
¼ teaspoon thyme, or oregano	Hard-boiled eggs, sliced

If the fish tastes a little too smoky, freshen it by soaking for an hour in cold water. Drain and pat dry with a towel.

Grease a baking dish lavishly with butter or bacon fat. Spread half the onion slices and the green pepper over the bottom of the dish, and lay the fish on top of them. Brush the fish well with melted butter and lay the remaining onions on top. Season with plenty of black pepper, thyme, and a few grains of cayenne. Pour milk around fish until almost covered. Salt lightly. Bake covered in 400° oven for about 20 minutes (longer if baking dish is glass or ceramic), or until fish flakes. Lift out the fish onto a serving platter, arranging onion slices and pepper rings on top. Thicken the remaining milk with a little *beurre manié* and pour over the fish. Garnish with chopped parsley or a dusting of paprika, and sliced hard-cooked eggs. Serve with lots of spinach.

Serves 4 to 6.

Baked Finnan Haddie and Kippered Herrings may be prepared as above.

Haddock

NEW ENGLAND CREAMED FINNAN HADDIE

Finnan haddie is haddock split or cut down the back to clean, and salt-smoke cured.

2 pounds finnan haddie	2 egg yolks, slightly beaten
Milk	2 hard-cooked eggs, finely chopped
2 tablespoons flour	Parsley
2 tablespoons butter	Paprika

Put the finnan haddie in a saucepan and add enough milk to cover it. Let it soak for about an hour, then put it over a low heat for about 20 minutes. Drain the milk off the fish and save.

Using the top of a double boiler, make a light *roux* of flour and butter, and stir in the warm milk from the fish, stirring constantly until lightly thickened. If sauce is too thick, stir in a little more milk or cream, and keep stirring over heat until smoothly thickened. Remove from heat, stir a little of the sauce into the egg yolks, mixing quickly and thoroughly, and quickly return the mixture to the sauce, stirring it to blend. Continue to cook another 5 minutes over simmering water, stirring frequently to keep an even texture.

Remove bones and skin from the fish, break the fish into chunks, add to the sauce, and gently stir in the chopped egg. Leave over hot water until heated through and serve, garnished with parsley and a sprinkle of paprika.

Hakes

The silver hake of the Atlantic and the Pacific hake are the most common of the hakes. They differ from the other cods in that they are very bony and have soft, fragile, perishable flesh. They are best salted and smoked.

Pollock

A favorite of sportsmen, this fighter of the cod family is sometimes, wrongly, called Boston bluefish. A good size, 4 to 15 pounds, the pollock has excellent flesh of a light brownish color. It's at its most attractive in a Manhattan-style chowder, or filleted or steaked and baked with Sauce Espagnole or colorful Tomato Sauce. (See also recipes for carp.)

Tomcods, Atlantic and Pacific

The tomcods are very small members (under 1 pound) of the cod family. The Atlantic tom occurs from Labrador south to Virginia and enters fresh waters in Quebec and the northeastern states. The Pacific tom's range is from California to Alaska. Delicious fish, they are at their best during cold weather at spawning time.

Tomcod are broiled, pan-fried, baked, or oven poached. They are delicious smoked. See Panfishes.

In Quebec tiny toms are netted through the ice and instantly frozen. Thawed and prepared like Whitebait, they are called *Poissons aux Chenaux.*

Corvinas   See DRUMS; WEAKFISH.

Crappies   See PANFISHES.

Crevalle jack   See POMPANOS AND JACKS.

Croakers

Croakers are small members of the drum family. Averaging around 2 pounds, they are widely distributed along the Atlantic and Pacific coasts; some have been reported in fresh water in Florida. Perishable, they should be dressed and iced promptly and frozen or pan-fried or broiled by basic methods; or salted, pickled or smoke cured.

Cusk   See CODFISHES.

Dolphin

The subtropical dolphin follows the warm currents along the Atlantic and Pacific coasts. A discriminating predator, the dolphin is a favorite of sportsman and gourmet alike, a catch yielding 5 to 10 pounds of excellent, firm flesh on the lean side, but rich. It broils well. Dolphin often appears on menus under its Hawaiian name *mahi-mahi*. (The pompano dolphin, a minimember of the family, is sometimes confused with young, small dolphins, but that needn't confuse the cook.)

FILLETS OF DOLPHIN WITH MUSHROOMS

½ cup butter
2 or 3 thin slices onion
2 cups sliced mushrooms
3 green pepper rings
2 pimiento pepper rings
2 pounds dolphin fillets
Salt
White pepper
1 tablespoon lemon juice

2 cups dry white wine
1 cup water
¼ cup flour
½ cup cream
Dash cayenne
Few chives, chopped
1 hard boiled egg
4 or 5 sliced black olives

Butter a large baking pan lavishly with ¼ cup of the butter. Spread the onion slices, mushrooms, and pepper rings over the bottom of the pan. Place the fish on the vegetables, salt lightly, and drizzle lemon juice, wine, and water over the fish. Closely cover with foil and poach in a preheated moderate oven at 375°F for about 15 to 25 minutes. (As the cooking time can be affected by how long it takes the dish to heat, prod the flesh with a fork after 15 minutes to see if it flakes.) Remove the fish carefully to a warm serving platter and keep it warm.

Melt the remaining butter in another saucepan and blend in the flour, stirring until it bubbles. Reduce the broth from the baking pan by half, strain, and stir into the roux. Cook until thickened. Blend in the cream and cayenne and let it heat through. Salt and pepper to taste. Add the strained mushrooms and onion.* Pour the sauce over the fillets, garnish with chopped, fresh chives, sliced hard-boiled egg, and sliced black olives. Serves 4 to 6.

* If the peppers are not unattractively limp, add them to the garnish.

Dolly Varden   See SALMONIDAE-TROUTS.

Drums   See also WEAKFISH; CROAKERS; SALTWATER BIG-GAME FISHES.

The drums are a noisy family of several species of fish, including the croakers, so collectively named due to sounds of varying amplitude made by twanging muscles against their air bladders; those without air bladders apparently grind their teeth.

The drums are predatory, medium-fatty fishes. Perishable, they should be dressed and iced as quickly as possible.

Drums of sporting and table interest include the red drum, croakers, spotted seatrout, weakfish, corvinas and white seabass. The family includes an inland member, the freshwater drum; spotted seatrout, and red drum, and some species of croakers have been reported inhabiting fresh water in Florida.

Eels and lampreys

The culinary history of eels and lampreys goes back thousands of years. Over the centuries they have been held in high regard in France and England. It was the annual custom for the City of Gloucester to present a lamprey pie to the British monarch. The importance of the eel to an Englishman has been such that even when England and Holland were at war the eel trade carried on uninterrupted, and the Dutch eel barges, holds bulging with the slithering live fish, ploughed up the Thames to the London markets.

Eel and lamprey are voracious predators, are both very fat, and have excellent flesh, although according to *Tante Marie's la Veritable Cuisine de Famille,* "eels and lampreys from fresh lakes and streams are preferable to those from moats and drains." Abundant in the Great Lakes–St. Lawrence River system and Atlantic estuarial waters, eel and lamprey offer high-quality food to North America, with no need to heed Tante Marie's cautionary advice. An offer unfortunately too generally rejected, especially in the case of the lamprey.

The common American eel is the most abundant of eels in North American waters and has long sustained a lucrative export fishery along the St. Lawrence, the runs well timed to meet the demands of the ethnic pre-Christmas trade. Also a popular sports fish, its table merits are well appreciated by French Canadians and easterners.

Besides being very lightly boned, a good reason the eel has such a high success rate on the table is its ability to live out of water a considerable length of time and thus reach the kitchen live, where it can be freshly killed for cooking.

The infamous reputation of the parasitic sea lamprey in relation to the devastation of lake trout in the Great Lakes has overshadowed its value as food, no doubt contributing to the prejudice of North Americans against eating it. Though good it should be, feeding as it does on the fine trouts.

During a period of research on lamprey control at Sault Ste. Marie, biologists reported no problem in disposing of quantities of captured lamprey, as the Finnish residents of the area actually lined up to take the delicacy off their hands.

There has been no recent commercial fishery of sea lamprey to speak of, other than for research laboratories and such. Incredibly, it has been imported from Europe for the gourmet trade.

A Pacific lamprey, neither so abundant nor disreputable as the sea lamprey, is a good food fish.

Eels and lampreys, though not related, are dressed similarly and recipes for both are interchangeable.

DRESSING EELS AND LAMPREYS

Eels and lampreys should be taken alive from fresh, clean waters and kept alive until time to cook, then killed, skinned, cleaned, and cooked at once. Eels have a tenacious hold on life. To kill either quickly, jab the point of a sharp knife or any sharp, pointed instrument into the spine at the back of the head to a depth of about an inch. This should render the fish motionless.

Lampreys require a plunge into boiling water, or scouring with coarse salt before skinning, to loosen the slimy sediment that clings to the skin, followed by rinsing in several cold waters.

With a sharp knife, cut the skin around the head, loosening the skin and drawing it down. Tie a stout cord tightly around the neck, looping it over a nail driven into a post, or nail the head directly to the post. With pliers, grasp the loosened skin at the neck and pull it down and off in one motion. Smaller specimens may be skinned by holding the head firmly in one hand and with a damp cloth in the other hand pulling the skin off. Cut off the head. Slit and clean the fish, scraping off surface fat. The light tail-fin bones may be pulled out by hand. The soft bone is easily removed, and filleting is a simple matter—simply slice the sides from the backbone.

Eel and lamprey are then fried, broiled, baked or stewed according to basic recipes for fatty fishes. Either is superb jellied, smoked, or pickled.

The rich, oily flesh of either fish is improved by a light parboiling in salt water or in a court bouillon.

SPITCHCOCKED EEL
(an English dish)

1 1 ½- to 2-pound eel	Shallot, finely minced
Salt and pepper	1 egg, beaten
Parsley, finely minced	Fine bread crumbs

Skin and dress the eel. Sprinkle with salt and refrigerate for an hour. Rinse in cold water and pat dry between towels. Remove the bone. Cut into 3-inch lengths. Season lightly with salt and pepper and sprinkle with parsley and shallot. Dip each piece in beaten egg and dredge in bread crumbs, working in a little more parsley and shallot. Spread the pieces on a plate and refrigerate until 20 minutes before serving time. Pan-fry in hot oil until crisply golden on each side.

Serve garnished with parsley lightly fried in butter, along with Piquant or Tartar Sauce, Sauce Espagnole or Tomato Sauce.

BROILED EEL

1 1 ½- to 2-pound eel	Lemon juice
Salt and pepper	2 tablespoons oil

Dress, bone, and cut as for Spitchcocked Eel above. Put on a plate, season with salt, pepper, a sprinkle of lemon juice and cooking oil. Refrigerate until 20 minutes before serving time. Move the eel to a heated, greased broiling rack and broil until golden on both sides. (See Chapter 3, Broiling.) Serve on a warm platter garnished and with sauces as above.

JELLIED EEL

1 2- to 3-pound eel, dressed	1 medium onion stuck with a clove
1 teaspoon salt	1 bay leaf
1 tablespoon lemon juice	

Dress eel as directed. Coil the fish, placing tail in mouth and tying securely. Put the coiled fish in the bottom of a deep saucepan and barely cover with water. Add the remaining ingredients.

Cover and cook gently until the flesh flakes. Do not replace lost moisture. Skim off oily surface liquid. Remove the eel to a large platter and take out the backbone intact without disturbing the flesh. Coil the fish in a pudding bowl and allow to cool while the stock is boiled down to one-half its original volume. Pour the stock over the fish and allow to set firmly. If it does not set firmly, reheat the stock and stir in 1 tablespoon gelatin moistened in cold water. Remove congealed fat, and turn the fish out on lettuce leaves on a serving plate.

Serve cold with Sauce Remoulade or Tarragon Sauce.

STUFFED EEL

1 3- to 4-pound eel	¼ teaspoon ground allspice
1 cup fine bread crumbs	⅛ teaspoon freshly grated nutmeg
1 cup hot milk	¼ teaspoon salt
1 cup finely ground veal	1 carrot, diced
1 cup raw shredded fish	1 onion, diced
Eel liver	1 green pepper, diced
2 egg yolks	Stick of celery, diced
¼ cup melted butter	½ cup white wine
½ teaspoon black pepper, freshly ground	

Skin and dress the eel, reserving the liver. Remove the bone.

Prepare the forcemeat stuffing: Add bread crumbs to milk and let soak a few minutes. Process veal, fish, and liver in blender with the egg yolks. Blend in the butter, then the milk and crumbs, and the seasonings. Blend at medium speed to a fine, pasty consistency. A little grated onion may be added.

Stuff the eel, spreading the stuffing lightly and evenly. Close the cavity with fine trussing pins and strong white thread, or sew it up with needle and thread.

Coil the fish, tying with string to secure. Put a sheet of heavy-duty aluminum foil on a baking pan, shiny side up. On the foil put a layer of diced vegetables: carrot, onion, green pepper, and celery. Lay the fish on the vegetables, and bring up the sides of the foil. Moisten with ½ cup of white wine and close the foil securely with a double fold, tucking the ends up securely.

Bake in a preheated 375°F oven for about 20 minutes per inch of thickness, or until the fish is cooked.

Carefully remove the fish to a serving platter. Remove the string and trussing. Fill the center with sautéed mushrooms and pour over all an Anchovy Sauce or other fish sauce and serve.

Variation: The stuffed eel may be served cold, galantine style, and an elegant dish it is. Let the eel cool in the foil, opening only enough to let steam escape. When cold remove from foil to serving platter.

Remove trussing and refrigerate the fish. Remove the grease from the pan drippings and use the pan juices, including vegetables, to make stock for aspic with which to glaze the fish. (See Chapter 3, Aspics.)

Fill the center with a Shrimp or Crabmeat Salad or a simple garnish and serve with a cold Mayonnaise Sauce.

DEEP-FRIED LAMPREY

2 pounds dressed lamprey, cut into 2-inch pieces
Court Bouillon No. 1
2 eggs

Fine bread crumbs seasoned with garlic salt, black pepper or a pinch of cayenne

Put lamprey into a saucepan; add court bouillon to cover. Cover and bring to a boil; remove from heat and let stand 20 minutes. Drain off the liquid. (Don't lift the fish up through it.) Pat fish between paper towels to dry.

Beat eggs until light. Dip each piece of fish into egg and roll in bread crumbs, pressing quite firmly. Arrange in a deep-fry basket, shake gently to get rid of loose crumbs, and deep-fry, or pan-fry *à l'Anglaise.* (See Chapter 3.)

MATELOTE DE LAMPROIE
(a lamprey Stew)

2 pounds dressed lamprey, cut into 2-inch pieces

Court Bouillon:
4 cups red wine
Few sprigs parsley
1 bay leaf
6–8 prunes, softened in water
2 small onions

1 or 2 carrots, cross-sliced
2 cloves garlic, bruised
Sprig of thyme
½ teaspoon cracked peppercorns
Salt

Sauce:

2½ tablespoons butter	20 white pickling onions
2½ tablespoons flour	½ pound button mushrooms

Tie the lamprey loosely in cheesecloth. Parboil as directed above, using lightly salted water. Drain.

Combine court bouillon ingredients in a kettle and simmer over a low heat for 1 hour. Cool.

When the court bouillon is cooled, add the bag of fish. Bring to a boil, turn down heat, and simmer gently until the fish flakes (about 15 minutes). Remove the bag of fish to a platter.

Prepare the sauce: In a saucepan melt the butter and, using a wooden spoon, stir in the flour, blending well. Stir over the heat until the bubbly mixture takes on a pale yellow color, then stir in 2 cups of the court bouillon, straining it through a fine sieve and reserving the prunes. Stir until the sauce is very smooth; if too thick add a little more court bouillon. (It should be a rather thin sauce–or thick soup.) Brown the white pickling onions in butter, and add with the mushrooms and the prunes. Taste and adjust seasonings. Simmer until the onions are tender.

Return the bag of fish to the sauce, letting it heat through thoroughly. Remove the fish, letting it drain over the kettle, and arrange on a large, deep, heated serving dish, removing the cheesecloth. Arrange the onions, mushrooms, and prunes around the fish and over it all pour the sauce. Garnish with croutons and serve hot.

Eulachon   See also SMELTS.

Eulachon, or candlefish, is a small delicate relative of the smelt, weighing only a few ounces. Now restricted, it supports one of the oldest of west coast fisheries. The importance of the eulachon to the economy of the Indians of the northwest coast of North America goes far back, with great value placed on the little fish as food, a source of cooking oil, of light, and as a medium of barter.

The eulachon is a very oily fish, and when dried and fitted with a wick from the inner bark of the cedar, burns like a candle. Hence the name "candle-fish."

The eulachon (also *olechan*) takes its name from the Chinook language of the West Coast Indians, interpretations of pronunciation over the years coming out *hooligan, houlikan,* and *yshuh.*

The catch is limited in Canada and the United States and is sold locally fresh and smoked.

A very perishable little fish, eulachon is superb when broiled fresh from the water, over hot coals. It is highly esteemed by Indians from California to Alaska.

Flatfishes   See FLOUNDERS.

Florida pompano   See POMPANOS AND JACKS.

Flounders (flatfishes)

One of the more curious phenomena of marine life is the flounder and the whole of its flatfishes. Actually there are two families of flounder, the left-eyed and the right-eyed. They start their independent life swimming about like any other newly hatched fry, but within a matter of days one eye begins to move to the other side until the fish has two eyes on the same side of its head. Those with eyes on the left side are called sinistrals, those on the right dextrals. Meanwhile, the fish has moved to the bottom of the ocean where, lying on its side, it can keep its world under inverted surveillance from below.

The flounder accounts for many of the world's most valuable fisheries, such as flounder, halibut, plaice, sole, and turbot. They come in sizes ranging from a few inches to 10 feet long. The flounders are lean and quite bony.

While they live close to the bottom, their preferences are generally higher on the marine food chain, and their white flesh has a fine flavor and delicate, even fragile, texture. It is fine-grained according to size.

Within a size range, recipes for various flounders are interchangeable.

Summer flounder and winter flounder

Also called respectively winter fluke and summer fluke, either may be known simply as fluke or plaice. Both Atlantic flatfishes, the summer flounder is left-eyed; the winter is right-eyed. The common catch is 2 to 5 pounds, sometimes larger, in inshore ocean and bays.

The flesh of the flukes is superb though bony, worth taking the trouble to fillet. (See *Soles.*)

BROILED SUMMER FLOUNDER

2 pounds summer flounder (fluke) fillets, cut in serving portions

See Chapter 3, Broiling. Flounder is lean and requires plenty of basting while broiling. Prepare a mixture of melted butter with lemon juice (or one of the hot butter sauces) and brush the fillets well on both sides. Arrange the fish on a preheated, greased broiling rack and dab with bits of hard butter. Broil quickly in the oven as directed. Don't overcook.

Arrange the fish on a hot serving platter. Pour off the butter from the drip pan, mix in a small handful of minced, fresh parsley, season with salt and pepper, and pour it over the fish.

Serve with lemon wedges, hot garlic bread, new sweet corn on the cob, and lots of butter.

Halibut

Halibut is a prized table fish on both the Atlantic and Pacific coasts. It commands the highest price of the flatfishes.

On the West Coast, the fishery is controlled by the International Pacific Halibut Commission of the United States and Canada. Under the Commission, the recovery of the halibut fishery on the Pacific Coast is a notable example of fishery management.

The biggest of the flounders, Pacific halibut is graded according to size: 5–10 pounds is chicken halibut; 10–40 pounds is small medium; 40–60 pounds is large medium, and so on up to "whales," which are 125 pounds and over.

On the Atlantic the grading differs: A snapper is 5–8 pounds; a chicken, 8–15 pounds; and so on to the 125-pound "whales."

Halibut most commonly taken by sportsmen are in the snapper and chicken range, which are also the finest table sizes. A dedicated predator, the halibut has glossy white flesh which is firm and flavorful. Inherently lean, its liver is rich in oils.

Halibuts are filleted or steaked. Either way simple cooking is best, with plenty of moistening, not unlike sole. Chicken halibut is superb deep-fried in batter. An esteemed market fish in Canada, its cookery reflects Scandinavian and French-Scottish cuisines.

Turbot is quite similar to halibut and is prepared by the same methods.

BAKED HALIBUT

2 pounds halibut fillets, or 4 steaks
½ cup salt pork, cut into coarse
    cubes
3 or 4 medium carrots, sliced thin
1 large onion, diced
2 tablespoons diced green pepper
1 cup diced mushrooms
1 large stick celery, sliced

1 teaspoon chopped dill weed, or ½
    teaspoon dill seed
Salt and pepper
2 tablespoons chopped fresh parsley
Butter
1 lemon, sliced
1 cup dry white wine

Wipe the fillets with a damp cloth and cut into serving portions for four.

In a flameproof oven dish, sear the pork until crisp and gold. Spread the carrots over the pork, and over them sprinkle the rest of the vegetables, the dill, and a little salt and pepper. Lay the fish over the vegetables. Dab well with butter, distribute the parsley and lemon slices over them, and pour on the wine. Cover closely and bake in a 400°F oven for about 15 minutes. Remove the cover, baste from the pan, and continue baking until lightly golden and the flesh flakes to a fork. Serve from the casserole with some of the vegetables and a few bits of the pork. Serve with a green salad and mashed potatoes.

HALIBUT IN SOUR CREAM

2 pounds halibut steaks
Salt and pepper
½ teaspoon mild curry
2 tablespoons cooking oil
2 medium onions, minced
8 small potatoes, barely cooked
6 medium tomatoes, firm and red,
    sliced

2 tablespoons lemon juice
¼ teaspoon sugar
Pinch cayenne
Pinch thyme or savory
2 cups sour cream
Paprika

Preheat oven to moderate, 350°F.

Wipe the steaks with a damp cloth. Sprinkle on both sides with salt, pepper, and curry. Heat the oil in a large frying pan and quickly sauté the fish until lightly browned but *not* cooked. Transfer to a large, heated, greased baking dish and keep warm, not hot.

Add a little more oil to the hot frying pan and in it lightly brown the onion and potatoes. Arrange them around the fish. Over everything spread the tomatoes.

Combine lemon juice, sugar, cayenne, and thyme or savory with the sour cream, mix well, and pour over the fish. Sprinkle paprika over top. Bake uncovered in oven for about 25 minutes, or until the flesh flakes to a fork.

The two preceding recipes are for large, lean fish of superior quality—not necessarily confined to halibut. They are equally fine for the freshwater great northern pike, walleye, dolphin, cod, snapper and winter-caught burbot (ling) loins.

Soles

More lines of cookery seem to have been written under the title "Sole" than any other basic item of food, unless it's sauces. On close scrutiny the extensive mileage appears to be the result of permutations and combinations of soles, basic simple cookery methods, and sauces.

Actually, the best of the North American table soles, whether obtained by hook and line or over the counter, are not of the true sole fraternity, but are right-handed flounders, i.e., their eyes are on the right side. Most plentiful on the West Coast, these are the butter sole, the Dover, petrale (brill), English (lemon), rex and rock soles, and diamond turbot. The winter flounder and witch flounder of the Atlantic are also right-eyed flounders, not that this matters to the cooking, but they are small and their delicate flesh is comparable with that of the fine soles and are cooked by the same recipes. In fact both are also known by the name "gray sole." Summer flounder or fluke, in the same cookery class, is left-eyed, and a little bigger than the winter. For that matter, the term "sole" is applied rather loosely to small members of the flounder family. Small soles may be pan-dressed and cooked whole; large soles are filleted and skinned like other flounders.

Delicate in flavor and in texture, the soles should be cooked by the simplest of methods and handled tenderly. Pan fry *à la meunière* or quickly sauté and finish in the oven, with one of the many fine white or cream fish sauces. Sole is excellent gently poached or steamed by the basic method. It is superb deep-fried in a crisp batter. Create your own combination and add to the list. Whatever you do with sole, above all, don't let it overcook. Garnish it with an eye to color.

FILLETS OF SOLE BAKED IN WINE SAUCE

1 pound sole fillets, fresh or frozen
2 tablespoons clarified butter, or
    salad oil
2 tablespoons finely minced onion
2 tablespoons flour

¾ teaspoon salt
Pinch white pepper
1 cup light cream or milk, heated
½ cup white wine

Defrost frozen fillets in their package. Wipe fish with a damp cloth, cut into serving portions, and arrange in a layer in a well-buttered shallow baking dish.

Heat the oil over medium heat and sauté the onion to a golden translucence. Stir in the flour and cook and stir until smoothly blended and bubbly. Add the salt and pepper, and in a slow and steady stream, stir in the cream, stirring constantly until thickened. Remove from heat and slowly stir in wine until blended.

Pour the sauce over the fish. Bake in a preheated 350°F oven for about ½ hour or until the flesh flakes to a fork. Spoon the sauce from the pan over the fish from time to time, keeping it well distributed over the fish.

This recipe is also excellent for fillets of walleye, winter caught lake whitefish, halibut, flounder, red snapper, etc.

Fluke   See FLOUNDERS.

Flying fish

Flying fishes really do fly. Taking off on the tropical breezes like a fleet of silvery toy planes, they soar at speeds up to 35 miles per hour on their gossamer, winglike fins.

Flying fish are one of the finest delicacies of marine food fishes. They are netted commercially and some are taken by angling.

Flying fish weigh less than a pound of lean, whitish, delicious flesh. They are bony, having ribs that fork into a second row of fine bones. They are plank-split butterfly fashion, and boned and broiled simply, in tropical tradition. (See also *Panfishes.*)

Freshwater drum   See also DRUMS.

The freshwater drum's range takes in the Hudson Bay, Great Lakes, and

Missouri drainage systems, and it occurs generally under various local names, such as sheepshead, drum sunfish, silver bass, grunter, and so on.

The freshwater drum is a fat fish; it may grow to great size but its average is around 3 to 5 pounds or less. Not noted for inherent fineness of flavor and texture at any time, the early spring- or winter-caught drum, freshly dressed and skinned, does credit to a savory Manhattan-style chowder or stew or to a salt cure and smokehouse treatment.

Goldeye

A category of freshwater fishes of greater or lesser sporting qualities, generally labeled "coarse," has been discussed in Chapter 3. The culinary potential of these too-often-scorned fish is best illustrated in the Cinderella story of the Lake Winnipeg goldeye.

Before its transformation in the smokehouse a half century ago, the goldeye was a coarse, abundant, nuisance fish in Lake Winnipeg. In 1900 its soft, unattractive gray flesh sold for a cent a pound as dog food. Now, in its gleaming golden jacket, smoked Winnipeg goldeye has earned worldwide prestige as an exotic delicacy and commands a price to match.

The momentous discovery that changed the goldeye's destiny was that smoke from smoldering willow wood gave the flesh of the fish a beautiful reddish-gold color and a distinctive exquisite flavor. When the willow supply failed to stand up to pressures of mass production, it was found that oak and maple give the same delectable flavor, but not the color. In today's production, food coloring provides the tint.

The Lake Winnipeg population of goldeye also failed to stand the pressure, and now the Winnipeg smokehouses import the goldeye from other waters. The name "Winnipeg goldeye," however, does not refer to the lake, but to the special process that was developed in Winnipeg and boosted the fish to fame and fortune.

Heat-smoked, the fish are already cooked and ready to eat. They may be refrigerated for a few days, but should not be freezer-stored, as freezing impairs their flavor and general quality. Eat them cold or warm them up in a moderate oven and serve with an herb butter. Or, as the purists dictate, simply eat them with a sprinkle of lemon juice.

Groupers   See NASSAU GROUPER AND RED GROUPER; SEA BASSES AND GROUPERS.

Grunion   See PANFISHES.

Grunts   See PANFISHES.

Haddock   See CODFISHES.

Hakes   See CODFISHES.

Halibut   See FLOUNDERS.

Herrings

Members of the herring family of table importance are the Atlantic and Pacific herrings, the pilchard (Pacific sardine), and the American and hickory shads. (See also *Shads.*) The anadromous shads live in fresh water as well as salt. The alewife is a herring. Freshwater or lake herring (cisco) are of another family (Salmonidae), not true herrings.

Of worldwide abundance, the herring has a long history of commercial importance. One of the first coastal fishes utilized by man, it probably sparked the ancient and universal practice of curing. Being a fat little fish (over 1 pound is a big one), the herring cures well, and salting, smoking, or kippering herring are still the favored methods of preparation.

Fresh herring is very good pan-fried. The scaled fish cooks better if scored along the sides with gashes about 1½ inches apart. (See also *Panfishes.*)

The Pacific herring has been an important item of food and barter to the West Coast Indians for many centuries.

SLOWPOKES
(a Newfoundland dish)

6 fresh herring or gaspereau (alewives), under 1 pound each, filleted and boned

Season each fish with salt, pepper, and lemon juice. Roll the fillet and secure with a toothpick. If handy, tuck an anchovy fillet inside the roll. Arrange the rolled fillets closely in a baking dish and add:
1 cup vinegar with 1 tablespoon sugar mixed in; *or* 1 cup juice from sweet pickles or pickled beets.

Combine 1 cup sour cream with 1 teaspoon lemon juice and pour over the fish. Add a trace of cayenne, and salt and pepper to taste.

Bake in a slow oven at 325° until the fish flakes to a fork.

Pan-size trouts or smelts, cleaned and boned, may be prepared in the above manner.

SMOKED HERRING, OVEN-POACHED

Cut the heads and tails from smoked herring. Cover with cold water and soak overnight. Put in a greased baking dish, cover with onion slices and a bit of thyme or other herb, add some pepper, and add milk to not quite cover. Cover the dish and bake in a 350°F oven for about 30 minutes. Serve the herrings in the milk, or move them to a platter and thicken the pan milk with a little *beurre manié* to make a sauce.

KIPPERED HERRING

See Codfishes: Smoked Cod Poached in Milk.

Hickory shad   See SHADS.

Inconnu   See SALMONIDAE-TROUTS.

Jacks   See POMPANOS AND JACKS.

King mackerel (Cavalla)   See SALTWATER
BIG-GAME FISHES.

Kokanee   See SALMONIDAE-TROUTS.

Lake herring   See CISCO OR LAKE HERRING.

Lake sturgeon

The sturgeons of North America belong to a family of ancient prehistoric lineage. Seven species are listed for the U.S. and Canada, and with the exception of the green sturgeon of the West Coast, are eminently edible. The freshwater lake sturgeon is the most common.

The lake sturgeon's range is wide, taking in three drainage basins, the Mississippi, the Great Lakes system, and the Hudson Bay.

The size of the lake sturgeon is legendary. Properly documented records reveal fish taken from North American inland waters at over 300 pounds; early unconfirmed reports have claimed catches at around 2,000. In any case, it's a big fish even at today's average of around 40 pounds.

The lake sturgeon is not as common as it once was when Hiawatha's "king of fishes" patrolled the inland deeps in vast number.

The destruction of the lake sturgeon in North America has been compared in wantonness to that of the passenger pigeon and the bison. Prior to the mid-nineteenth century, when both value and diminishing number were becoming vaguely apparent, the huge fish were netted by the thousands. Considered worthless, net-tearing monsters who fed on more valuable fishes, they were thrown on the banks to rot or carted away for various extravagant uses. Piled like cordwood, they were dried and burned, or used as fertilizer, although some were rendered of their copious oils which were marketed in Detroit. According to research by W. J. K. Harkness, sturgeons were reportedly used to fire the boilers of the Great Lakes steamboats, a supply piled ready on the dock at Amherstburg.

The French Canadians utilized sturgeon meat in stews and soups, and pickled it, parboiling to rid it of its excessive oils. This is the basis of the cookery of fresh sturgeon.

However, it was not until the late 1800's that smoked lake sturgeon and the roe (caviar) began to get the attention they deserved, and sturgeon market fishery, along with valuable commercial by-products, became an important aspect of the fishing industry. The sturgeon is now protected and fishery controlled by international regulation.

Far from being the threat to "other valuable fishes" that the early settlers believed it to be, the general fare of the sturgeon is mostly small animal life that it takes from the bottom, and it has been known to feed on spillages of wheat and corn near grain elevators. It is wise to fish sturgeon from clean, fresh waters.

The flesh of the sturgeon, even with excessive oils removed, is still a rich dish. Its excellent flavor has been described as more like chicken than fish, but it is perhaps more like domestic duck than chicken. Certainly, when from cold northern waters in the spring of the year, it is superb fare when properly cooked. It should be parboiled and boiled or poached; it is far too rich for most tastes to fry.

Fat, coarse of grain, and flaky, sturgeon is a superior smoker and is excellent pickled. (See Chapter 7.)

The sturgeon has a tough, armorlike skin. It should be skinned as soon as the fish comes from the water, otherwise traces of its muddy haunts are imparted to the flesh. The fish should be dressed at the same time. The roe should be reserved; it is highly valuable as caviar.

One average-size sturgeon provides about 25 pounds of excellent bone free fish for the freezer. To freeze sturgeon, cross-cut the dressed fish into family-size portions (about 2 pounds). Pull out the spinal cord of each piece immediately and wash the fish. Do not cut into individual serving portions. (See Chapter 2, Freezing Fish.)

STURGEON IN ASPIC

2-pound center cut of sturgeon, fresh or frozen	1 tablespoon gelatin
	½ cup white wine
1 lemon, juice and rind	1 medium cucumber, thinly sliced
Fish stock	2 hard-cooked eggs, sliced
1 carrot, sliced	Ripe olives, parsley, lemon slices

Thaw frozen fish.

Parboil in water to which the juice and rind of 1 lemon has been added. Follow directions in Chapter 3, Parboiling.

Pour or ladle off the oily surface water; lift the fish. Discard the water.

After the water is discarded, cover the fish with the hot fish stock, add the sliced carrot, and simmer gently until the flesh flakes. Skim off oil. Remove the fish and let it cool, then chill. Boil the stock down to about 2 cups. Skim off any oil. Dissolve the gelatin in a little cold water, stir into the hot stock, and stir over heat until well blended. Strain through a cloth-lined sieve, saving the carrot slices. Add the wine and let cool until slightly thickened—that is, pourable but not set.

Pour a little of the aspic over the bottom of a serving platter and set the fish on it. Lightly glaze the fish with a little more of the aspic and decorate the top with slices of the cooked carrot, the cucumber, and the egg. Pour the remaining aspic over the fish and refrigerate to set. Serve well chilled, garnished with olives, parsley and lemon slices around the edges, and with Beetroot and Horseradish Sauce on the side.

Lake trout   See SALMONIDAE-TROUTS.

Lake whitefish

Long valued by Indians and Eskimos, lake whitefish has only in the past few years been recognized by anglers and consumers for the fine fish that it is.

Lake whitefish is one of the cisco group of the trout family. (See *Cisco or lake herring.*)

According to northern Indians, it is the perfect food. On a diet of whitefish, all goes well. Without it, ailments.

Lake whitefish has always been important as dog food in the North, where the Indians partially dry or "hang" it to make light work for the dogs who must carry it. A ten-day requirement for six dogs being 120 fish, weight is a consideration when the whitefish up there run to 8 pounds, of which 90 percent is water.

The fish are dried by hanging them from a scaffolding of willows. Slit through the tail, they are threaded on a willow stick and hung to dry well off the ground. The slit must be "just right or the fish will fall off."

The recent recognition of the lake whitefish is in measure due to the increasing popularity of ice-fishing, for the whitefish is a winter fish. In summer the bottom-feeding whitefish is fat and sluggish and as a fresh food and angling item it is best ignored.

Winter-caught whitefish is another matter. The post-spawning fish is leaner and hungrier and provides a good sport and tasty flesh. The winter whitefish is an important commercial fishery.

The fat summer and fall whitefish, however, is an excellent smoker and much is smoked commercially.

Lake whitefish is extremely delicate and perishable and should be handled gently. Winter whitefish freezes well, and ice-fishing conditions make it an ideal stock item for the home freezer.

A superior table fish, the 4- to 5-pounders are as delicious as they are beautiful when stuffed and baked whole under a tomato sauce. Their fine, delicate flavor is also shown to advantage by steaming whole over water with white wine and serving chilled as a cold entrée.

While the lake whitefish grow up to 15 pounds, 3 to 5 pounds is about the average catch.

Lake whitefish and mountain whitefish are different species, although both belong to the trout family. The lake whitefish occurs inland in fresh water from the border states northward, and also in the Atlantic. The mountain variety is strictly a freshwater fish, its range that of the Rocky Mountains (it's also called Rocky Mountain whitefish). It is a good smoker, and best prepared in that manner. The winter catch is superior to the summer catch.

LAKE WHITEFISH BAKED IN SAUCE ESPAGNOLE

1 3- to 5-pound winter-caught lake whitefish, dressed or pan-dressed	2 cups Sauce Espagnole
	White wine
Wild Rice Stuffing	Melted butter

Refer to Chapter 3, Baking. Prepare stuffing and Sauce Espagnole. Prepare and stuff the fish and bake as directed. Baste frequently with a mixture of white wine and melted butter until the fish is just beginning to brown, but is not quite done. Pour half the Sauce Espagnole over the fish and finish cooking uncovered. Carefully move the fish to a warm platter and keep in a warm oven. Stir the remaining Sauce Espagnole into the pan drippings, and cook and stir for about 5 minutes.

Garnish with fresh parsley, lemon wedges, and black olives around the fish. Serve the pan sauce in a sauceboat on the side.

Lake whitefish may be filleted and chunked, and deep-fried.

WHITEFISH FILLETS À LA VIEILLE GARE

4 tablespoons butter	1½ pounds lake whitefish fillets
1 tablespoon chopped onion	Salt and pepper
½ cup mushrooms, chopped	White bread crumbs
½ cup dry white wine	Parsley, chopped

Melt 2 tablespoons butter and fry onion in it over a low heat until soft but not colored. Add mushrooms and cook for 1 minute. Add white wine and boil rapidly for another minute. Lay fish fillets in a buttered, shallow ovenproof dish. Season and pour wine mixture over them. Sprinkle evenly with bread crumbs and dot with remaining butter. Cook near top of preheated oven at 400°F or 450°F. For thick fillets, 20 minutes should see the fish just cooked and crumbs golden and crisp. Sprinkle with chopped parsley. Serve hot in the cooking dish.

Jean-Claude Forgeront,
Chef des Cuisines,
La Vieille Gare, St. Boniface, Manitoba

WHITEFISH IN ASPARAGUS SAUCE

2 pounds fillets winter-caught
    whitefish, skinned
Salt and pepper
½ cup white wine
½ teaspoon prepared French-style
    mustard

½ cup cream
1 cup Asparagus Sauce
½ cup grated cheddar cheese

Wipe the fillets with a damp cloth, cut into serving portions. Season the fish with salt and pepper, and sauté quickly on each side. Place in bottom of a well-buttered glass or ceramic baking pan.

Deglaze the sauté pan with the wine and mix in the mustard. Blend in the cream and asparagus sauce. Pour over the fish. Bake in a preheated hot oven (400°F) for about 20 minutes, or until bubbly and the fish is cooked. Sprinkle cheese over top and return to oven until cheese has melted.

Serve with fresh cooked asparagus tips, dressed with hot Lemon Butter.

The above recipe may be used for any of the delicately flavored lean white-fleshed fish like walleye, sole, and the young of the cod family. Also for Florida pompano and red snapper.

WINTER WHITEFISH SALAD
(or other delicately flavored white-fleshed fish)

5 pounds dressed winter-caught
    whitefish (or 3 pounds
    pan-dressed)
2 cups sour cream
2 tablespoons lemon juice
1 teaspoon salt

¼ teaspoon white pepper, or more
    to taste
⅛ teaspoon cayenne
½ cup diced celery heart
¼ cup diced pimiento

If the fish is lean, steam over white wine and water, or poach in a fish fumet. (See Chapter 3, Steaming; Poaching.) If fatty, poach in Court Bouillon, No. 1 or 2. Let the fish cool, skin it, and remove bones. Break the meat into chunks. Cover with a damp cloth and refrigerate.

Blend sour cream, lemon juice, and seasonings and chill for at least an hour. Then into the mixture blend celery and pimiento. Blend the fish into the dressing and refrigerate until needed.

WHITEFISH PRAIRIE MOUSSE

1 tablespoon plain gelatin	2 tablespoons finely diced sweet
¼ cup cold water	gherkins
¼ cup boiling water	1 tablespoon lemon juice
1½ teaspoons salt	Dash white pepper
1 cup stiffly whipped cream	Cucumber, washed and sliced very
2 cups flaked steamed lake whitefish	thin
1 tablespoon prepared horseradish	Lettuce, watercress, or parsley sprigs
½ cup finely diced celery	

Soak gelatin in cold water. Add boiling water and salt and stir well. Let cool. Fold in the whipped cream, then fold in the whitefish. Add next five ingredients and blend.

Lightly oil a 3-cup fish mold. Pour in one-third of the fish mixture, spread with a layer of cucumber slices; repeat, ending with a layer of fish. Chill until firm. Turn out onto a serving plate. Garnish with greens, adding black and green stuffed olives, and decorate with anchovies if desired.

Lamprey   See EELS AND LAMPREYS.

Largemouth bass and smallmouth bass

The most popular freshwater game basses, the largemouth and the smallmouth, are not basses at all but belong to the sunfish family. They are distributed widely over North America under a profusion of folk names. Largemouth collectively takes in black bass, Alabama spotted, Florida largemouth, green bass, green trout, Oswego bass, lake bass, and mossback, to mention some; the smallmouth goes by black perch, brown bass, black bass, river bass, tiger, gold and redeye bass, and bronzeback.

Generally running 2 to 4 pounds in weight, these lean, scrappy game fishes have excellent firm flesh. The skin may tend to have a bitter taste, although this is usually not the case in small smallmouths. They are generally at their best filleted and skinned, then cooked by simple basic methods for lean fish. Recipes for walleye fillets may also be used.

Black and white crappies and rockbass are "panfish" members of the sunfish families.

STUFFED FILLETS OF BASS

4 smallmouth or largemouth bass,
    1 ½ to 2 pounds each, filleted
    and skinned
1 tablespoon butter
¼ cup finely minced onion
4 slices stale bread
½ cup milk

¼ teaspoon thyme or chervil
Salt and pepper
1 egg, beaten
Flour
1 egg yolk, beaten
½ cup fine, dry bread crumbs
Oil for deep frying

Wipe the fillets with a damp cloth.

Melt the butter and cook the onion until translucent. Soak the bread in the milk until soft and wet, and squeeze dry, rubbing and crumbling the bread with your hands. Mix the bread with the onion, add seasonings, and mix with the beaten egg to bind. Dividing the mixture evenly, spread it over the fillets and roll up paupiette fashion, fastening with a toothpick. Dust the rolls with flour, dip in beaten egg yolk, and roll in the bread crumbs. Arrange in deep-fry basket (see Chapter 3, Deep-frying) and plunge into hot fat. Fry until golden brown all over. Toothpicks may be removed before serving.

Serve with Tomato Sauce.

Yields 8 paupiettes.

BASS BAKED IN SOUR CREAM

2 pounds largemouth or smallmouth
    bass fillets, skinned
Flour, seasoned
2 hard-cooked eggs, sliced
½ cup clarified butter
½ pound mushrooms, sliced

4 medium potatoes, raw, sliced
Salt and pepper
½ cup Velouté Sauce
½ cup sour cream
¼ cup grated cheese

Cut the fillets into four portions. Dust in seasoned flour and sauté quickly in greased frying pan over brisk heat. Put the fish in a lavishly buttered baking dish. Lay a few slices of egg on each portion.

Melt the half cup butter and lightly fry the mushrooms in it. With a slotted spoon remove the mushrooms and pile them on the fish. In the same butter brown the potatoes until almost cooked and arrange them around the fish. Season everything with salt and pepper to taste.

Combine Velouté Sauce and sour cream, heat through while blending well, and pour it over the fish and potatoes, covering everything. Sprinkle cheese over the sauce, and bake in a preheated moderately hot oven at 400°F for about 20 minutes, on until bubbly and brown.

Serves 4.

Ling   See BURBOT.

Lingcod

The lingcod is a Pacific fish, ranging from Alaska to California. While no relation to the cod, this lean predator is cooked in much the same way as fresh cod. (See *Codfishes*.) Lingcod grows to monstrous size, but the young, small and slim ones (under 10 pounds) are the best table fish.

Little snook   See SNOOKS.

Mackerel   See ATLANTIC MACKEREL AND PACIFIC MACKEREL; SALTWATER BIG-GAME FISHES.

Madtoms   See CATFISHES; PANFISHES.

Marlin   See SALTWATER BIG-GAME FISHES.

Minnows   See PANFISHES; WHITEBAIT.

Mountain whitefish   See LAKE WHITEFISH.

Mullet

Of worldwide distribution, from ancient times the mullet has been a highly esteemed food fish of Europe and the Middle East, especially red mullet. According to C. E. Francatelli's nineteenth-century *Modern Cook* (T. B. Peterson, Philadelphia, 26th ed.), the generic term *mullus* from which the name derives is said to have reference to the scarlet color of the sandal or shoe worn by the Roman consuls and in later times by the emperors, which shoe was called *mullus.* The mullet provides one of the earlier examples of fish farming, having been successfully cultivated by the Egyptians and Romans. The *Modern Cook* goes on to say that mullets should never be drawn; that it is enough to take out the gills only, "as the liver and trail are considered the best parts of this fish."

North American striped mullet is the variety most abundant along the southern half of the California coast and along the Atlantic coast, Florida accounting for the major landings and market. Mullet is the Ama-Ama of Hawaii, and a popular food fish of the Southern states. (In some northern regions suckers are mistakenly called mullets.)

The catch averages 2 to 3 pounds. Mullet flesh is rich in food values; it has a sweet nutlike flavor. The lean ones are best broiled or simply pan-fried and served with a Lemon Butter Sauce. The fatter mullets may be poached in a white wine or sherry fumet (or champagne). (See Chapter 3.) Fat mullets are best smoked.

The epicurean delights of the entrails of the mullet notwithstanding, we generally prefer to clean the fish we eat. However, mullet roe is a delicacy (see Chapter 5).

MULLET POACHED IN WINE

4 small mullets, pan-dressed	Juice of ½ lemon
Fine Herbs Sauce	Anchovy essence (optional)
½ cup sherry, or white wine	Fresh parsley

Wash and pat dry dressed mullets and place them in a well-buttered baking dish. Pour half the Fine Herbs Sauce over the fish, and add sherry or white wine.

Half an hour before serving time, put the mullets into a preheated hot oven, at 425°, to bake, basting them with their own sauce until done. Remove the fish and arrange on a warm serving platter and keep warm. Add a little wine to the pan, swishing it around to deglaze the sides, then mix it into the remaining sauce. Add the lemon juice and a few drops of anchovy essence, if handy, and pour the sauce over the fish. Serve at once, garnished with a few sprigs of fresh parsley.

Muskellunge

Also called maskinonge in Canada, the muskie got its name from the Ojibways, meaning "ugly fish."

The muskie and its close relative the northern pike (see also *Northern pike*) are known to sportsmen for their spunk and to cooks for their bones. Each grows to an impressive and challenging size, but is both more manageable in the kitchen and palatable on the table when it tips the scale at a modest 10 pounds or less.

Most abundant in regions of the Great Lakes, the muskie averages around 10 pounds, and 30 is not uncommon. At these sizes the voracious predator may not be considered the prize in the kitchen that it is on the end of a line, but it should not be overlooked. Skinned and filleted, its lean flesh is excellent in flavor and does justice to a fish stew or chowder.

Mutton snapper   See RED SNAPPER.

Nassau grouper and red grouper

Probably best known of the groupers to anglers and commercial fishermen and preferred by cooks are the Nassau grouper and the smaller of the reds taken in shallow inshore waters around southern Florida. Both are lean fish.

The Nassau's average catch is 3 to 4 pounds. It is rather bony and has a tough, bitter-tasting skin. Its skinned fillets, when cut in chunks, make an excellent chowder or "deep fry." Red grouper is treated the same way. (See also *Sea basses and groupers*.)

Northern pike

According to Walton, the northern pike is "too good for any but anglers, or very honest men." It is of circumpolar distribution and ranges widely and in abundance in North America from the border states northward through Canada and Alaska. Also called Great Northern, and jackfish, it averages 2 to 4 pounds but may go to 40 pounds; it is best under 5 to 6 pounds.

The flesh of the pike is excellent, long held in high esteem in Europe. The fish, according to its size, may be baked or steamed whole, or filleted and cooked by basic methods for lean fish. Boning a pike is complicated and is best demonstrated by an expert. Methods whereby the bones are disposed of in the preparation process, such as in stews and chowders, are good for the big specimens. A salt cure and pickle cure which soften the bones are also recommended.

PIKE WITH ANCHOVIES

1 2–3 pound pike, dressed and scaled	1 large onion, sliced
Lemon juice	½ cup melted butter
Salt	1 dozen anchovy fillets

Wash the fish and pat dry with paper towels. Rub cavity with lemon juice and salt, and tuck in a couple of slices of onion.

Put the remaining onion slices in the baking pan. Pour in half the melted butter, and lay the fish on the onion. Score the top side of the fish with slits about ½ inch deep and insert anchovy slices. Brush with melted butter, reserving about 2 tablespoons.

Bake in a hot oven, basting frequently from the pan, until the fish flakes.

Pound 3 or 4 of remaining anchovy fillets to a paste, mix with remaining melted butter, and spread over the fish. Garnish with fresh parsley and serve with buttered boiled potatoes and a green salad.

GREAT NORTHERN PIKE IN ASPIC

For dramatic presence on the evening buffet, a whole 4- to 5-pound pike, appropriately garnished and served on a gleaming silver platter, is an imposing production.

1 4- to 5-pound pike	1 medium cucumber, unpeeled and
½ cup white wine	sliced thin
2 quarts Fish Stock No. 2	Pickled pimiento
1 tablespoon gelatin	Green Sauce
Black olives	

The pike should be dressed whole, head and tail on, scaled, and all but the pectoral fins cut out.

Handling carefully, steam the pike (see Chapter 3, Steaming), adding ½ cup white wine to the water. Steam until the flesh flakes to a fork, and remove from the steamer.

Meanwhile, reduce 2 quarts of fish stock by half and clarify it. (See Chapter 3, Aspics and Jellied Stock.) Mix a tablespoon of gelatin in a little cold water and stir into the hot stock. Stir over the heat until well dissolved. Let cool until slightly thickened but not set. Pour a little of the aspic over the bottom of a silver platter, and put it in the refrigerator to set. Reserve the remaining aspic at room temperature.

Run the point of a knife around the shoulders of the pike, just behind the pectoral fins, and around the caudal peduncle in front of the tail, and carefully remove the skin from the body. Carefully lay the fish in the middle of the aspic-coated tray. Pour a thin coating of aspic over the fish. Now cover the exposed flesh of the fish with rows of cucumber slices, overlapping shingle style to resemble the scales of the fish, starting at the tail and working toward the neck, one row up the middle, then a row on either side until covered.

Surround the fish with half-round scoops of a fine, moist potato salad, evenly spaced. Put a plump raisin or green cherry in each eye. Using the remaining aspic, pour it evenly over the entire fish and the potato salad. Start with a thin layer, let it set, and repeat until it is covered with a thin coat. Garnish each scoop of salad with a black olive or a small piece of pimiento, alternating colors.

Chill in refrigerator until needed. Serve with Green Sauce.

NORTHERN PIKE IN WINE SAUCE

4 pounds pike fillets	½ cup peeled chopped tomatoes
½ cup flour	½ cup dry white wine
Salt and pepper	½ cup sautéed sliced mushrooms
3 tablespoons cooking oil	2 tablespoons chopped parsley
¾ cup chopped onion	

Roll fish in the flour, which has been seasoned with salt and pepper. Sauté fillets and onion in hot oil until fish is browned on both sides and flakes easily. Remove fish and keep warm.

Add tomatoes and wine to the onions in the skillet and cook 5 minutes. Stir in mushrooms and parsley. Heat through. Pour sauce over the fish, sprinkle with a little parsley and serve.

Jean Power
Mississauga, Ontario

BAKED PIKE

See *Codfishes:* Cod baked in Film; *Flounders:* Baked Halibut, Halibut in Sour Cream.

Northern puffer

This fascinating slender little fish when annoyed blows himself up (or rather blows up a built-in balloon device attached to his stomach) like a small beach ball. Hence the name. Puffers, or blowfish as they are also called, are getting more and more attention from anglers along the northwest Atlantic coast as their table merits become appreciated. When skinned, which is done easily, the puffer reveals along its back delectable, edible loins, not unlike a chicken drumstick in appearance, which piece (and often the fish itself) is commonly known as a "sea squab." This is all of the puffer that is edible. Viscera are toxic.

Skinning the puffer must be done carefully, and it should be skinned and dressed as soon as caught. Gloves should be worn as the fish has a rather nasty, prickly skin. Care must be taken that the knife does not penetrate the viscera, or any other part of the puffer.

Skinning a puffer. Lay the fish on a cutting board, belly down, grasping it firmly by the head. With a sharp knife cut through the backbone just back of the head, but don't cut right through. Still holding the head, flip the fish over on its back and, pressing the fish down with the other hand, pull the head back and slip off the skin inside-out like a glove. Carefully cut away the loins (the part between the dorsal and lateral lines) in one solid round piece of flesh with the bone running up the middle. This is a sea squab. Rinse the piece well. Discard everything else.

Although the fish is a bottom feeder, the edible part of the puffer is fine, firm, and delicately flavored. Sea squab commands a high price at the market. It is pan-fried, deep-fried, or broiled.

Northern redhorse   See SUCKERS.

Ocean perch   See REDFISH.

Ouananiche   See SALMONIDAE-TROUTS.

Pacific cod   See CODFISHES.

Pacific herring   See HERRINGS; PANFISHES.

Pacific lamprey   See EELS AND LAMPREYS.

Pacific mackerel   See ATLANTIC MACKEREL AND PACIFIC MACKEREL.

Pacific permit   See POMPANOS AND JACKS.

Pacific pompano   See PANFISHES.

Panfishes

The panfishes are those fine flavored, succulent *little* sport fishes too small to be considered game fish, and small enough to fit into a frying pan. They are usually well under a pound in weight. For cooking purposes, small game fishes of "keeper" length may be considered panfish if they fit the pan.

The panfishes are the small herrings, cods and scrods, whitings, grunts, snappers, butterfish, flying fish—the surf perches, the freshwater perches of the temperate bass family, and the basses of the sunfish family which includes, besides sunfish, the pumpkinseed, bream, the crappies and bluegills; the perch family itself and the pickerels of the pike family. Brown bullheads (mudcat, mudpout, catfish, madtom) are panfish. Smelts are dealt with separately.

Panfish are very perishable. The whole essence of their goodness is in their freshness. They require prompt on-the-spot cleaning and cooling, and then into pan or freezer.

For more on panfish, see Chapter 1 and Chapter 3.

—Mace

DILLED PANFISH

3 or 4 pan-dressed panfish, fresh or
frozen
Salt and pepper
½ cup clarified butter, or margarine

1 tablespoon crushed dill weed,
preferably fresh
Juice of 1 lemon

If frozen, thaw fish in refrigerator. Wash in cold water and pat dry between towels. Cut through ribs to one side of backbone (plank split), and flatten the fish. Sprinkle with salt and pepper. Melt butter in frying pan, add dill weed, and let it heat through until the butter is bubbly. Place 2 of the fish, flesh down, in the hot butter. Fry for 2 or 3 minutes until lightly browned, turn carefully, and continue cooking until flesh flakes (another 2 or 3 minutes). Carefully lift the fish to a warm serving platter and keep in warm oven. When remaining fish have been cooked, turn heat down to low and stir the lemon juice into the dilled butter. Pour over the fish and serve.

Variation: Substitute capers or wild sorrel (sourgrass) for dill.

Perch   See WALLEYE AND SAUGER; PANFISHES.

Pickerels   See also WALLEYE AND SAUGER.

The pickerels, which include redfin, grass pickerel, and chain pickerel, are the small members of the pike family. Their range extends from the Great Lakes regions southward. They are quite tasty when scaled or filleted and skinned depending on size, and cooked by basic methods for lean fish. (See *Panfishes.*) Although they should not be, the pickerels are persistently confused with walleye.

Pike   See NORTHERN PIKE.

Pilchard   See HERRINGS; PANFISHES.

Plaice   See FLOUNDERS.

Pollocks   See CODFISHES.

Pompanos and jacks

Members of this family of fatty fishes range in size from about 2 pounds to a big-game 50 pounds. The smaller members, the Florida pompano, the Pacific permit, and the very young crevalle jack (about 2 pounds or less) are at their table-best when simply cooked—pan-fried à la meunière, broiled, or baked. Fatty, they also smoke well.

The Pacific pompano is of another family, the butterfishes. The pompano dolphin is a dolphin—a lean fish.

Florida pompano

Due to the presence of other species in the Atlantic called pompano, the name Florida pompano has been adopted for the Atlantic pompano (*Trachinotus carolinus*), since Florida is the major source of commercial pompano.

The little Florida, which averages 1 to 2 pounds, is considered one of the finest fish in the ocean. It is exported fresh as far inland as Toronto markets, where it meets a ready demand.

Certainly, with its silvery pink skin, it is one of the most beautiful fish.

The exquisite flavor and firm, rich flesh of pompano lends itself to simple cookery with understated seasonings. It is cooked whole or filleted, and is broiled, or fried à la meunière or à l'Anglaise. (See Chapter 3.)

Pompano and trout (small size) recipes are interchangeable.

FLORIDIAN POMPANO, SHRIMP-FILLED
(an adaptation of a Southern classic)

1 2-pound Florida pompano, scaled and filleted, skin left on	1 cup minced, cooked shrimp
1 cup Mushroom Sauce, heavy	1 tablespoon brandy
¼ cup heavy cream	Salt, pepper, paprika
	¼ cup sherry

Wipe the fillets with a damp cloth.

Mix half the cream into the Mushroom Sauce until well blended. Mix in the shrimp, then the brandy. Sandwich the filling between the two fillets, skin side out, and close the edges with a needle and thread or small lacing pins. Put into a well-greased shallow baking dish, just big enough to take it comfortably, mix the sherry in the remaining cream and pour it over the fish. Bake in a preheated oven until the flesh flakes to a fork, about 40 minutes, spooning the pan sauce over the top occasionally. Serve very hot, garnished with sliced cucumbers which have been marinated in salted water with a little vinegar.

The whole pompano, boned, may be prepared as above.

Variation: Stuff with Wild Rice and Partridge Stuffing, using chicken or available wildfowl.

Pompano dolphin See DOLPHIN.

Porgies, scup, sea bream

The porgy is a family of popular little sport fishes of the Atlantic Coast, including scup and sea bream. From less than 1 pound to 2 pounds, the fatty porgies are bottom feeders. They are pan-fried or broiled, whole or filleted, by conventional basic methods and served with a zesty sauce. All the porgies are good smokers.

Pumpkinseed See PANFISHES.

Rays See SKATES.

Red drum See also DRUMS; SALTWATER BIG-GAME FISHES.

Red drum is a large, medium-fatty coarse fish, running to 40 pounds, found along the eastern seaboard to Texas. It is also known as channel bass and redfish. More noted for angling than epicurean value, the big drum with its coarse, medium-fatty flesh takes to a salt and smoke cure better than to cooking, and those under 20 pounds may be so used. Small red drums under 10 pounds may be filleted, cubed, and deep-fried, or parboiled and made into a savory chowder.

Redeye bass See LARGEMOUTH BASS AND SMALLMOUTH BASS; PANFISHES.

Redfish, or ocean perch   Also called rosefish, red perch, red bream, and Norway haddock.

The redfish, a deepwater fish of the northwest Atlantic, is a commercial rather than a sport fish, and was virtually unknown on the inland markets until modern technology took over its processing. Redfish run from 1 to 5 pounds. A delicious, relatively inexpensive fish, in appearance it is not unlike the freshwater perch, but it is fatter and its flesh is stronger and coarser. Redfish is marketed in frozen fillets under the name ocean perch.

A fatty fish, ocean perch is excellent deep-fried, baked, and in chowders. Like the perches, it is bony. Machine-filleting is not perfect, watch for and remove bones when preparing the fish.

The Pacific cousins of the ocean perch are bigger. Also a commercial fish, these go chiefly to the fish-and-chips trade.

Red grouper   See NASSAU GROUPER AND RED GROUPER.

Red snapper

The red snapper, a superb table fish, is an important commercial fish in the United States. Ranging from the Atlantic coast and the Gulf of Mexico south into the tropical Atlantic, the red snapper finds its way to an eager market as far off as central Canada.

There are several snappers, and while of excellent fish flesh, they are not the reds the occasional purveyor would have you believe. A distinctive color, the real red snapper is marketed in its gorgeous red-orange skin, defying substitution. (Comparatively insignificant groupers have been known to appear on menus as red snapper.) Nor is the rockfish of the West Coast to be confused with the red snapper, as it is sometimes called. The bigger blackfin snapper of tropic fishery is sometimes marketed as red snapper.

The red snapper grows to 30-odd pounds. It is lean with delicately flavored, firm, rich flesh. Both head and throat are especially good. The throat flesh is rich and delicate; the heads are much in demand for chowders.

Blackfin and the smaller mutton snappers are popular gamefishes. The mutton, 5 to 10 pounds of firm, white flesh, is cooked like the reds or other lean, fine fish of comparable size. It, too, has the finely fleshed head, cheeks, and throat.

Both the red and the mutton snappers make beautiful rich chowders and aspics. They respond to simple basic methods of cooking lean fish. It's hard to beat the native "Florida broil" method of skewering a small snapper fresh from the water, still in the round, on a spit and broiling it over a deep bed of coals. (See Chapter 1.)

DILLED RED SNAPPER

2 pounds large red snapper fillets or steaks	Milk
2 tablespoons flour	2 tablespoons cooking oil
2 tablespoons cornmeal	6 heads fresh dill
1 teaspoon salt	2 medium ripe, firm tomatoes, peeled and sliced
Pepper	¼ cup red wine

Wipe the fillets with a damp cloth. Combine dry ingredients. Dip the fillets in the milk and dredge in the flour and cornmeal mixture. Heat the oil in a heavy skillet and quickly brown the fillets on both sides. Reduce the heat. Arrange half of the dill on the fish, cover with tomato slices, and put the remaining dill on top. Salt and pepper generously. Add wine to the pan. Cover and cook over medium heat for about 20 minutes, or until flesh flakes to a fork. Move to a serving platter. Serve immediately, garnished with additional fresh dill.

Red snapper takes well to recipes for the freshwater walleye, winter lake whitefish, bass and pikes of comparable size or cut.

RED SNAPPER, SOUTHERN-BAKED

1 large red snapper 5–7 pounds, in the round	1½ cups red wine
4 cups moist Basic Stuffing	Flour
¼ teaspoon dill seed	¼ cup tomato paste
Bacon fat	Hot water
3 or 4 strips fat bacon, sliced thin	Salt and pepper
	Fresh parsley, finely chopped

Split and bone the whole fish, in the same operation cleaning it, leaving head and tail on. (See Chapter 2, Boning Fish.) Wash and pat dry.

Add the dill seed to the stuffing. Stuff and close the cavity with thread or trussing pins and string. Score the fish with 3 or 4 diagonal gashes and rub well with bacon fat. Tuck narrow strips of fat bacon in the gashes.

Place the fish in a greased baking pan. Pour 1 cup of wine over it and bake in a preheated, moderately hot 400°F oven, with a piece of aluminum foil over it for the first 15 to 20 minutes. Remove foil. Dust lightly with flour. Baste from the pan occasionally and bake until the flesh flakes to a fork and is crusty brown. Remove the fish to a heated serving platter and keep warm.

Reduce pan juices by half. Stir flour into the pan drippings, in an equal amount by a good guess, and stir over heat until blended and bubbly. Mix the tomato paste and ½ cup wine and stir into the *roux;* stir and cook until thickened. Stir in hot water to desired consistency. Add seasonings and serve sauces with the fish.

RED SNAPPER IN ASPIC
(a beautifully colorful, light, and delicious late supper dish)

1 red snapper, 4–5 pounds, dressed (head and tail on), scaled, all fins but the dorsal cut out	½ cup red wine 6 cups clarified fish stock 1 envelope plain gelatin
Lemon	Garnish
Fresh dill, thyme, or fennel branches	

Wash the fish and pat dry with towels. Rub the cavity with a wedge of lemon and tuck in the fresh seasonings. Prepare and steam as directed in Chapter 3, pouring the wine over the fish.

Meantime make the aspic: Reduce the stock by half. Soften the gelatin in a little cold water and stir into the hot stock. Stir over the heat until well blended, then remove from heat and let cool to a pouring consistency. Pour a little of the aspic over a polished silver serving platter and put it in the refrigerator to set. Reserve the remaining aspic at room temperature. (Don't let it set.)

The fish should now be cooked. Test it with a fork. Remove the steamer from the heat and let the fish cool in the steamer. Carefully lift and unwrap the fish and remove the herbs. Lay it on the aspic-coated platter. Put a half black olive in each eye. Cover with a damp wrapping and refrigerate until cold, then pour the remaining aspic evenly over the fish and chill until needed.

Garnish with parsley and other greens, and cooked shrimps or crabmeat, or ripe and stuffed olives, with lemon or grapefruit wedges, but don't overdo it. Serve Horseradish Sauce No. 1 in a side dish.

To carve, run knife along the backbone as you would to fillet. Slice down and lift portions from the bone. Don't overlook the throat and cheek meat, the best parts.

Rock bass   See PANFISHES.

Rosefish   See REDFISH, OR OCEAN PERCH.

Sablefish

The sablefish, also called Alaska blackcod and Pacific blackcod, is not a cod but belongs to the sablefish family, which includes the skilfish. It inhabits the deep waters of the West Coast from Alaska to California, and is fished commercially rather than by angling.

The rich flesh of the sablefish is extremely oily and quite perishable. It salt-cures and smokes beautifully and the majority of the commercial catch is treated in this way, appearing on the market as smoked Alaska cod.

The sablefish is excellent in flavor and, when parboiled to remove excessive oil, makes a superb chowder. It is broiled or baked by basic methods for fatty fish (see Chapter 3).

Smoked sablefish may be served simply in salads or as an hors d'oeuvre.

The liver of the sablefish is rich in vitamins A and D.

Salmonidae-trouts

Salmonidae, the family of trouts and salmons, are treated here from a culinary aspect and grouping is not meant to reflect an attempt at scientific classification, other than to call them *en famille* "the trouts," as they appear in the third edition, 1970, *A List of Common and Scientific Names of Fishes from the United States and Canada*.

Of general distribution, the trouts and salmons are the most important family of freshwater fishes from both a sporting and a culinary point of view. They dominate the freshwater sport-fishing scene not only by sheer strength of number, but also by their sporting quality on the line and sparkling merits on the table.

The trouts are essentially anadromous, leaving the seas for fresh river head-waters on their annual spawning migrations—except for those who would if they hadn't become locked in the countless bodies of fresh water left by the receding glaciers in the formation of North America. These do the best they can to satisfy the primitive urge, and some put on notable displays, but few phenomena in natural history can match the spectacular and awesome migra-tion of the Pacific salmons up streams and waterfalls and over man-made obstacles to their tryst.

The introduction of exotic trouts to the Great Lakes has met with consid-erable success, some far-ranging. First of the exotics was the brown trout, introduced from Germany in 1883 with a planting of fry in the Père Marquette River, a tributary of Lake Michigan.

The rainbow came next. Introduced from the West Coast into Lake Superior by the United States Fish Commission in 1895, its appearance in Lake Huron was recorded in 1905. Seemingly at home in inland waters, it has since flourished to the joy of anglers all over North America. Adaptable as they are to fish farming, plans are under way in central Canada to farm the rainbows on a massive-scale put-and-take basis in vast areas of now nonproductive inland waters, thus creating an important commercial fishery.

In the wild the rainbow has a lovely, firm red or rosy flesh; rainbows from stock ponds tend to be pale and less flavorsome.

The Pacific salmons are come-latelies to the Great Lakes region. Kokanee, or landlocked sockeye salmon, was introduced in the 1960's by Ontario, and while natural reproduction has been observed, whether they will continue on their own is undecided.

The coho was planted in Lake Michigan in 1966, 660,000 yearlings strong. By 1967 they had traveled into Lake Huron. Subsequent plantings in Georgian Bay are supporting a modest commercial fishery and a growing sport fishery. Chinooks are currently being planted in Lake Huron by the State of Michigan.

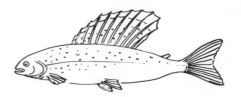

The arctic grayling, an odd member of the Salmonidae family with an enormous dorsal fin.

Pink salmon are taken in Lake Superior and have apparently made it there more or less on their own. Their presence posed a mystery until a story unfolded that could account for it. It seems that in 1956 pink salmon were raised in a Port Arthur hatchery for experimental stocking in Hudson Bay tributary rivers. Some 21,000 fingerlings that wouldn't fit into the plane were dumped into a sewer leading into a local river, and it was concluded that from this obviously sturdy pioneering stock six generations had spawned and hatched in the lake and its tributary streams. With this encouraging example, plantings have been continued on an experimental basis. They are reportedly making slow but steady progress and extending their range into the Upper Great Lakes by natural reproduction.

The introduction of the Pacific salmons to inland fresh waters is in a continuing experimental stage. Anglers are requested to cooperate by reporting capture of these exotics, many of which will be found tagged. (The request is extended to include the hybrid splake.) Refer to provincial or state fishing regulations.

The establishment of the splake as a self-propagating hybrid is a marvel of applied biology.

Splake is a hybrid of the early-maturing shallow-water brook or speckled trout and the late-maturing deep-water lake trout, hence the name. It has all the culinary attributes as well as the fighting spirit of these two fine game fishes. Catches have been made of up to 16 pounds.

Splake, or by its more lyrical Indian name, wendigo, has long been on record as an accidental cross-breed. The now established strain is the result of a controlled, selective cross-breeding program begun in 1957 by the Ontario Department of Lands and Forests (now Ministry of Natural Resources) biologists in the hope that the hybrid would fill the void left by the devastation of lake trout by the sea lamprey, and eventually would restore to the Upper Great Lakes a viable trout fishery.

In simplified form, the idea was to outwit the predator by genetics and simple arithmetic by establishing a deep-water trout capable of inhabiting both deep and shallow water, that could reproduce itself, and could do so early enough in life to ensure its posterity before the lamprey could destroy it. Its success appears assured.

Splake have now been spawning naturally for several successive years in former lake trout areas. Moreover, they have been found to grow faster than either parent species, and to the delight of anglers splake frequent both shallow and deep waters. A creel census in 1972 in the Georgian Bay area estimated a total sport catch of approximately 10,000 fish.

Following an international agreement in 1965 by which Ontario would furnish the highly selected brood stock, United States and Canada have initiated a joint splake-planting program in Lake Huron.

Whatever the reason behind the name "splake," it was not aesthetic. On a menu it is not in the same class with the Indian "wendigo," and wendigo it shall be here.

Sadly, the Atlantic salmon has not shared in this story of optimism. Rather the reverse. This great, noble fish, which rated recording in the art of the caveman, has not fared well in the past century of progress.

Stories abound of the salmon teeming practically every river flowing into the sea on the East Coast as far south as the Delaware, and the abundance extended inland to include Lake Ontario. However, early efforts to protect the fish in Lake Ontario failed and 1897 saw the last record of Atlantic salmon in the lake.

The landlocked Atlantic salmon, or ouananiche as it is called, still provides game fishing in eastern Canada, protected by sport-fishing regulations.

The family Salmonidae-trouts is considered for convenience as freshwater fish, since its game members are angled in waters that are subject to game-fishing regulations, and what with transplanting programs many of the coastal species are now inhabiting inland fresh waters. (And practically all follow a general pattern in cookery)

This is a family of fatty fishes, and those from extremely cold waters are often excessively fat. Except for their cousins the bottom-feeding lake whitefish and cisco, they are energetic predators, firm of flesh and fine of flavor. The flesh ranges in color from varying shades of pink to the fiery red of the Arctic char.

All the trouts, and especially the big ones with coarser-grained flesh, smoke beautifully.

The game members of the trout family are grouped here as follows (local names are in parentheses):

I. Pacific salmons—genus *Oncorhynchus*
   Chinook* (tyee, king, spring, quinnat)
   Chum* (keta)
   Coho* (silver trout, silver salmon)

Pink* (humpback)

Sockeye*

    Kokanee: landlocked sockeye (silver, red salmon, walla, redfish, blue-
back)

II. Trouts—genus *Salmo*

Atlantic salmon*

      Ouananiche (sebago, landlocked Atlantic salmon, salmon trout, lake
salmon)

Brown trout

Cutthroat trout (cranbrook trout, lake trout)

Golden trout

Rainbow trout* † (sea trout, steelhead, kamploops, California and Pacific
trout)

III. Trouts—genus *Salvelinus*

Arctic char* (sea trout, Hudson's Bay salmon, Quebec red)

Brook trout (speckled, mountain, mud trout, red trout, speckled char)

Dolly Varden (red trout)

Lake trout* (Great Lakes char, gray trout, mackinaw, togue, salmon trout)

Splake or wendigo (brook trout and lake trout hybrid)

IV. Inconnu* (sheefish, connie)

 V. Arctic grayling

For cooking purposes, they are regrouped according to the Size Guide given
in Chapter 3: small, medium and big; it does not necessarily imply the average
size of the catch. All catches are not average; put your fish into whichever
group it fits and cook it accordingly.

TRIMMING THE FATTY TROUTS

The concentration of fat is along the abdomen and, particularly noticeable
in lake trout, over the backbone. In excessively fat fish these parts should be
trimmed when dressing the fish as follows:

Abdomen: Trim away the fatty flesh from either side of the lower part of
the cavity and particularly around the vent.

Backbone: Cut through skin along to one side of the dorsal line, leaving
dorsal fin undisturbed (or cut the fin out, as you wish). Slip knife under the
skin, folding it back. Scrape out fatty strip over the backbone and replace
the flap of skin.

* Available on market.   † Available commercially from hatcheries.

Small trouts: 1 to 4 pounds

Small trouts include young Atlantic salmon (grilse), brook trout, young chinook salmon, young coho, sockeye, cutthroat trout, golden trout, Arctic grayling, ouananiche, kokanee, young rainbow, splake, and young lakers and chars of "keeper" size. CONSULT FISHING REGULATIONS.

Cook small trouts simply. When pan-size, fry or broil whole; others, split, fillet, or pan-dress and fry, broil, or bake. Salt and/or smoke, or pickle.

TROUT WITH ALMONDS

2 fresh trout, pan-size	2 tablespoons slivered almonds
Flour seasoned with salt and pepper	Lemon slices
2 ounces clarified butter	Parsley, chopped
Juice of ½ lemon	

Clean the trout through the gills but leave the head on. Dry the fish and roll it in seasoned flour. Melt 1½ ounces butter in a frying pan that is large enough to hold the fish flat. When hot, put in the fish and fry over low heat for about 5 minutes on each side until golden brown and crisp. Watch that they do not stick to the pan while cooking. Lift to a hot serving dish and sprinkle with lemon juice.

Add remaining butter to pan and fry almonds until golden, stirring frequently. Spoon over trout and serve immediately. Garnish with slices of lemon and chopped parsley.

Serves 1 or 2.

Jean-Claude Forgeront,
Chef des Cuisines,
La Vieille Gare, St. Boniface, Manitoba

BAKED FILLETS OF TROUT OR SALMON

1½ pounds fillets, of medium-size trout or salmon	Milk
1 cup seasoned flour	Butter
Dash tarragon	2 tablespoons white wine

Grease the bottom of an oven-to-table baking dish.

Add tarragon to seasoned flour.

Dip each fillet in milk and dredge in the flour. Lay the fish in the baking dish.

Using the remaining flour make a *beurre manié*. Smear this over the fish, lightly spreading it on with a table knife. Cover with foil, dull side out, and bake in a preheated 350°F oven for about ½ hour. When half cooked, remove the foil, sprinkle white wine over the fish, and continue baking until brown and crusty. Serve with lemon wedges, horseradish, and a bright salad.

TROUT EN PAPILLOTE

1-pound trout or salmon, dressed	Minced parsley and sliced black
Butter	olives
Mushroom Sauce	

Traditionally and by meaning, *en papillote* is meat or fish cooked in an oiled paper package. The method is reminiscent of the primitive practice of cooking in grape or papaya leaves and cornhusks, and not unlike the modern camper's use of aluminum foil. (See Chapter 1.) *En papillote* is a method ideally suited to the cooking film which allows the fish to brown through the film while keeping in all moisture. Small whole fish or fillets are cooked in individual portions in this manner.

1. Aluminum foil: Cut a piece of aluminum foil double the size of the fish, or fillets side by side, leaving plenty of margin for folding over the fish. Butter the foil. Lay the foil over a long baking pan. Lay the fish on the foil and pour Mushroom Sauce (see *Sauces*) over each portion. Dab with lots of butter and garnish with minced parsley and sliced black olives. Bring the edges of foil together in a loose package and pinch in a double fold; close ends the same way. Bake in a preheated medium hot oven (400°F) until the foil swells from the steam inside. Move the package to warm serving plates and serve with foil folded back.

2. Cooking Film: Cut off large piece of film and prepare the fish in the manner described above. The film should be large enough to allow for a good double fold. Fold and twister-tie the ends. Bake as above until the film has puffed up and the fish may be seen to be a golden brown.

Small bluefish and Florida pompano are prepared as above.

WINDBLOWN TROUT

Pan-size trout, under 1 pound   Flour
Salt   Butter (optional)

The cleaned fish should be as fresh as possible. Skin them from the gills down; remove gills and eyes. Cover each fish entirely with salt, rubbing it well into cavity along backbone. Shake off excess salt. Run a string through the eyes and hang the trout up, well-spaced, overnight in a breezeway or in a dry, clean, cool place with a brisk circulation of air. If outside, the weather should be cool and dry.

Next morning, dredge the fish lightly in flour and broil crisp in oven broiler or in hinged grill over hot coals. Serve very hot, with or without a pat of butter on each. This indoor-outdoor recipe is an old Scottish breakfast dish, superb in camp or castle.

This recipe may be used for other small panfish that are firm of flesh, such as perch.

TRUITE AU BLEU
(Quebec style)

For brook trout, rainbow, or other   Hot vinegar
    freshwater trout 2 pounds or   Court Bouillon No. 1
    less

It's the sticky waterproofing on the skin of the trout which, on contact with the hot vinegar, turns blue in this process. Therefore the coating must not be disturbed in handling. It's important that the fish be freshly caught and delivered alive to the kitchen. It is cleaned, but is not scaled or washed. Small fish may be gibbed. (See Chapter 2, Cleaning Fish.) Cleaning is done about 10 or 15 minutes before serving.

Prepare Court Bouillon No. 1, using, instead of wine and water as directed, 2 cups tarragon vinegar and 2 cups water. While this is cooking kill and clean the fish. Sprinkle each one with hot vinegar and in turn quickly plunge it into the boiling court bouillon. Cook at a low simmer and as soon as the fish, now curled and blue, flakes to a fork, lift each carefully and drain. Serve, garnished with fresh parsley or watercress, with Hollandaise Sauce on the side.

Medium-size trouts: 5 to 9 pounds

Medium-size trouts may include sockeye salmon, coho salmon, young chum and chinook salmon, pink salmon, rainbow trout, brown trout, Atlantic salmon, lake trout, splake, Arctic char, and Dolly Varden.

To cook, trim excess fat. Bake or poach whole. Bake, poach, or broil fillets and steaks.

BAKED WENDIGO BORDEAUX

1 4–6 pound wendigo (splake), or
    other medium-size trout

Stuffing (see *Stuffings*)
½ cup *beurre manié*
1 ½ cups Bordeaux
Flour
Pinch of cayenne

Leave the tail on the dressed fish and remove the head if desired. Wipe the fish all over with a cloth moistened with vinegar or lemon juice. Stuff with a well-seasoned, medium-dry basic rice or Wild Rice Stuffing.* (See Chapter 3, *Stuffings.*)

Stuff the fish lightly, leaving room for the stuffing to swell, and close with pins, skewers, or sew it up.

Place the fish and the *beurre manié* in a baking pan, sprinkling the butter around the pan. Add 1 cup Bordeaux. Cover with cooking foil, tying it down around the pan. Bake in a 400°F oven for about 40 minutes. Uncover, baste, and dust the fish lightly with flour; bake another 10 to 20 minutes until golden and done, basting from the pan.

Remove the fish to a hot platter and keep warm in the oven. Strain the pan sauce. Add another ½ cup Bordeaux, blend in a little browned flour; stir over heat for a moment or two. Add a pinch of cayenne and let the sauce boil down gently for about 10 minutes.

Garnish the fish on the platter and serve the sauce separately.

LAKE TROUT EN CROUSTADE

1 5- to 7-pound lake trout or other
    trout, filleted and skinned
Water
Wine, red or white
1 teaspoon salt
1 tablespoon clarified butter
3 green onions, chopped

1 cup cooked wild rice
¼ cup sliced mushrooms
Pastry, 2-crust pie-size
Salt and pepper
Juice of 1 lemon
1 tablespoon butter

Place fillets on greased rack in poacher. Add water and wine in equal parts, enough to just cover the fish. Add salt. Cover, bring to a bubble, reduce to a low simmer and poach for 15 minutes, or until the fish flakes. Remove fish and let it cool.

Melt clarified butter and sauté onions, then combine with wild rice and mushrooms.

Roll the pastry to a thin oblong shape. Place one fillet on one half area of the pastry, sprinkle with salt, pepper and half the juice of the lemon. Heap the wild rice stuffing on the fillet and spread toward edge. Dab with butter. Season other fillet the same way and lay it, seasoned side down, on the stuffing. Fold the pastry over the fish, pinching the edges together to seal. Place in a foil-lined biscuit pan. Bake in a 425°F oven for 30 to 35 minutes, until pastry is golden brown. Slide foil and fish to a warm serving platter, and carefully tear away the foil. Serve with green peas and tossed salad.

Serves 4 to 6.

Mrs. Cathy Brown,
White Gables Camp, Temagami, Ontario

BUFFET SALMON
(an impressive luncheon or supper fish)

1 whole salmon, 5 to 10 pounds, or
    char, lake trout, Dolly Varden,
    inconnu, or other big trout of
    similar size
1 bottle (26 ounces) dry red table
    wine
Few sprigs of parsley
1 bay leaf
1 medium onion, sliced
2–3 carrots, sliced

1 lemon, sliced
Sugar
Peppercorns
1 teaspoon salt
1 quart water plus additional water
½ cup potted lobster *or* 1 3½-ounce
    can lobster paste
4 ounces cream cheese
Pinch of cayenne
Garnish

Refer to Chapter 3, Poaching in Court Bouillon.

Remove the eyes, leaving the head and tail on the dressed fish. Trim the fatty parts around cavity. Wrap the whole fish in wet cheesecloth, trussing if desired or necessary to fit the kettle. If excessively fat, parboil.

Into a large, deep kettle or roasting pan put the wine, parsley, bay leaf, onion, carrots, lemon, a dash of sugar, a few peppercorns, and salt. Add 1 quart of water, bring to a boil, reduce the heat, and simmer for 1 hour, and then cool it.

Carefully place the wrapped salmon in the cold court bouillon. If necessary to curl the untrussed fish to the shape of the kettle, let the tail take an upward curve. Add enough water to cover the fish. Bring to a boil, then cover the pot, reduce the heat, and simmer gently for 1 to 1½ hours, depending on the size of the fish, until the flesh flakes to a fork.

Remove the pot from the heat. Skim off oily liquid from surface, and lift the fish to a platter and let it cool in the wrap. Remove the wrap, taking the skin from the top-side but leaving head and tail intact.

Combine potted lobster with cream cheese and a pinch of cayenne. Mix to a smooth paste. Thin if necessary with sour cream. Extra paste may be necessary for a larger fish.

Arrange the salmon on a large china or highly polished silver platter or tray. Put red cherries in the eyes and a wedge of lemon in the mouth. Spread the lobster paste over the exposed flesh of the salmon. Decorate lightly with hard-boiled egg slices and black olives, covering the seam at head and tail where spread meets skin.

Garnish the platter with deviled eggs with a bit of anchovy on top; tomatoes stuffed with shrimp salad; asparagus tips; cucumber slices, radishes, black olives, and lemon wedges. Garnishes may be used to help support the tail of the fish, making the whole thing an artistic arrangement.

Big trouts: 9 pounds and up

The big trouts may include the chinook salmon, chum salmon, coho salmon, Atlantic salmon, Arctic char, lake trout, and inconnu.

Trim fat and cook simply by basic methods for fatty fish; see Chapter 3. Bake whole or in part. Poach in court bouillon, parboiling excessively fat fish first. Fillet or steak, and bake or broil. Chunk and deep-fry, or make chowder or stew. Salt and/or smoke.

The following recipes may be applied to any of the big trouts and also to fatty young saltwater fishes of comparable size and cut—little tunny and skipjacks, Spanish and king mackerels, bonite, albacore, swordfish, drums, etc.

MAGNIFICENT ARCTIC CHAR IN GALANTINE

1 whole Arctic char, 8–12 pounds, or big salmon or trout	4 cups aspic
4 quarts Court Bouillon No. 3	Garnish

Remove eyes and gills, if not already done, leaving the head and tail on the cleaned fish. Trim excess fat from front and backbone. Truss the fish if desired or necessary to fit the kettle. Wrap the fish in wet cheesecloth, leaving long tabs of cloth at each end for handling. (See Chapter 3, Steaming and Poaching.)

Prepare 4 quarts of Court Bouillon No. 3 and let it cool.

Carefully lower the char into the court bouillon. Add cold water to cover. Parboil and poach as directed for Buffet Salmon above, which is essentially the basic method for poaching fatty big fish. Cook for 1 to 1½ hours in all, depending on the size of the fish and whether it is trussed. (The trussed takes longer.) Allow 10 minutes per inch of thickness, or cook to 140°F by meat thermometer inserted in thickest part. When done, that is when the flesh in the thickest part flakes to a fork, carefully lift the fish from the court bouillon, and let it cool on a large platter. Don't let the fish overcook.

When the fish is cooking, make about 4 cups of aspic from clarified stock. Coat the surface of a huge silver tray with aspic and chill it to set. Lacking such a tray, use a cutting board covered with aluminum foil. Unwrap the fish and carefully transfer it to the chilled, glazed tray; refrigerate until well chilled, covered with the damp cheesecloth.

Keep an eye on the aspic. It should be refrigerated until thickened slightly but will still pour. It must not be allowed to set or it will not pour evenly, if at all. If the aspic has begun to set, melt it down slowly and start over.

Remove the cheesecloth from the chilled char, taking the skin from the sides of the fish, and leaving head and tail intact. Put cherries, ripe olive halves, or a bit of truffle (or black olive) in each eye, and lemon in the mouth (if it should be open).

In a thin, even stream, pour half the aspic over the entire fish, coating it thinly and evenly. It should set on contact with the chilled fish. Put a collar around the neck and a cuff around the tail where flesh meets skin by sticking rings of stuffed olives into the aspic.

Let the aspic set, then pour the remainder of the aspic over the entire fish. Refrigerate until ready to serve.

Garnish with slices of hard-boiled egg, cherry tomatoes, ripe olives, cucumber slices, lemon wedges, or whatever takes your fancy, and punctuate with fresh parsley sprigs.

Serve a cold mayonnaise sauce or two on the side.

To carve, run knife along dorsal line, then cut down at right angles, lifting out portions.

A party on a platter!

Inconnu

Inconnu—the unknown—was so named by the early French explorers of the Far North who simply didn't know what kind of a fish it was. Described as "looking like a 20- to 40-pound overgrown whitefish," the inconnu was long thought to be an accidental cross-breed of the whitefish and lake trout. A member of the Salmonidae-trouts family, it is now established as a species in its own right with the scientific name *Stenodus leucichthys*.

In trout family fashion, the inconnu is a predator and a fat one. It is at its best as food under 10 pounds, and soon after it enters the rivers of northern Canada and Alaska to spawn in the fall. Then it is clear, light pink, firm and palatable of flesh. Like other trouts after spawning the flesh becomes paler and flabbier in texture, and the flavor not so good. An 8-pound inconnu is a common catch; it can go to 50 pounds.

Thanks to marketing developments in far northern freshwater fisheries, the famed inconnu is reaching the markets of Canada and the United States, usually in steak form. It is cooked like similar cuts of Arctic char, lake trout, and salmon. The fish jellies well and is particularly successful in galantines and aspics.

INCONNU IN CREAM WITH WILD RICE

4 inconnu steaks, or skinned fillets,
    fresh or frozen
Lemon juice
Flour
1 tablespoon clarified butter, or
    cooking oil
¼ cup white wine
1 cup light cream

Beurre manié
Pinch dry saffron, crushed and
    steeped in a bit of wine
Pinch or sorrel
½ cup sliced mushrooms, cooked in
    butter

If frozen, defrost frozen steaks in their packages. Trim excess fat from the steaks. Wipe with a damp cloth and sprinkle both sides with lemon juice. Dust lightly with flour.

Heat the butter in a large skillet and fry the steaks, turning as each side browns. Cook until flesh just flakes to a fork. Carefully lift with a spatula to a warm serving platter and keep in a warm, not hot, oven while making the sauce.

Deglaze the pan with wine, swishing it around the edges. Stir in the cream and cook gently to reduce it by about a third. Sprinkle the *beurre manié* over the cream and stir until blended and thickened. Add seasonings. Pour the sauce over the fish; garnish with mushrooms.

Serve at once with mounds of hot, steamed wild rice.

BARBECUED TROUT STEAKS
(lake trout, char, salmons, inconnu)

The big trouts, high in fat, broil especially well, and the chunky big steaks barbecue quickly to a sweet succulence under a saucy, crusty coat, whether the sauce is complex or a simple butter and lemon juice mix. (See Chapter 3, Broiling.)

6 trout or salmon steaks, 1½ inches thick (about 3 pounds)	Barbecue Sauce No. 2 *or* Savory Barbecue Marinade

If frozen, the steaks should be thawed in their package in the refrigerator. Pat them between towels to remove any condensed moisture. Trim excess fatty flesh. Have a barbecue rack or hinged wire grill well greased and quite warm. Dip each steak in the sauce, place on the grill, and cook about 4 inches from charcoal coals. Brush frequently with the remaining warm sauce during the cooking, and give the steaks about 5 minutes on each side, until the flesh flakes to a fork. Don't let it overcook. Serve at once with a tossed green salad.

TROUT ON A SPIT

2 pounds trout steaks, 1½ inches thick	Bay leaf
	Parsley
¼ cup lemon juice	Paprika
¼ cup olive oil	Salt
1 clove garlic, crushed	Olives, pitted
Onion juice	Pickled onions

Rub 6 long skewers with oil. Cut fish into 1½-inch cubes. Mix all the other ingredients except olives and onions into a marinade. Spread the fish over a large glass or earthenware pie plate. Pour the marinade over the fish, turning the pieces so all are well coated. Cover and refrigerate for 2 or 3 hours, turning a few times.

Remove the pieces of fish and put on long skewers, spacing pieces with pitted olives and/or pickled onions. Lay the skewers over dripping pan and broil under high heat (see Chapter 3, Broiling), basting with the marinade during cooking. Cook until crisp and golden. Serve with lemon wedges. The fish may also be broiled over the barbecue.

BARBECUE-SMOKED LAKE TROUT
(or other king-size fine fish)

12- to 15-pound lake trout

A large kettle-type charcoal barbecue is required for this preparation.

Soak in water overnight a large (10-gallon at least) tub full of hardwood chips—cherry, apple, pear, hickory, oak, maple or any other unpainted suitable hardwoods (for example, broken hockey sticks).

Fire the entire area of the barbecue pan with charcoal briquets, two layers deep; burn until all are white hot or beginning to build up ash.

Meanwhile prepare the big trout. Dress the fish. It will likely be necessary to cut off the head and tail to fit the fish into the barbecue. Scrape the skin and cut off the inch or so fatty part from around the cavity and the strip of fat along the backbone. Wash and wipe dry. Rub cavity with lemon and sprinkle the fish with salt, pepper, and nutmeg (or any spices you wish) inside and out. Tuck into the cavity a sliced onion, a sliced green pepper and/or green tomato, a few branches of fresh fennel, dill, savory or parsley. Cut a piece of heavy duty aluminum foil, a little larger than the fish, lay it on the barbecue rack and lay the fish on it; fold up the edges of the foil forming a pan to contain the juices.

Back to the barbecue: lift the chips from the tub, shake off excess water and spread them directly on the hot coals, smothering them entirely. This makes beautiful moist smoke. Place the rack with the fish into position on the barbecue over the chips. Close the cover and keep it closed, and don't peek too often.

The 15-pound trout takes about 3 hours to cook, about 30 minutes for each inch thickness at the thickest part of the dressed fish. After 2 hours look in and test it. When the flesh flakes to a prod with a fork it is done. Better still, use a meat thermometer inserted before cooking, in the thick shoulder area and cook to 140°F.

If there isn't a breeze, you may find with this type of barbecue that you have to fan a bit through the vents in the bottom to encourage the coals.

Any big fish may be smoke-cooked in this manner. Lean fishes like walleye require larding—tuck about ¼ pound butter in chunks in the cavity, oil the fish well all over and lay a few thin strips of bacon over the fish.

Remove stuffing, carve, and serve from the rack with barbecued stuffed ripe or green tomatoes along with a salad. (Put tomatoes in with the fish for last half-hour of cooking.)

Mrs. Lorene Wilson,
Scarboro Rod and Gun Club,
Scarborough, Ontario

Salmons   See SALMONIDAE-TROUTS.

Saltwater big-game fishes   Albacore; blue tuna; king mackerel (kingfish, cavalla); big billfishes including marlins, sailfish, spearfishes; jewfish; giant sea bass; big drums; and swordfish are all big-game fishes.

Big-game saltwater fishing and kitchen cookery are not generally compatible pursuits. For one thing, the "out of the water and into the pan" advice is obviously not practicable. For another, the size of a trophy fish, which can run into hundreds of pounds, puts it outside the "fine" range of table fishes. More importantly, as the mercury contamination problem continues to unfold, the great predaceous sea-rovers have revealed concentrations of mercury above and beyond the tolerance of humans. And the bigger the fish, the greater the concentration.

The younger of these fishes, say under 20 pounds, are probably the safest bet as table fish. In any case the monsters are no culinary prize, and the smaller the better. However excellent of flavor and firm of flesh, the smaller of the species have a comparatively finer grain and more palatable texture. A 20-pounder is still coarse-grained.

This group of fishes is a fat one, and probably the finest hour of a coarse-grained, fatty fish is when it emerges from the smokehouse. (See Chapter 7.)

DRESSING THE BIG-GAME FISH

The fatty fishes are quite perishable. For the best quality meat, the rough dressing and butchering should get under way immediately and the meat put on ice. Game-fishing boats are equipped to handle the job on board.

Fish over 10 pounds are steaked or cut into meal-size portions. (See Chapter 2, Catch to Kitchen.)

Recipes for the 10- to 12-pound salmons, trouts, and chars may be applied to the big-game fish of comparable size and cut.

Sauger   See WALLEYE AND SAUGER.

Scads   See ATLANTIC MACKEREL AND PACIFIC MACKEREL.

Scrod   See CODFISHES; PANFISHES.

Scup   See PORGIES, SCUP, SEA BREAM.

Sea basses and groupers

The sea basses and groupers constitute a most fascinating family of fishes, with a wide diversity of characteristics. Some species are food fishes of world-wide importance, while others are known to cause tropical fish poisoning. Within the family they may range in size from an ounce or two to half a ton. Chameleonlike, some lie around the bottom blending into the background with their mouths open optimistically, while others roam the oceans pursuing the active life of the hunter.

As a family their love life seems to be rather loosely defined, to say the least. Some are transsexual—born as females and switching to male. Others are self-fertilizing hermaphrodites. However, spawning is a group affair, and it all seems to come out all right and the family flourishes.

All have a preference for warm tropical and subtropical waters.

(See also Black sea bass; Nassau grouper and red grouper; saltwater big-game fishes.)

Sea bream   See PORGIES, SCUP, SEA BREAM.

Sea lamprey   See EELS AND LAMPREYS.

Searobins

Taken in shallow coastal waters during the summer months, searobins are usually under two pounds.

The searobin, although of a different family and nontoxic, like the puffer presents a thorny dressing problem. It, too, is a bottom feeder, and has lean, tasty, delicate flesh when fresh and properly prepared.

The searobin is skinned and dressed by the same method as the puffer, but does not skin as easily. The skin must be cut away. (See *Northern puffer.*) Cook searobin by the same methods as sea squab but serve with heartier sauces, such as Sauce Espagnole.

Sea squab   See NORTHERN PUFFER.

Seatrout   See DRUMS; WEAKFISH.

Shads

Shad are big herring. Anadromous, they spawn in fresh water. The American shad of 5 to 8 pounds is a catch familiar to anglers from the Gulf of St. Lawrence to Florida. The smaller hickory shad is a Southern fish, considered inferior in quality to the American.

The American shad has delicately flavored, light, creamy flesh. It is very oily and very, very bony.

The consensus of opinion after a couple of centuries of shad cookery is that the bony shad is next to impossible to fillet, so that it is best baked whole "stuffed like a chicken," and close attention given servings offered to young children. And it does bake beautifully. (See Chapter 3, Baking.)

Shad also makes a fine chowder. Whole or pan-dressed, the fish is tied in cheesecloth and parboiled to float off excessive oils, then simmered until the bones can be removed and chowder made from the boned flesh and resulting stock.

Both American and hickory shad respond to a salt and smoke cure, the salting process softening the bones. (See Chapter 7.)

Shad roe is a delicacy. (See Chapter 5.)

Sheepshead

The sheepshead is a member of the porgy family. A saltwater fish of the Atlantic coast, the sheepshead has moved into the fresh waters in Florida where it is a popular sport and food fish. It may grow quite large, but the general run is around 4 to 5 pounds, a good table size. The flesh is excellent, rather fatty, and the fish is filleted or pan-dressed and baked whole according to basic methods for fatty fish, or made into stews and chowders. Recipes for lake whitefish may be used for sheepshead of comparable size. It smokes well.

The more generally distributed freshwater drum is sometimes mistakenly called sheepshead.

SHEEPSHEAD FILLETS BAKED IN WINE SAUCE

1 3- to 4-pound sheepshead, scaled and filleted (skin on or off)	Butter
Fresh dill or parsley branches	3 large, firm tomatoes, sliced
Lemon juice	1 cup White Wine Sauce

Wash the fillets and pat dry with paper towels. Grease a large baking dish and lay the dill on the bottom. Rub the flesh side of the fillets with lemon juice and lay them, flesh side up, on the dill branches. Dab with butter. Arrange the tomato slices shingle style over the top of the fish, and pour the White Wine Sauce over the tomatoes. Bake in a 350°F oven for 45 to 50 minutes, depending on thickness of the fillets. Cover lightly with foil for the first half hour, spoon some of the sauce over the fish, and bake uncovered until the flesh is flaky and the dish browned. Serve in the baking dish, garnished with fresh dill heads or parsley.

Excellent for fillets of trout, salmon, summer caught Spanish and big Atlantic mackerels. Garnish with fried pine nuts.

Silversides   See PANFISHES; WHITEBAIT.

Skates

There are big and little skates, and even winter skates, distributed widely throughout the oceans, all looking more like fat kites than skates. The barndoor skate of the northwest Atlantic is the largest used on this continent, having a wing span (actually an overgrown pectoral fin) of 5 to 6 feet.

Taken commercially rather than by sport fishing, the wings are used as food. Cut into rounds with a cookie-cutter sort of tool, the wings of the barndoor and other large skates have in the past been marketed as scallops. This illegal practice was stopped and the label is now "mock scallops."

The only resemblance to the shellfish meat is in appearance after the meat is cut, and it's easy to spot the difference. The mock scallop is crossgrained and the real scallop's grain runs vertically. The frozen mock product also may have a faint characteristic odor of ammonia.

Large skates are sold wings only; the small ones are sold whole.

The flesh of the skate is gelatinous rather than fatty, and the smaller ones are finer in grain than the large. The gelatinous nature of the skate lends itself well to aspics and soups. Its flavor is delicate and highly esteemed in many parts of the world.

The wings of rays are sometimes used in the same way as the skate wings. Caution is essential in handling rays as the barbs on the tail can cause serious injury.

Dressing skates. Wash well and skin the fish. Eviscerate and wash again. Lay the skate flat on a cutting board and with a sharp knife separate the fleshy parts (the wings), cutting along both sides of the backbone in a curving direction following the line of the wings. Cut the larger wings into long strips, cutting right through the cartilaginous or finny parts. Leave small wings whole. Put to soak in cold water with a little salt and refrigerate for 2 hours or overnight, changing the water once or twice. Use the bones and fleshy trimmings to make stock or fumet, soaking in a couple of changes of salted water first.

When eating whole skate wings, the flesh is stripped from the wings with a fork rather than cut.

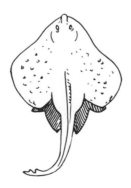

SKATE IN COURT BOUILLON

Roll the strips of skate and tie with string. Cook in a sharp court bouillon, (No. 1) using a *dry* white wine or substitute with vinegar (see Chapter 3, Poaching). When the flesh flakes, drain well. Chill. Arrange on a round serving platter lined with lettuce or watercress and garnished with fresh parsley. Serve with Lobster, Shrimp, or Oyster Sauce, or Fine Herbs Sauce.

SKATE AU BEURRE NOIR

Prepare the wings, cut into strips, or leave the smaller wings whole and cook in a court bouillon as described above. Drain and place the wings on a warm silver serving dish, garnish with sautéed parsley, and pour hot Brown Butter Sauce with capers generously over the fish.

FRIED SKATE

Prepare the wings as described above, cut into strips, or leave the smaller wings whole. Drain the fish and pat between towels to dry. Pan-fry *à l'Anglaise* (see Chapter 3, Frying), seasoning the crumbs with salt, pepper, and a pinch each of cayenne and curry. Serve with Sauce Espagnole or Tomato Sauce, or any sauce recommended for Skate in Court Bouillon.

Skipjack   See SALMONIDAE-TROUTS (of comparable size)

Smallmouth bass   See LARGEMOUTH BASS AND SMALLMOUTH BASS.

Smelts

The rise to popularity, if not fame, of the smelts of North America is another rags-to-riches sort of fish story on a par with the Winnipeg goldeye. Both stories feature the treatment of a "coarse" fish, if in different ways.

The gastronomic success of the millions upon millions of pounds of smelt served annually on the North American table is due in large measure to, and a shining example of, the value of prompt and chilly processing of the fresh fish. The fatty smelts and their close relatives are as delicate and perishable a little fish as will be found. Netted inshore at night during their winter and spring spawning runs, the fish, generally under 10 inches in length, are head-dressed and frozen under conditions favorable to culinary perfection. (See Chapter 2.)

Anadromous like the trouts, to which they are distantly related, smelts occur in both salt water and fresh. Once considered a nuisance fish, smelts are now an economic asset.

The most common and commercially important of the North American smelt family is the American (rainbow) smelt. Of growing importance on the Atlantic coast is the capelin. The eulachon, also a smelt, is one of the oldest fisheries of the British Columbia-Alaska coast. Surf smelts and smeltlike silversides are taken on the West Coast.

Formerly considered a fodder fish, the American smelt was introduced to Crystal Lake, Michigan, in 1912 as food for the landlocked salmon. Here it thrived and moved on through Lake Michigan and into the rest of the Great Lakes, where it has established itself in legendary number. In 1972 a biologist estimated two billion of the little fish in Lake Ontario alone. Despite tremendous fishing pressures, there is apparently no sign of decline.

The smooth, silvery fish are easily and quickly dressed. With a sewing scissors, cut off the head just below the gills, slit open, and clean with a forefinger. Wash well and cook or block-freeze in meal-sized lots. (See Chapter 2.) Smelts are commonly around 7 inches in length. Larger ones are easily boned. Loosen the backbone at the neck end with the tip of a knife, slip a finger under and raise the bone, lifting it away from the flesh. Smelts are not skinned.

The smelts are fat, oily fishes. Delicate in texture and flavor, the fresh smelt has a sweet, fresh fragrance and flavor attributed to a volatile oil which is dissipated during storage.

The flesh of the smelts when cooked is pearly white (the French call them *éperlans*—"pearly fish").

Recipes abound for cooking smelts and capelins and other small, oily, smeltlike delicacies, but the fine, light flavor of the fish is best captured when the fish are crisply fried or broiled by the simple, basic methods for panfish. (See Chapter 3, Pan-Frying *à la meunière* and *à l'Anglaise,* and Broiling.) The very small ones are exquisitely delicious when dusted with flour and deep-fried, like whitebait.

All the smelts are excellent pickled and smoked.

SMELTS BAKED IN WHITE WINE

2 pounds smelts   ½ cup fine bread crumbs
1 cup chopped celery   Salt, pepper, and cayenne
¼ cup minced parsley   1 cup sliced mushrooms
½ cup white table wine   6 tablespoons butter

Dress the smelts, wash, and pat dry between towels. In the bottom of a greased baking dish arrange a layer of chopped celery and parsley and over this lay the smelts. Pour wine over smelts, then sprinkle with bread crumbs seasoned with salt and pepper and a trace of cayenne. Arrange mushrooms on top and dot with butter. Bake uncovered in a very hot 500° oven for about 10 minutes or until the flesh flakes, basting once with juices from the bottom of the pan.

SMELTS IN SOUR CREAM

1 pound smelts, head-dressed   1 tablespoon finely minced chives
Flour   ½ cup fish fumet
Salt and pepper   ½ cup sour cream
Butter, clarified   1 teaspoon finely minced pimiento
1 tablespoon finely minced parsley

Dredge the smelts in flour seasoned with salt and pepper until it sticks. Heat butter about ¼ inch deep in a large frying pan. Gently sauté the fish a few minutes on each side, moving them about gently and turning carefully. The fish should be barely light gold, not browned, and slightly underdone.

Add parsley and chives to heated fumet. If no fumet is on hand, use a light meat stock or a chicken bouillon cube. Stir in the sour cream, mix well, blend in the pimiento, and pour over the smelts. Let heat through without disturbing the fish, and serve from the pan to individual plates, spooning the sauce over the fish.

Snappers   See RED SNAPPER; PANFISHES.

Snooks

The snooks are popular sport fishes of the warm waters around Florida and the Gulf of Mexico, as well as in the inland freshwaters of the region.

Favoring other fish as food, with the odd shellfish for variety, the snook's flesh is quite firm and of good flavor, especially when the fish is caught in spring before spawning and is within the kitchen-size range.

Promptly dressed, filleted, and skinned, the snooks bake and broil well by the basic methods for fatty fishes, and are excellent in fish stews and chowders.

Sockeye salmon   See SALMONIDAE-TROUTS.

Sole   See FLOUNDERS.

Spanish mackerel

Spanish mackerel is commonly caught in summer months along the mid Atlantic coast northward to Chesapeake Bay. It averages 9 to 10 pounds though it may run much more. Like other mackerels, it is extremely fatty and definite in flavor. It responds particularly well to a salt and/or smoke cure.

The big mackerel should be cooked by a method whereby it is parboiled to float off excessive oils and modify the flavor. (See Chapter 3, Parboiling.) Small ones broil or bake well.

Recipes for lake trout or char of comparable size may be used.

Spearfishes   See SALTWATER BIG-GAME FISHES.

Speckled trout   See SALMONIDAE-TROUTS.

Splake   See SALMONIDAE-TROUTS.

Spotted sea trout   See DRUMS; WEAKFISH.

Striped bass

The striped bass, a river-spawning, handsome, big rover, belongs to the family of temperate basses, which includes the white perch and the freshwater white and yellow basses, little more than panfish.

The migratory striped bass has a long and prestigious history of feeding the North American people, dating back to the Plymouth colonists. With an original distribution from the Gulf of St. Lawrence to northern Florida, apparently concentrated from Massachusetts to the Carolinas, the striped bass was the basis of a vital fishery that the far-sighted colonists in 1639 saw fit to regulate by law, prohibiting its use, along with that of the cod, for fertilizer. In the early 1880's some four hundred striped bass were transplanted from the Atlantic to the Pacific waters around San Francisco, where they flourished so well that within ten years a commercial fishery was established. Today the striper roves the West Coast from the Columbia River to Southern California.

Striped bass is anadromous, spawning in fresh water. A landlocked, transplanted population is fairly widespread.

An active voracious predator, running up to 10 pounds or more, the striped bass is lithe in muscle and firm in flesh and is highly esteemed by cook and angler alike.

A medium-fatty fish, striped bass responds magnificently to recipes for trout and salmon in the 5- to 10-pound range. A more bony fish than these, the striper is better filleted than steaked. It bakes and poaches well whole, and excellent results are obtained from a salt-pickle and smoke cure.

The stripers should be scaled carefully so as not to tear the skin.

STRIPED BASS BRANDY BRAISE

1 4- to 5-pound dressed striped bass, or section	2 sticks celery, cut into chunks
	1 green pepper, sliced thick
Butter	Bouquet garni
Salt and pepper	2 tablespoons brandy
Thyme or parsley, minced	1 cup dry white wine
2 onions, sliced	2 tablespoons melted butter
2 carrots, sliced	

Prepare the fish for cooking. Rub the inside of the cavity with a mixture of butter, salt and pepper, and minced thyme or parsley. Arrange it in a baking dish on a bed of onion, carrots, celery, and green pepper. Add a bouquet garni. Warm the brandy in a long-handled butter melter, and ignite it as you pour it over the fish.

Moisten the vegetables with the dry white wine, and pour the melted butter over the fish.

Bring to a boil on top of the stove, then put into a moderate oven, about 375°, and cook uncovered for 40 to 50 minutes, or until the flesh flakes to a fork, basting frequently with pan juices.

Remove the bass to a warmed serving platter and keep warm.

Remove the bouquet garni and reduce the brew left in the pan to boil off moisture, and in it make a Sauce Espagnole or Velouté Sauce. Season to taste and, if the vegetables are now looking less than presentable, strain; pour over the fish and serve.

POACHED STRIPED BASS

3- to 4-pound center cut striped bass, or tail end

Wash the fish and pat dry with paper towels. Put into deep kettle in Court Bouillon No. 2 to cover, bring to a boil, reduce to a simmer, and cook as directed. (See Chapter 3, Poaching.) Let drain.

Prepare in one of the following ways:
1. Lay the hot fish on a linen napkin on a serving platter; garnish brightly with parsley, lemon wedges, and thin strips of pimiento pepper. Serve with Clear Lemon Butter Sauce and boiled parsley potatoes.
2. Lay the fish in a warmed serving platter. Peel off the skin. Pour Hollandaise Sauce over the fish and garnish with lots of hot, freshly cooked spinach around the edge and hard-boiled egg slices and ripe olive rings on top. Serve with boiled potatoes on the side.
3. Drain and cool the fish, covered with a dampened napkin. Remove the skin and arrange the fish on a serving platter. Garnish with fresh parsley or dill. Serve with one of the cold mayonnaise sauces, such as Tarragon or Remoulade.

Recipes for striped bass, salmon, and trout of comparable size and cut are interchangeable.

Sturgeon   See LAKE STURGEON.

Suckers

Suckers, or buffalo fish, are widely distributed across the continent and generally frequent warm, shallow, turbid rivers and lakes. The northern redhorse and white sucker from the clear, clean, cold lake waters in the spring of the year before spawning are the best table suckers, and even these could not be called the most flavorsome of fish.

The fatty, bony suckers should be promptly dressed and skinned. Lightly parboiled and made into savory stews, chowders, and casserole dishes, whereby the bones are removed in the process, sucker provides tasty fare. The cheeks of the sucker are succulent morsels and the heads should be included in the stock.

The coarse-grained fillets of the larger suckers smoke splendidly and after a bone-softening salt cure and treatment in the smokehouse they emerge epicurean fare. Consider the Winnipeg goldeye.

Summer flounder   See FLOUNDERS.

Sunfishes   See LARGEMOUTH BASS AND SMALLMOUTH BASS; PANFISHES.

Surfperches   See PANFISHES.

Swordfish   See SALTWATER BIG-GAME FISHES; SALMONIDAE-TROUTS, BIG TROUTS.

Tautog

The tautog, a member of the wrasse family ranges the northwest Atlantic Coast from Nova Scotia to South Carolina. Though it grows to quite a size, 3 pounds is average.

A lean fish, the tautog has rather soft, bland flesh that reflects lazy, indiscriminate feeding habits. A few years ago it would have been called a "coarse" fish.

Taken from shallow waters in the spring before spawning, the fresh tautog can provide tasty fare in a deep fry or stew or chowder.

Tomcods   See CODFISHES; PANFISHES.

Trouts   See SALMONIDAE-TROUTS.

Tullibee   See CISCO OR LAKE HERRING.

Turbot   See FLOUNDERS.

Walleye and sauger

The walleye, so-called because of its large flat eyes, is a member of the perch family. It goes by other names: pike-perch, walleyed pike, yellow pickerel, pickerel, doré, jack salmon, jackfish, golden pike, opal eye, and probably more.

By any name it is an attractive, succulent fish, and its firm, white, flaky, delicious flesh places the lean, predatory walleye and its smaller cousin the sauger among the most desirable of table fishes.

Indigenous to the Northern states and Canada, the walleye is adaptable to transplanting and stocking. It is now widely available to anglers in practically all but a few far western and southern states. In some areas a common catch may be around 5 pounds; the average is 2 to 3.

The sauger, known also as sand pike and sand pickerel, is not the popular game fish that the walleye is, but its flesh is considered the better of the two by many. Sauger is fished and marketed commercially. Its maximum weight is around 2 pounds. Both fish respond to plain basic methods for lean, fine fish, either whole or filleted according to size and recipe. (See recipes for sole and flounder.) Walleye is delicious stuffed with Vegetable Stuffing and baked in baking film with white wine.

WALLEYE FILLET PROVENÇAL

4 walleye fillets
2 tablespoons seasoned flour
Oil and butter for frying
1 medium onion, finely sliced
1 clove garlic, crushed
¾ pound tomatoes, crushed

1 teaspoon fresh herbs, parsley, chives
Salt and pepper to taste
Black olives for garnish
White wine (optional)

Roll the fish in seasoned flour. In a frying pan, heat oil and butter. Fry fish quickly until golden brown on both sides. Drain, arrange in a shallow serving dish, and keep hot.

Strain off surplus oil and butter, leaving 1 good tablespoon in the pan. Fry onion until tender and add the garlic, tomatoes, and herbs. Toss quickly over brisk heat for 3 minutes. Season and add olives. If using white wine, add to sauce. Pour over the fish.

Serves 4.

Jean Claude Forgeront,
Chef des Cuisines
La Vieille Gare, St. Boniface, Manitoba

FILLETS OF WALLEYE STUFFED

2 pounds fillets walleye or pike, skin   Melted butter
    on   2 tablespoons white wine
2 cups moist stuffing   Pine nuts
1 lemon, plus lemon for garnish   Parsley
Flour

Prepare 2 cups of moist stuffing. (See Chapter 3, Stuffings.)

Lay one half the fillets, flesh up, in the bottom of a large, well-greased baking dish, or on a baking sheet covered with a large sheet of baking film.*

Squeeze ½ the lemon over the fish. Heap the stuffing in the middle and with a light hand spread it over the fillets.

Squeeze the other half lemon over the flesh side of remaining fillets and lay them, skin side up, over the stuffing. Dust lightly with flour, brush with melted butter, and drizzle white wine over all. Sprinkle a few pine nuts over the top. Cover the dish (if no cover, use aluminum foil) and bake in a preheated moderate oven at 350°F for about 30 minutes, or until the flesh barely flakes to a fork. Remove cover for last 10 minutes or until fish is cooked and nicely browned. Serve from baking dish, garnished with fresh parsley, with lemon wedges on the side.

Weakfish   See also DRUMS.

Weakfish, which goes by the local names gray weakfish, squeteague, and yellowfin, is a member of the drum family. It usually runs from 1½ to 3 or 4 pounds, though it can go to 12 or 14 pounds. On the fat side, its flesh is quite perishable and it should be dressed and iced as quickly as possible. Scaled, or filleted and skinned, it has a fine, delicate flavor and is excellent baked, poached, broiled, or fried by any of the basic methods in Chapter 3.

Seatrout and corvinas are treated by the same methods as weakfish. All three may be prepared like trouts of comparable size. Excellent pickled or smoked.

---

* If baking film is used, close the film with a double fold, tucking ends under the fish. Baking time will be about 30 minutes. Open the wrap carefully and let steam escape. Test with a fork–if it doesn't flake readily, baste and return it to the oven to cook for a few more minutes in dry heat. The fish will cook through the film and keep marvelously moist. Move the fish in the film to a deep serving platter and garnish as above.

WEAKFISH IN WHITE WINE

2 weakfish, about 2 pounds each, dressed and scaled	Bouquet garni
Lemon juice	1 small onion, thinly sliced
Salt	½ cup dry white wine
Parsley	Butter
	White Wine Sauce

Wipe the dressed fish with a damp cloth, and rub inside with lemon juice and salt. Tuck a few branches of parsley inside. Place in a well-buttered baking dish with a bouquet garni of thyme, fennel, parsley, summer savory, and dill (or as you fancy) and onion. Pour the wine over the fish. Dab with butter, cover with cooking film, and bake in a preheated 350°F oven for about 25 minutes, or until flesh flakes to a fork. Move fish to a heated platter and keep warm.

Make a White Wine Sauce, using the juices from the fish as part of the liquid. Remove the parsley from the cavity of the fish. Garnish the platter with branches of fresh parsley or fresh fennel, and serve the sauce in a sauceboat.

Wendigo   See SALMONIDAE-TROUTS (MEDIUM-SIZE TROUTS)

Whitebait

Smaller still than panfish is a size range of fishes generally termed "whitebait" (bait-size). These are the tiny, little more than an inch long members of the herring family (sardines and pilchard), anchovies, smelts, silversides, whitings, minnows, and the fry of other fishes.

Deep-fried whitebait is a gourmet's treat of worldwide fame, rare because it is seasonal and the little fishes must be out-of-the-water fresh, and preferably alive. The exquisitely tasty dish is believed to have originated in England some two centuries ago with a fishmonger who became purveyor of whitebait, every day of the season, by appointment to King George IV during his reign.

WHITEBAIT

(English and French Style)

1 ½ pounds whitebait	Salt
Fat for frying	Lemon wedges

Wash and dry the fresh fish by patting between towels. Dust the fish with flour and place in a small-mesh deep-fry basket. Shake gently to rid of excess flour.

Plunge the basket into deep, hot fat (see Chapter 3, Deep-Frying) for about 30 seconds, or until fried crisp. Drain on paper and serve hot, heaped on a napkin. Sprinkle generously with salt. Serve with lemon wedges.

Serves 4.

White bass   See PANFISHES.

White crappies   See SUNFISHES.

White perch   See PANFISHES.

White seabass   See DRUMS.

Whitings   See PANFISHES; WHITEBAIT

Winter flounder   See FLOUNDERS.

Yellow bass   See PANFISHES.

☙ 5 ❧

Fish Roe and Giblets

Roe

Caviar, the celebrated luxury preparation of sturgeon roe, has rather over-borne any claim to fame by lesser producers of fish eggs, or any other preparation thereof. However, while Imperial Europe was teasing its impeccable palate with the salted delicacy, Indians of North America, who had never heard of caviar, were weaning babies on fish eggs, including sturgeon's.

The roes of healthy North American fishes of the cold and temperate waters are generally edible, with the exception of those of the puffer (blowfish) and the gars.

The roe consists of an ovarian sac containing the eggs, the package varying in shape and size from species to species, and the size varying with the size of the fish and the maturity of the eggs. Each female fish produces two roes.

Used at the prespawning stage, the roe is wholesome-looking, clear, and well formed, with no sign of shriveling or cloudiness. The sac is firm and clear, smoothly and closely filled with a translucent mass of eggs. Failure to meet these qualifications may indicate pesticide contamination and the roe should not be eaten.

CAVIAR

Caviar is the roe of the sturgeon, although the name has been applied to the eggs of other fish. However, what is commonly meant by caviar is the salted roe of the sturgeon. It has been reported that caviar produced from the lake sturgeon of North America is of the finest, the eggs being somewhat larger than those of the marine species. It was the discovery of the North American source of high-grade roe by the European caviar industry that virtually saved the lake sturgeon from extinction on this continent.

Caviar roe is taken from the prespawning sturgeon as they congregate in tributary rivers in the spring. In making caviar the eggs of the roe are separated from the ovarian sac by pressing them through a mesh of matching size. The eggs, called "berries" in the industry, are then salted, forming their own brine. When the brine is drained off, caviar remains, ready for an involved commercial grading and packing process.

The highest-grade caviar is made from hard roe, that is, the nearly full-size, not yet fully matured eggs. The mature eggs just before spawning are too soft to go through the mesh unbroken.

Size and color are important in grading caviar. Color depends on the stage of maturity and grading is complicated by the fact that the size of the eggs may vary in different parts of the sturgeon's range.

Roes of fishes other than sturgeon—for example, salmon, cod, haddock, tuna, mullet, whitefish, etc.—may be salted into a caviar product and can be every bit as delicious. The paddlefish yields a fine caviar. Products from other fishes are identified as salmon caviar, etc., on the label.

The quality of caviar, like the quality of fish flesh in general, depends more on handling and care in processing the delicate, perishable eggs than on the kind of eggs used. In top-quality caviar, the berries are round, none crushed, and glistening in their own fat. There is no odor of fish or salt.

Caviar must be served cold and kept cold until eaten, thus it is better served in a bowl in ice with thin, dry toast on the side than spread as a canapé. It is never, never cooked or subjected to any preparation involving heat.

HOMEMADE CAVIAR

Use roe of prespawning sturgeon or other fish.

The roe is extremely perishable. Take the roe from the fish as soon as it is killed and process at once.

Cleanliness is of utmost importance throughout the process. Keep hands well washed and sterilize all utensils and equipment with the care given an infant's bottles.

You will need a screen or sieve of a size to allow the eggs just to pass through without breaking; a glass or boil-proof plastic bowl; a French wire whisk; small glass jars with covers; and for every 2 pounds of roe, 1 ounce of fine, noniodized salt.

Put roe on the sieve or screen over the bowl. Gently moving them about with the whisk, separate the berries from the sac and fluid and let them fall into the bowl. Wash the berries gently in several cold waters, moving them around with the whisk as necessary until all the frothiness can be drained off and the clean, whole berries remain. Let drain for a few minutes on thick paper toweling or on a clean linen towel.

Rinse out the bowl and return the berries to the bowl, alternating a layer of berries with a layer of salt in proportions given above, finishing with a layer of salt. Pack the caviar immediately in prepared jars, level with the top so that there is no air space. Cover and keep in the bottom of the refrigerator for 2 weeks, when it will be ready to use and at its best. The salted caviar may be kept several weeks at a near-freezing temperature, but must not be allowed to freeze or the berries will break.

Turn the bottles every few days or so to prevent oil settling at the top.

To keep the caviar at peak quality, pack in small jars and, once opened, use it all. Don't store caviar again once opened.

COOKING FISH ROES

Roes must not be overcooked as, like other eggs, they become tough. A light poaching or parboiling, until they just begin to coddle or turn opaque, helps float off some of the oiliness (something like pork sausages) and eases the apportioning of the roe.

Fish roes are a rich dish and should be served on dry toast with a tart, piquant sauce or a condiment like green tomato pickle. Tabasco or Worcestershire sauce adds a nice touch. Otherwise, serve with nothing more than sliced tomatoes, a salad or greens, and a dry white wine.

Most recipes for roes of carp, cod, shad, herring, pike, salmon, trout etc. start with poached or parboiled roe. To parboil, wash the roe and pat dry between towels. Drop the roe into boiling salted water to which lemon juice has been added—about 1 tablespoon to a quart of water. Turn down heat and cook until roe just begins to turn opaque. Lift with a slotted spoon and plunge into cold water. Drain. Separate the roe into pieces.

Pan-fried roe à la meunière. Dip each piece of parboiled roe in beaten egg, dust with seasoned flour, and lightly pan-fry in clarified butter until crisp and brown, turning once. Serve on toast with hot melted butter with a bit of lemon juice and onion juice mixed in.

Or, dust with seasoned flour only and pan-fry as above.

Baked roe. Place parboiled roe in buttered baking dish. For 1 pound of roe, brown 1 tablespoon fine herbs in ½ cup Noisette Butter and pour over roe. Add ¼ cup sherry. Cover and bake in a moderate 375°F oven for about 10 minutes.

Serve on dry toast, spooning the sauce over the roe.

Oven-browned roe. Prepare buttered toast, trim and cut in half, arrange on baking sheet and keep warm. Fry a small amount fine, dry bread crumbs in butter and set aside.

Wash the roes in water and pat dry between towels.

In a frying pan heat clarified butter, about ½ inch deep, adding 1 tablespoon lemon juice to approximately ½ cup butter. Poach the roes in the butter, covered lightly, until just opaque. Put on toast, cutting the larger roes in half. Sprinkle each with fine dry bread crumbs fried in remaining butter, lemon juice, and salt and pepper. Brown quickly in a 425°F oven, no more than 10 minutes.

Garnish with minced parsley. Serve with sliced firm, red tomatoes and a green salad.

Sturgeon roe. Large roes, such as those of sturgeon and paddlefish, are poached. Bring a kettle of water (enough to cover the roes) to a boil. Add salt and lemon juice or vinegar, about 1 tablespoon to 1 quart of water. Drop the roe into the boiling water, lower heat, and let simmer for about 10 minutes until roe is opaque.

Drain the roe. Break the sac and serve the eggs on toast with Tartar or Caper Sauce.

SOFT ROES

The soft roe, or milt, is the sperm of the male fish. A smooth white substance, it is considered a nourishing and highly digestible delicacy. Much favored are the milts of carp, herrings, and mackerels, though like roes, the milt of other fishes may be used.

To prepare soft roes for cooking, wash them well in cold water, drain and strip the small vein found on one side.

Cook and serve the soft roes like other roes; poach quickly, or parboil for about 2 minutes and pan-fry, bake, or oven-brown.

Giblets

Whether called variety meats, offal, or innards, most healthy fish of the cold and temperate waters have some eminently edible internal organs. These are the liver, the sounds (air or swim bladder), the tongue, the heart, and, included here for convenience, the cheeks.

These variety meats of fish, especially those of the cods, have been used over the centuries in Scottish and French cookery, which has influenced the cookery of the Canadian Maritimes and Quebec, trailing off across Canada in the wake of the early settlers and explorers. They are important in Jewish cookery, especially in the preparation of gefilte fish, and for this market fresh-water whitefish, northern pike, walleye, sauger, mullet (sucker), and carp are packed in the round (i.e., not dressed), and except for the intestine and bones, practically the entire fish is utilized.

The fishes providing these delicacies have usually been the cods, trouts, and salmons in both old country and new.

Best known generally as a table delicacy are the tongues and cheeks of the cods, which find a ready market both at seashore and inland in fresh, frozen, and salted forms. When of any size or number at all, they are worth attention in any fish.

As was said above, *most* of the healthy temperate and cold-water fishes with which this book deals have edible innards. (This is not necessarily so in tropical fishes.) The puffer (blowfish) is a notable exception. Check individual fishes locally.

All the variety organs are extremely perishable. Remove the organs as the fish is dressed and immediately cook or freeze, or rub all sides with a mixture of ½ cup salt and 1 or 2 tablespoons brown sugar, cover, and refrigerate.

TONGUES

FRIED TONGUES WITH PORK

1 pound fish tongues   Flour
¼ pound salt pork, diced   Salt and pepper

Wash tongues well and pat dry between towels. Dice the pork coarsely and sear in a hot skillet to a crisp gold. Remove the pork and drain on paper towels. Keep warm.

Dredge the tongues in flour seasoned with salt and pepper and pan-fry *à la meunière* in the hot pork drippings. (See Chapter 3, Frying.)

Serve with the pork cubes and a zesty Tomato Sauce, or green tomato pickles.

Cheeks may be fried in the same way, with or without the tongues.

SCALLOPED SALTED TONGUES AND CHEEKS

1 pound salted tongues and cheeks   Butter
1 cup Béchamel Sauce, or Cream   Fine bread crumbs
    Sauce

Freshen the salted tongues and cheeks by soaking in cold water for a few hours. Drain and rinse in fresh water. Cover with cold water and simmer gently for about 5 minutes. Drain and place in a casserole. Pour the Béchamel or Cream Sauce over them, sprinkle with bread crumbs which have been lightly fried in butter, and brown in a 350° oven until bubbly and brown.

Variation: Mix crumbs with a little grated Parmesan cheese, sprinkle over sauce, and brown in oven.

SOUNDS AND LIVERS

The sound is the air or swim bladder which is found lying under the kidney in most fishes. It is a balance organ occurring in fishes of recent origin, in terms of fish history, most developed in bottom feeders and large fishes of deep waters. The size, of course, also varies with the size of the fish.

The sound is richly supplied with blood and is gelatinous. Sturgeon sounds in the past were an important source of isinglass used in the clarification of beverages, especially fine wines.

The liver of fish is highly regarded—its choice depending on whether one prefers it rich and oily or lean and delicate. Some like the big, rich cod, haddock, ling, and skate livers; others prefer the smaller sweet, exquisitely flavored livers that are to be found in pikes, pickerels, walleyes, and smaller trouts. However, a lean fish does not necessarily mean a lean liver: cod, burbot, haddock, and halibut livers are very oily. *Larousse Gastronomique* credits the lamprey and eel with having the most nourishing livers.

The liver of a healthy fish is a clear, bright red, smooth and without lesions, nodules, or other deformities. Extremely perishable, it should be removed as the fish is dressed out and washed and cooked immediately, or salted for a day or two of storage, or frozen. When removing the liver, take care to do so without breaking the gall bladder. Remove the gall bladder.

FISH SOUNDS POACHED IN MILK

Fish sounds   Egg Sauce or Piquant Sauce
Milk

Wash the sounds and soak overnight in equal parts of milk and water. Wash, then simmer gently in fresh milk and water until tender. Drain well on a towel. Cut into pieces. Heat in Egg Sauce or Piquant Sauce.

TONGUES AND SOUNDS, NEWFOUNDLAND STYLE

1 pound tongues and sounds of   ¼ pound salt pork
    codfish, or other fish   1 medium onion, minced
Milk   1 cup Egg Sauce

Wash tongues and sounds in several waters, soak overnight in milk and water, and simmer as directed in foregoing recipe. Drain. Cut up the sounds and slice the tongues, if desired, and put into casserole.

While fish is cooking, cut the salt pork in small cubes and fry with minced onion until the pork is crisp and golden. Add pork and onion to the fish. Pour hot Egg Sauce over all, garnish with minced parsley, and serve.

(Cheeks are sometimes substituted in this recipe for the sounds.)

PAN-FRIED LIVER OF FISH (lean)

Wash the fresh or semithawed liver. Drain and pat dry. Dredge in seasoned flour and quickly pan-fry *à la meunière*. Fish livers, like chicken livers, cook very quickly.

BAKED LIVERS OF FISH (oily)

Cod, halibut, haddock, or burbot   Salt and pepper
    livers

Wash livers well. Place whole in a pie plate. Score lightly. Season to taste and bake in a 350°F oven for about 20 to 25 minutes, or until tender. Baking renders out excessive oils, which are further absorbed by draining the livers on heavy absorbent paper before serving. Serve hot with plenty of tart pickle or relish.

❧ 6 ❧
Shellfishes

While there is no substitute for an aromatic clambake on the wet sands of a Pacific beach, or just idling on a wharf in the salty breezes off the Atlantic waiting for the lobster boats, shellfish of the North American coasts are as close as the local fish market or grocer's freezer. Thanks to modern fishery technology in the jet age, live lobsters leave their northwest Atlantic waters in the morning to be served the same night in a restaurant on the Pacific coast.

Scientific fisheries management, and modern packing technology applied under rigidly controlled and supervised conditions, are combining with rapid-transit facilities to open up an inland market for Atlantic and Pacific shellfish, and are delivering to markets across the continent on a year-round basis a product of unprecedented quality.

Shellfish in North American cookery fall into two categories:

Crustaceans	*Molluscs*
lobster	oysters
crab	clams
shrimp (prawn)	conchs
spiny lobster	mussels
crayfish	scallops
	periwinkles
	abalones

All are saltwater creatures, except crayfish and a freshwater clam (mussel).

Many dishes feature shellfishes in combination with each other or with fish. Here is a fine recipe that combines halibut with four types of shellfish:

LA PETITE MARMITE DU BON PECHEUR
(a dish of mixed shellfishes)

6 Alaska king crab legs, or lobster tails	12 jumbo shrimp, raw
1 tablespoon olive oil	24–30 mussels
3 large shallots, or 1 medium onion, finely diced	3 cups white wine
	Pinch saffron
1 small bay leaf	1 cup light cream
1 pound halibut, cut into 12 pieces	12 littleneck clams
	Salt and pepper

Cut the crab legs, in the shells, into 2-inch pieces, or cut the lobster tails, in the shells, into sections.

In a large, fireproof casserole or Dutch oven heat oil and fry shallots or onion until light gold, adding a bay leaf. Lightly brown the halibut. Add the crab legs or lobster pieces and shrimp. Fry until heated through. Add mussels, white wine, and saffron. (Dry saffron on a piece of paper in a *warm* oven for a few minutes. Pound in a mortar with a pestle. Steep in a little hot water and add to dish.) Heat to a boil, blend in the cream, and add the clams. Cover and cook until the clams open. Immediately lift out all the seafood with a slotted spoon and set aside.

Reduce the pan juices by one half. Thicken with a little *beurre manié,* if desired. Season to taste with salt and pepper. Return the seafoods to the sauce, arranging the opened clams on top with the shrimp and crab showing through. Let the dish heat through, and serve immediately with boiled new potatoes sprinkled with parsley, or rice.

Tony Roldan,
Executive Chef,
Westbury Hotel, Toronto, Ontario

Lobster

A captivating, bizarre appearance and an unsurpassed quality of red-dressed, firm white meat has made the American lobster of the northwest Atlantic one of the most famous of edible crustaceans.

The abundant lobster of the Atlantic coastal waters, from the shores of Belle Isle to North Carolina, has provided the most important northwest Atlantic inshore fishery over the past century. An efficient fishery, all is utilized, from the meat to selling shells as fertilizer to farms.

Whole lobsters have been known to weigh in at around 40-odd pounds; the average taken now is a pound to a pound and a half. However, newly discovered lobster grounds in the deep offshore northwest Atlantic waters are said to offer a prospect of catches of the future averaging 25 to 30 pounds.

American lobsters from the cool Atlantic coastal waters are unsurpassed for flavor, and the American lobster is strictly an easterner. (The spiny lobster of the west Atlantic and its close relatives in California support commercial fisheries. These are more like crayfish than the true lobster.) Efforts to transplant lobster to the West Coast have been unsuccessful—apparently it just vanished without a trace.

Lobsters are marketed live or cooked in the shell, and cooked and the meat canned or frozen. A live lobster should be lively; a cooked lobster's tail should be curled and spring back into a curl on straightening.

The natural color of a live lobster ranges from greenish blue to brownish olive, but due to chemical action upon application of heat, the shell rapidly changes to scarlet during cooking.

A 1-pound lobster cooked in the shell will yield approximately ¼ pound of meat, or ⅔ cup when chopped. It should be an adequate serving along with a salad.

When serving cooked lobster (particularly canned), be sure to remove the thin piece of cartilage usually lodged in the meat of the claws. (It gets between the teeth.)

FREEZING LOBSTER   Freeze only freshly caught, freshly cooked lobster meat.
Boil the live lobster in salted water or steam. Cool quickly in shells. Pick meat from shells and package in recipe- or meal-size quantities. Pack closely in freezer containers or glass jars, allowing about one inch headroom. Freeze hard, uncovered. Add cold water to cover the meats by about ¼ inch. Freeze hard. Seal tightly and store in freezer.

BOILED LOBSTER, AND HOW TO EAT IT BLUENOSE FASHION

Fill a large, deep kettle with enough water to cover the lobsters. If you have enough lobsters (or large ones, say 4 pounds), use a wash boiler. For each gallon of water add 1 cup salt, unless you're by the seashore, in which case use clean sea water. Bring the water to a rapid boil. Grasp each lobster

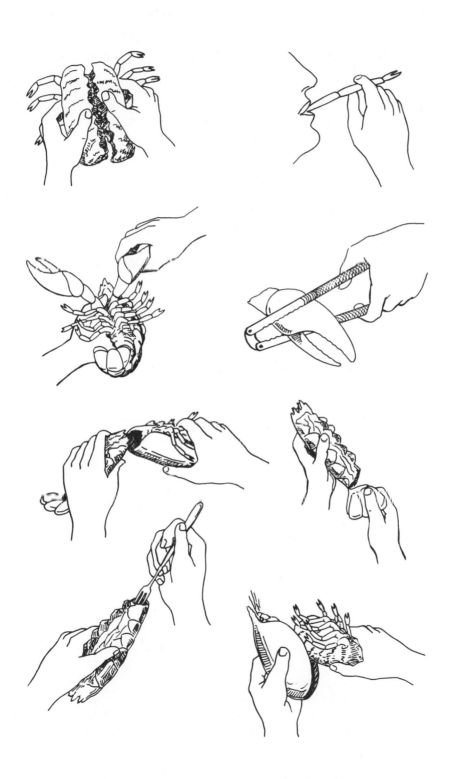

firmly behind the head, under the claws, and plunge it head first into the boiling water. Be sure it's submerged. Cover the kettle. Let the water return to an easy boil. Allow 15 to 20 minutes for 1½- to 2-pound lobsters, and an extra 5 minutes for each pound over that weight. The lobsters will turn a bright red. Don't let them overcook. Immediately lift. (The lobsters may be cooled off under running cold water.) Turn them on their backs and drain. To serve cold lobster, refrigerate until needed.

To serve lobsters hot, omit the chilling, but do run them quickly under the cold water, as the shells are too hot to handle. The meat will stay hot inside the shell long enough to eat it.

Now to eat the lobster. A seaside expert may get so accomplished at eating a whole lobster as to be able to dissect it with bare hands. However, the novice may need a knife, a lobster or pickle fork, and some practice. Twist off the claws and pull each open until the little pincer comes off. Crack the claws with a nutcracker or a good whack with the handle of the knife, draw out the meat and eat, not overlooking the meat in the pincers.

Take a firm grip on the body and tail piece and bend the tail back up over the head until it separates. Pull off the legs and swimmerets and suck the meat out of them. Pull off the tail fans. Insert the fork where the fans came off and push the tail meat out. Eat it, and chew the meat out of the fans.

Unhinge the back from the body. Cut the body up the middle, or crack it apart. Remove the dark vein that runs up midbody; discard the spongy, gray-green lungs on either side of the back and the small sac, or "lady," behind the head. This is the stomach. (To the fanciful, the tiny calciferous structure in the stomach resembles a robed lady. Legend inevitably has accredited the lobster a special if obscure patronage of the Virgin Mary.) Don't discard the bright green matter, which is the liver (tomalley), or the red ovaries (coral), in the hen. These are considered by many to be the most delicious parts of the lobster. Suck the meat from the small claws for the last succulent remains of the lobster meat.

Serve boiled lobsters with hot melted butter, lemon wedges, frosty pitchers of foaming beer, and lots of hot, crusty French bread, plain or garlic.

STEAMED LOBSTER

Plug the claws of the lobster, that is, insert a small piece of wood between them and tie with a string. Put them in a deep sink or dishpan and cover with hot (tap) water. This treatment will make the lobsters sluggish and more tractable, and presumably resigned to their fate in the steamer. If you wish you can kill the lobster immediately before cooking by sticking the point of a sharp knife between the eyes.

Meanwhile put about an inch of water in the bottom of a roomy steamer, adding a jigger or two of white wine if handy, and bring to a boil. Pile the lobsters on the steamer rack and lower into the steamer. Sprinkle with salt, ½ teaspoon for each. Cover tightly and let steam. Allow 20 to 25 minutes for 1½- to 2-pound lobsters, and an extra 5 minutes for each pound over that. Remove from steamer immediately.

Eat or use like boiled lobster.

LOBSTER ON THE HALF SHELL

A tidier way to serve boiled or steamed lobster.

Prepare boiled lobster as directed above.

Place the drained lobster on a cutting board, back down. With a sharp knife or kitchen shears, cut through the shell and underside of the tail and body. Spread tail and lift out meat. Remove the back vein, stomach, and lungs. Remove but don't discard the tomalley or coral if present.

Turn the lobster over and cut up the back. Crack the large claws. Extract the meat. Repack the body shells with lobster meat, adding the tomalley and coral. Serve with mayonnaise on the side, or serve as you would whole boiled lobster, i.e., with melted butter, beer, and French bread.

Lobster tomalley and coral are delicious poached and eaten with hot Lemon Butter on toast

POTTED LOBSTER

LOBSTER BUTTER

Potted lobster is made from debris—legs, claws, shells, coral, and tomalley—of cooked lobster. Shells and coral give a lovely creamy rose color, and with tomalley, a meaty flavor and smooth texture.

Traditionally, everything is combined with butter and pounded in a mortar with pestle until the blended mass can be passed through a fine sieve. It can also be made in a blender.

You need 1 cup lobster debris and ½ cup melted butter, hot and ready.

While the butter is melting, chop everything into small, chunky pieces or put through food chopper. Scald blender and dry quickly. Add hot butter and lobster and blend at top speed. Press through a fine sieve. Pack in little custard cups.

Serve with canapés, hard-boiled eggs, to garnish a cold dish, or to enrich bisques or soups.

STUFFED LOBSTER

2 2-pound lobsters	1 cup heavy cream
½ pound mushrooms	3 tablespoons sherry
2 tablespoons butter	Tomalley and coral, if present
1 tablespoon flour	2 tablespoons chopped parsley
Salt and pepper	

Cut the boiled lobster and remove meat. (See illustration.) Reserve drained shells. Dice the meat. Wash mushrooms and trim; cut into small, thin slices. Bring water to a boil in the bottom of a double boiler.

Meanwhile, melt the butter in the top part of double boiler and cook the mushrooms until browned. Sift flour over the mushrooms, adding a dusting of salt and pepper, and stir until smooth. Remove from the heat. Blend in the cream and place the pot over the boiling water for 7 or 8 minutes, stirring often. Remove from over the hot water and blend in the sherry. Press tomalley and coral through a sieve and blend into sauce. Add lobster meat. Fill the shells with sauce.

Before serving, place under broiler for a few minutes to color. Arrange on small shallow platter and garnish with parsley. Serve at the table from the shell.

STUFFED LOBSTER TAILS

6 medium-size lobster tails, freshly boiled, or frozen	Pinch tarragon
2 tablespoons butter	1 tablespoon minced parsley
2 tablespoons flour	1 teaspoon minced chives
2 cups milk	Salt and pepper
4 tablespoons soft bread crumbs, rubbed fine	3 hard-cooked egg yolks, sieved
	Paprika

If not cooked, drop lobster tails into boiling salted water; simmer 15 to 20 minutes. Remove from heat and cool. Remove lobster meat and cut into cubes.

Melt butter, add flour, and blend until smooth; add milk and cook until thickened. Add crumbs, tarragon, parsley, chives, lobster, salt and pepper.

Wash shells and wipe dry, and fill with lobster mixture. Arrange in baking dish. Put into hot oven at 400°F for 10 minutes to heat. Before serving, sprinkle sieved egg yolks over top and garnish with paprika.

LOBSTER À L'AMERICAINE

The controversy over the origin and name *lobster à l'Americaine* that flourishes in culinary circles is enough to testify that the dish is one worthy of attention. Claims exist that it was originally *à l'Amoricaine* from Brittany and imported to America by some long-forgotten cook, where it caught on and became corrupted to *Americaine.* This is doubtless the case, since, except for the native cookery of the North American Indians, our cuisine, like the people, came from somewhere else. The corruption of the name was almost inevitable, as the prize of the lobster world, *Homarus americanus,* or the American lobster, was already here, destined to bring the dish to its peak of succulence and worldwide prestige.

2 1½–2-pound hen lobsters, live	1 teaspoon chopped parsley
6 tablespoons olive oil	¼ teaspoon tarragon
Tip of a clove of garlic	½ cup dry white wine
Salt and pepper	¼ cup fish fumet
1 medium onion, diced	2 tablespoons cognac
4 or 5 shallots	Cayenne
4 tomatoes, peeled, seeded, and	2 tablespoons plus ¼ cup butter
coarsely chopped	Lemon
1 tablespoon tomato paste	Parsley, chopped

Place the lobsters, backs up, on a small tray, so as to catch the juices. Grasp firmly below the head and under the claws with one hand. With the other hand slip the point of a sharp knife under the head shell and sever the vein at the base of the neck. Twist off the claws, legs, and tail fans. Separate the tail from the body and cut the tail into small slices, following the markings on the shell. (Refer above to Boiled Lobster, and How to Eat It Bluenose Fashion.) Cut the head in two. Split up underside of body; remove and discard the sac or stomach and gritty lung substance around it. Remove the coral (in uncooked lobster it is green) and the tomalley (gray-green) and save for later use along with the juices from the lobster. These will be used for thickening. Turn body over and split through the back.

Heat the olive oil in a large saucepan, along with the garlic tip. When it starts to bubble, take out the garlic. Season the lobster with salt and pepper and put the pieces, including the claws, legs, and fans, into the pan. Brown quickly on all sides over a brisk heat. Remove the lobster. To the pan add onion and cook until almost tender. Add the shallots and cook and stir for a minute. Add the tomatoes and tomato paste with the chopped parsley and tarragon, and blend. Lay the pieces of lobster on top of the vegetables, and moisten with wine, fish fumet, and the cognac. Season very lightly with a few grains cayenne.

Bring the mixture to a boil and cover and cook for about 20 minutes, until lobster has turned red. Remove the lobster, drain. Pick the meat from claws and tails. Pack the halves of shells with meat. Arrange on a large platter, garnishing the edges with claw and leg shells. Keep warm while preparing the sauce.

Reduce the sauce in the pan by half. Mix the coral, tomalley, and lobster water (actually, its blood) with about 2 tablespoons of butter, and rub through a fine sieve. Whisk the mixture into the sauce over a high heat, and whisk until smoothly thickened. Remove from heat and, still whisking, add ¼ cup diced butter; whisk to blend well. Season with a few grains of cayenne and a squeeze of lemon juice, and pour the hot sauce over the lobster. Garnish with chopped parsley and serve at once.

Serves 4.

LOBSTER NEWBURG

4 tablespoons butter	½ teaspoon salt
2 tablespoons coral, if available	2 eggs, beaten
¼ cup dry sherry, or Madeira	1 cup cream
Pinch of freshly grated nutmeg	2 cups lobster meat, boiled or canned
Pinch of paprika	

Melt the butter in the top of a double boiler. Add the lobster coral,* and stir over boiling water for about 3 minutes. Stir in the wine, cook a couple

* If there is no coral, omit this step and use 3 eggs instead of 2.

of minutes, then add the nutmeg, paprika, and salt. Leave over the hot water.

Blend the beaten eggs into the cream and stir into the sauce. Cook and stir until the sauce is thickened. At no time let this dish boil. Add lobster meat and heat through.

Serve on hot buttered toast or a mound of fluffy boiled white rice, or on crisp, hot waffles.

This recipe may also be used for Crab Newburg.

Crab

The crabs best known to the North American table are the large Alaska king and the Dungeness of the Pacific coast; and on the East Coast the blue crab, from Cape Cod to Florida; the sweet little stone crab down to the Gulf of Mexico; and the queen or snow crab, come lately to fame in the northwest Atlantic.

Crabs have two phases of interest to the cook: the soft-shell and the hard-shell. The soft-shell is a stage in the cycle after molting, while the crab is building its new shell; after that it is a hard-shell crab.

Debate on the relative merits of soft-shell and hard-shell crabs is lively; many connoisseurs consider the soft-shell to be a delicacy, while others think it to be at its least appetizing stage and its flesh not yet its most succulent and firm. Either way, to be at their best crabs must be cooked, or the hard-shells fast frozen almost as soon as taken from the water.

Crabs are protected in many areas. Inquire locally regarding regulations before taking your own.

SOFT-SHELL CRABS

The earlier in the molting stage, the better-flavored the soft-shell crab. The soft-shell crab when cooked remains green; if it turns red, it is no longer a soft-shell, but a hard-shell crab. Soft-shell crabs are eaten shell and all.

Dressing soft-shell crabs. Stick a small, sharp, pointed knife in between the eyes to kill the crab. Lift up pointed edge of back covering, peel it back, and dig out the spongy matter underneath. Turn it over and pull the apron from the front. Wash well under cold running water. Dry in a towel.

Broil, or fry in deep fat.

Broiling. Dust the crab with flour. Dip in melted butter, to which a bit of lemon juice and tarragon have been added. Broil over coals or in oven, basting frequently. As one side browns, baste, turn, and broil the other side. Serve at once with salt, pepper, melted butter, and lemon juice.

Deep-frying. Dress the crabs and prepare the same way as deep-fried scallops.

HARD-SHELL CRABS

Large hard-shell crabs like Alaska king and the Dungeness or Pacific edible are usually boiled, though they may be steamed. The small crabs like the blue crab are steamed. Either way the method is the same as for lobster.

Boiling hard-shell crab. Cooking time is about 10 minutes per pound. The crab is cooked when the apron begins to rise.

Steaming hard-shell crab. Put the crabs into a hot-water bath to incapacitate them, then pile them into the steamer following the instructions for steamed lobster. Should any claws fall off in the bath, put them on top of the pile. Sprinkle with 1 teaspoon salt and a good pinch of cayenne pepper per crab. Cover tightly and steam. As soon as the aprons begin to rise (about 20–25 minutes), remove rack and crabs. Be careful not to overcook.

Turn the crab over on its back, and with a sharp knife, cut the sinews of the legs close to the body and carefully break them off. Take each leg and break it into five pieces as shown. Discard all No. 1 pieces with the exception of the two biggest, which you use as picks to get the meat out of Nos. 3 and 5. All Nos. 2 and 4 should be piled in a separate heap and cracked with nutcrackers, after which the meat may be easily extracted.

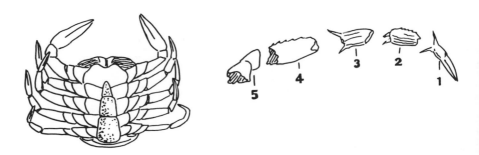

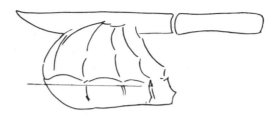

When all crab legs have been disposed of, take the meat from the body. Lift the triangular appendage shown in the first drawing, and, following right around, pull off the entire main shell. The body will now be left, which is covered with spongy gills and olive-green crab fat. All gills and fat should be removed, and the remaining shell, which is filled with snowy meat, should be held under cold running water and rinsed off. Cut the meaty body into four sections, first vertically, then laterally as shown by the line. Use the pincer-picks to extract the meat.

Once cooked, immediately do one of three things: eat it; fast-freeze it; chill and refrigerate the meat.

Once you know how to eat them, the other two steps are simple. Roger Phillips, an engineer of West Vancouver who for the past twenty-five years has been dedicated to the hobby of observing, gathering, and cooking the riches of the British Columbia coastal waters, has charted the procedure for extracting the last bit of succulent meat from a crab. With his generous permission, his skill in the frustrating art is passed along in the accompanying sketches.

Freezing hard-shell crab. The meat of the hard-shell crab is packaged and frozen by the same method as lobster meat. (Soft-shell crabs are not frozen.)

SNOW CRAB MOUSSE

1 envelope plain gelatin
¼ cup lemon juice
1 teaspoon salt
¼ teaspoon paprika

Dash of fresh ground black pepper
2 cups crab meat, frozen or canned
1 cup heavy cream, chilled

Chill a mixing bowl and a rotary beater or whisk in refrigerator while preparing gelatin.

Put 4 ounces cold water in a soup plate, sprinkle the gelatin over it and let soften (5 to 10 minutes). Place the bowl over boiling water and stir until the gelatin is thoroughly dissolved. Remove from heat.

In a second mixing bowl combine lemon juice, salt, paprika, and pepper. Mix well and stir in the gelatin. Place in refrigerator until thickened but not set, stirring occasionally. Blend in the crab meat, mixing gently.

Meanwhile, using the chilled bowl and beater, whip the cream to medium stiffness so that it heaps softly. Gently fold the whipped cream into the crab mixture and turn it into a lightly oiled 1-quart mold. Chill for at least 3 hours and turn out onto a serving platter. Garnish with parsley and a few thin slices of radish or colorful garnish, and serve with Sour Cream Cucumber Sauce on the side.

CRAB BISQUE
(a modified version)

1 medium onion, sliced	1 pound fresh or frozen crab meat,
4 cups milk	or 2 7-ounce cans
4 tablespoons butter	1 tablespoon chopped pimiento
4 tablespoons flour	½ cup heavy cream
½ teaspoon salt	Pinch cayenne
	2 tablespoons dry sherry

Heat the onion and milk together in a saucepan; don't let it boil.

Heat water in bottom of double boiler. Separately, in the top of the double boiler, melt the butter. Stir flour into the butter, add salt, and cook and stir to a bubbly *roux*. Place over hot water, now boiling. (The water level should not reach the top part of the double boiler.) Strain the hot milk to remove the onion and stir it into the *roux,* and, stirring constantly, let it cook until slightly thickened. Add the crab meat and pimiento and continue to heat for about 10 minutes. Just before serving, blend in the cream, cayenne, and sherry. Adjust seasonings to taste. Let it heat through and serve at once.

Serves 4 to 6.

CRAB CREAMS

Crisp golden shells curling around a creamy mound of crab filling make this a dish of elegance that belies its simplicity. It is an attractive luncheon or late supper dish.

Shells

2 eggs, well beaten

1 teaspoon salt

1 cup flour (approximately)

Cooking oil

Crab Filling

3 tablespoons clarified butter

½ cup sliced mushrooms

2 tablespoons flour

1½ cups milk, or milk and cream
    mixed

½ teaspoon salt

⅛ teaspoon white pepper

Pinch cayenne

2 cups, or 3 5-ounce cans crab meat

¼ cup medium-dry white wine

To the beaten eggs, add salt and sift in just enough flour to make a stiff dough. Knead it very lightly and work with fingers until smooth. Watch the quantity of flour and don't overwork. Too much of either will toughen the results. Even so, this is not a short pastry, and the shells are not as tender as they are usefully decorative.

Roll the pastry very, very thin without cracks or breaks. Cut into 6 rounds about 3 inches in diameter. Heat cooking oil in saucepan and deep-fry the rounds of pastry, one at a time. Each takes only about 15 to 20 seconds. As the pastry browns it will mound in the middle and ripple at the edges, forming a scalloplike shell. When nicely brown, turn with a kitchen tongs and quickly brown the other side. Lift the shell, let it drain a moment, and lay it on thick paper toweling in oven to keep warm. Fry the rest of the shells.

The shells may be made in advance and frozen. Put directly from freezer into a moderate oven to avoid condensation of moisture on them.

Melt the butter over a medium-low heat and sauté the mushrooms until tender. Remove the mushrooms with a slotted spoon, and drain on thick paper towels. The remaining butter should now equal the flour. Make a *roux:* With a wooden spoon, stir flour into the butter and stir and cook until all is smooth and bubbly. Heat the milk and gradually stir into the *roux;* stir until thickened. Stir in salt, pepper, and cayenne. Add the crab meat, the mushrooms, and the wine and gently blend while it heats through. Remove from heat.

Place each shell on a dessert-size plate and fill with the crab, dividing it evenly. (There should be 6 shells.) Stick 1 or 2 pieces of claw in each and sprinkle a bit of fresh parsley leaf on top. Tuck a few sprigs of parsley under the edges of the shells to relieve the bareness of the plate, or place shells on paper doilies.

Variation: Use above recipe with lobster instead of crab. If the tomalley and coral are present, stir into butter before the flour, which should be reduced to 2 tablespoons.

Shrimps and Prawns

The universally esteemed shrimp is one of the most widely distributed shellfishes, supporting valuable fisheries around the world. Most famous and abundant are the big shrimps that grow in the Gulf of Mexico and off Key West, Florida, where hundreds of millions of pounds are harvested annually.

Shrimps, generally thought of as warm-water inhabitants, thrive hundreds of varieties strong in the cold waters. Twenty-nine varieties are recorded off the northern Atlantic and Pacific coasts of North America.

Most important of the cold-water species is the pink shrimp of circumpolar distribution from the mouth of the Columbia River on the West Coast up and around the North Pole and down to Massachusetts Bay. Long an important fishery on the Pacific coast, this delectable little shrimp has only lately been discovered in abundance in the northwest Atlantic, and a good future for its fishery has been predicted.

Not all the cold-water shrimp are small. The giant red of the Pacific grows as long as eight inches and is second in size only to the prawn. It occurs from the Bering Sea to the Washington coast.

The Pacific prawn is the largest of the shrimps. Deep-fried in batter, it is favored in Oriental cookery.

The color of the shrimp *au naturel* may vary from gray-green to light brown to light pink. When cooked the shells turn red and the meat varying shades of pink.

The meat of the shrimp is firm in texture. Its parchmentlike shell fits the body tightly, and if the flesh has drawn away from the shell, the shrimp is not fresh.

Only the tail of the shrimp is eaten.

For cooking purposes, shrimp are divided according to size: small, medium, and large or jumbo. The jumbo, which includes the prawn, may grow a tail as long as four to five inches, while the cold-water pink may have a tail not much bigger than the curl of a button hook.

Cold-water pink shrimp are marketed frozen or canned, in both cases cooked, and there is nothing to be done with the succulent little morsels but eat them.

Market shrimp are usually steamed on board the boats after capture, the meat removed and iced or flash-frozen on board.

Shrimp come to the kitchen raw or cooked, and all should arrive fresh. The black vein running along the back is not inedible, but for appearance's sake it may be removed from the larger shrimps.

Fresh shrimp have a mild, lingering odor of the sea. A trace of iodine may be detected in the warm-water shrimps, especially when frozen. (This is not noticeable in the cold-water shrimps.)

Freezing shrimp. Whether raw or cooked, freeze only strictly fresh shrimp.

If raw, wash the shrimps; remove head and sand vein. Wash in brine: 1 teaspoon coarse pickling salt (uniodized) to 4 cups cold water. Drain well, package, and freeze as directed for lobster.

If cooked, prepare the shrimp as above, then bring a pot of salted water to a boil, deep enough to cover the shrimp. Immerse the shrimp quickly, and the second they turn red, remove them from the water. (A deep-fry basket is useful here.)

Shell and devein if necessary. Rinse under cold running water, drain, and package and freeze as directed for lobster.

Shrimp packed commercially for market are processed fresh, frozen, and canned. They are always cooked, at least partially. If not fully cooked, i.e., pink in color, a few minutes in boiling water will be sufficient.

Thawing frozen shrimp. If frozen raw, drop into boiling water, adding 1 dtablespoon lemon juice or vinegar per cup. Simmer until pink.

If frozen cooked, thaw in refrigerator *in package;* or drop into boiling water, remove from heat, and let steep until thawed.

Cooking shrimp. Shrimp is one of the most exquisitely delicate in flavor of seafoods. It should be very simply prepared and served, and nothing should be allowed to overpower the flavor of the shrimp. We say prepared rather than cooked, for after the initial cooking, shrimp must only be heated. Overcooking is disastrous to shrimp, as they lose flavor and become tough and stringy.

Whether shrimp are bought fresh, frozen, or canned, a shrimp that is pink is cooked; if cooking your own, the moment it turns pink it is done and must be cooked no more.

When shrimp are used in hot dishes, such as casseroles, everything is cooked before the shrimp go in. The dish stays in the oven just long enough to heat through and lightly brown the top, best done quickly at a high temperature.

Note: One pound of fresh or frozen whole shrimp tails yields ½ pound shelled shrimp, cooked or canned.

One pound cooked, peeled shrimp yields 1 pound edible meat.

BOILED SHRIMP

Put 1 pound fresh shrimp in a deep saucepan, cover with water, and bring to a boil. Add 1 tablespoon salt. Tie a small handful of pickling spices in cheesecloth and add, along with ¼ cup cider vinegar, to the water. Let boil for 5 minutes. Remove the spice bag and plunge the shrimps into the boiling water. Bring to a boil again and immediately reduce the heat and let simmer for 3 to 5 minutes, depending on the size of the shrimp, until the skins turn red. Remove immediately and rinse in cold running water. Shell and devein. Refrigerate for immediate use or freeze until needed.

COOKED SHRIMP IN ELEGANT STYLE

2 quarts water	1 bay leaf
1 cup white wine	1 teaspoon salt
1 stalk celery, cut up	1–2 slices lemon
Few peppercorns	2 pounds frozen cooked shrimp

Make a court bouillon in a small stock pot, using all ingredients except the shrimp. Bring to a boil and let simmer for about 10 minutes. Drop the frozen shrimp into the brew.

Reduce the heat to warm, and let the shrimp steep in the hot court bouillon for about 10 minutes. Lift out the shrimp with a slotted spoon, letting them drain a moment over the pot. Peel and devein quickly, if necessary.

To serve hot, nest the shrimp in the fold of a white linen napkin, with hot Lemon Butter in a side dish.

To serve cold, chill in refrigerator, covered with a damp cloth, and use in salad, or serve on crushed ice in a nest of lettuce or watercress, with a lemon wedge at the side, and a bowl of fish dip or hot Drawn Butter. (Dip cold shrimp in hot butter.)

DEEP-FRIED SHRIMPS, PRAWNS, SCAMPI

For cooking purposes, prawns, or by their Italian name *scampi,* are overgrown shrimps, and are grouped together with big shrimps as "jumbo."

Jumbo shrimp are time-honored favorites for deep-fried shrimp. Strict attention to the rules of deep-frying is essential. (See Chapter 3, Deep-Frying.) Batter should be light as a cloud, so fragile that the instant it hits the hot fat it crusts quickly, sealing in the tender nugget of precooked shrimp meat, and giving it only time to heat through.

The shrimps may be fried in the conventional deep-fry kettle, or by the more elegant tempura method.

The deveined shrimps should be at room temperature. A vegetable oil is recommended for deep-frying purposes.

EGG-WHITE BATTER FOR SHRIMP

2 egg whites	2 tablespoons cornstarch
2 tablespoons white wine	Pinch of salt

Beat egg whites with a whisk until barely frothy. Mix the cornstarch and salt in the wine and whisk into the egg whites. Whisk to a frothy, fluid stickiness.

GOLDEN GLAZED JUMBO SHRIMP

20 jumbo shrimp, boiled, fresh, or frozen	Lemon juice
	Oil for deep frying
Egg-White Batter, for Shrimp, double recipe above	

Have shrimp at room temperature. Wash in cold water, score along back, and remove vein. Pat dry on a towel. Sprinkle with lemon juice and let stand while mixing batter and heating oil. (See Chapter 3, Deep-Frying.)

Dust each shrimp lightly with flour, then coat in batter and deep-fry until crisp and golden. Fry only a few at a time to maintain the heat of the oil. Drain on a paper-lined cookie sheet in a warm oven.

Variation: Beery Shrimp Puffs. Substitute Beer Batter for Egg-White Batter.

SAUTÉ OF JUMBO SHRIMPS OR PRAWNS

12 large shrimps, or 8 prawns	2 or 3 leeks
Peanut oil, or other vegetable oil	A few fine shavings of ginger
Egg-White Batter for Shrimp	1 clove garlic, minced fine
2 green peppers, seeds removed and coarsely diced	2 tablespoons soy sauce
	1 tablespoon sugar
4 tiny chili peppers, seeded and halved, or ¼ teaspoon hot pepper sauce	1 teaspoon salt
	2 tablespoons cider vinegar
	Dash monosodium glutamate

Shell and devein the shrimps or prawns. Cross-cut the large shrimps in two, the prawns in three pieces, making a small slash in each piece to prevent shrinking.

Heat oil about 2 inches deep in a wok or deep-frying pan to 360°. Prepare Egg-White Batter for Shrimp. Dip the shellfish in batter and deep-fry to a light gold. Fry a few at a time. Place on absorbent paper and keep in a warm oven.

Heat ¼ cup of the oil in a sauté pan or wok, and over a high heat sauté the peppers, leeks, ginger, and garlic for 1 minute. Stir in the remaining ingredients, bring to a boil, add the fried shrimp, and serve at once.

SHRIMP TEMPURA

The tempura is a Japanese refinement of the deep fry, an elegant tableside preparation using a wok or tempura pan. Tempura is a method rather than a recipe. Jumbo shrimp is traditional in the tempura, along with bite-size chunks of other firm-fleshed fish, including octopus and squid, and firm vegetables. The foods are dipped in a light batter such as Egg-White Batter for Shrimp or one of the two following Tempura Batters, and deep-fried in hot oil, all set up at table or buffet, along with a sweet-and-sour dip sauce.

Whatever the arrangement, it must provide for the high, constant heat required for deep-fat frying. For buffet service, the charcoal hibachi or gas-fueled burner with wok or tempura pan are aesthetically most satisfactory, as well as efficient. Otherwise a presentable deep-frying electrical appliance will perform efficiently at the table.

A *wok* is a concave metal frying pan which rests on a frame over the heat. Center depth makes it particularly good for small-quantity deep-frying.

TEMPURA BATTER NO. 1

3 egg yolks   ½ cup flour
¾ cup water   ¼ teaspoon salt
⅓ cup cornstarch

Stir egg yolks to mix (don't beat); stir in water. Combine cornstarch, salt, and flour; mix into liquid and stir lightly.

TEMPURA BATTER NO. 2

1 cup flour   1 tablespoon crushed dried shrimps
⅓ cup cornstarch   ¼ teaspoon salt
2 teaspoons baking powder   2 eggs
⅛ teaspoon ground ginger   1 cup water
Pinch of mace   1 tablespoon evaporated milk

Mix dry ingredients thoroughly and make a well in the middle. Beat eggs with water and milk and pour into the well. Mix from the middle out until all the flour mixture is taken up, resulting in a light batter. Don't overmix.

Variation: A delightful little cocktail nibble may be made from the above recipe by increasing crushed dried shrimps to ¼ cup and soaking them in an extra ¼ cup water. Fold into the batter. Drop a teaspoonful at a time into hot, deep fat. When crusty brown, lift and drain on paper towels.

Shrimp flakes or dried shrimps are available at Chinese and Japanese grocers.

BUTTERFLY SHRIMP

1 pound (2 cups) large shrimp,   1 egg, beaten
    cooked   2 tablespoons milk
Flour   Bread crumbs

Shuck and devein shrimp, leaving fan on tail. With a sharp knife cut the outside curve along the line of the vein, deeply but not through the shrimp. Open the shrimp out flat to spread the wings. Dust lightly with flour.

Dip the shrimp in a binding mixture of 1 egg beaten with 2 tablespoons milk, press both sides in fine, soft bread crumbs, and deep-fry.

Or dip butterflies in Egg-White Batter for Shrimp and deep-fry.

POTTED SHRIMP

1 pound cooked shrimp	Salt
2 tablespoons lemon juice or vinegar	White pepper
¼ pound softened butter	Watercress or parsley
⅛ teaspoon ground mace	

Peel and devein shrimp. Chop fine. Put butter into blender, turn to medium speed, add shrimp, mace, salt and white pepper to taste. Blend for about 10 seconds until smooth. Pack in a small, deep bowl, chill well. Turn out and garnish with watercress or fresh parsley.

Variation: Substitute crayfish or crab for shrimp in above recipe.

Crayfish

The crayfish, also known as crawfish, crawdad, and by other local names, is a freshwater crustacean related to the spiny lobster and shrimp. Its appearance is like a miniature lobster. It spreads itself generously throughout North America—in fact, in almost all fresh waters of the world except in Africa, and its delicate flesh is highly prized by Europeans and discerning Americans. (This is the famous *écrevisse* of French cuisine.)

While over one hundred known species of crayfish grow in the United States and Canada, many are not of worthwhile eating size, and generally are more useful as bait for bigger fish.

In Louisiana, crayfish country of renown, they are farmed extensively. A market-crayfish of good size grows in Wisconsin, and a fairly large Pacific species in the western coastal streams. Although American crayfish are small by European standards, they are fine of flesh. American crayfish are marketed mostly in frozen form, under the name "Écrevisses."

Whatever size, crayfish can prove an important item of food in northern wilderness survival fare. They are fun for the kids to catch and cook in camp.

Crayfish may be cooked as in shrimp recipes. Like shrimp they are a delicate food, best cooked with very light seasonings.

The bisque and simple "crayfish boil" are two favorite crayfish preparations of the Southern states.

Crayfish are kept alive and frisky up to cooking time. If kept in cool, fresh, running water for a few days, they can go straight into the pot. If freshly caught, they should be scrubbed and rinsed well in several waters and cleaned. To clean, grasp the middle tail fin, give it a firm, gently pulling twist, and draw out the vein and stomach.

BOILED CRAYFISH

Clean the crayfish.

The kettle should be big enough, when filled two-thirds with water, to accommodate the crayfish without crowding. This may be anything from a quart-size saucepan to a copper wash boiler.

Add the water, bring to a boil, and add a little vinegar—about 2 tablespoons to the saucepan. Don't add salt yet. Throw in the crayfish a few at a time so that the water remains at a rolling boil. Add 1 tablespoon salt for each estimated gallon of water.

Hot crayfish: Cook not more than 5 minutes for the largest. Remove and drain the fish. Serve in the shell with clear Butter Sauce to which a little fresh dill has been added. Crayfish are eaten with the fingers. (A fingerbowl is a thoughtful accessory on the table.)

Cold crayfish. To eat cold or freezer-store, boil only about 1 minute and let the crayfish cool in the stock. Lift and drain. To extract the meat, separate the tail from the body, bending it across the back to crack. Draw meat from tail and body.

Freezing crayfish. See Freezing Shrimp, earlier in this chapter.

CRAYFISH BISQUE

20 medium-size crayfish (adjust quantity according to size)
6 tablespoons butter
2 cups *mirepoix:* about ⅓ to ½ cup each diced onions, carrots, green pepper, celery, mushrooms
Bouquet garni of fresh parsley, thyme, peppercorns, and celery leaf
Salt and pepper

Cayenne
2 tablespoons cognac, or brandy
½ cup white wine
6 cups white consommé (veal or chicken)
1 cup cooked white rice (preferably cooked in white consommé or crayfish stock)
1½ cups heavy cream
Potted crayfish

Clean and wash the crayfish.

Make the *mirepoix:* Melt 2 tablespoons of the butter in a large, covered kettle or Dutch oven, and sauté the diced vegetables until soft. (Chill the remaining butter.) Add the crayfish, bouquet garni, and seasonings. Over a high heat sauté the crayfish until the shells begin to turn red.

Warm the cognac or brandy in a long-handled butter melter or small saucepan, pour over the crayfish, and ignite it. Add the white wine. Cover and let simmer for a few moments until shells are bright red.

Remove the crayfish with a slotted spoon, letting them drain over the pot. Shell the crayfish, reserving 8 or more shells for garnish. Return remaining shells to the pot and mince or chop remaining crayfish meat and set aside.

Reduce liquid in pot by about half. Add 1 cup of consommé and simmer over low heat for 10 minutes. Pour into blender, shells and all. Process at low speed for about 10 seconds. Add another cup of the consommé and the cooked rice and blend to a fine, smooth purée. Pour into the top of a large double boiler. Dilute with remaining consommé, bring to a boil, and simmer for a few minutes, then keep hot over boiling water. If the soup is at all gritty, strain it through a fine sieve lined with cheesecloth.

Just before serving crumble the remaining chilled butter into fine bits and sprinkle over the bisque. Add the cream, blend gently, then add the chopped crayfish meat. Adjust the seasonings.

Pour the bisque into a tureen. Stuff the shells with Potted Crayfish (see Potted Shrimp) and use as garnish.

Oysters and Clams

Top-quality oysters and hard-shell clams have hard, well-cupped shells. When alive the shells of both are tightly closed, or snap tightly closed when disturbed. A gaping shell indicates that the little creature inside is no longer alive and is not edible.

Clams and oysters for the table should be gathered from areas of clean, unpolluted waters. Check with fisheries officials regarding regulations, local water quality, and good gathering spots.

Oysters and clams are marketed alive in the shell and as shucked meat fresh, frozen, and canned.

Storing oysters and clams. Oysters and clams kept at temperatures just above freezing and below 40°F will stay alive for quite some time. Store in the shell (oysters deep shell down) at the lowest possible temperature short of freezing. At 34°F they should keep alive and well up to 4 months; and at 40°F for several weeks.

The molluscs will die if allowed to dry out. Protect them with damp packing; keep it damp, but don't let water collect in the container. Check from time to time and discard any with gaping shells.

Shucked oysters and clams should be plump and have clear, fresh-smelling liquor. Pack shucked meats in their own liquor, in covered cartons or clean covered glass jars, and store in refrigerator or surrounded by ice for immediate use (1 to 2 days).

Freezing oysters and clams. Freeze only freshly gathered oysters and clams. Scrub well, shuck, and collect and reserve the liquor. Wash oysters and clams in a brine of 4 tablespoons pickling salt to a gallon of cold water, drain, and pack in freezer containers, covering with oyster or clam liquor and filling about three-quarters full. Label contents and date. Freeze at once. Add a little more water and freeze to cap with ice. If using glass jars, leave the covers loose until contents have frozen, then tighten.

An empty, straight-sided can lined with a tough plastic bag makes an excellent container. Shuck as directed, putting meats and liquor into the plastic bag. Set in freezer. Freeze hard, add salted water to cover if necessary. Freeze and seal the bag with a twister.

The bag may be removed by running a little hot water over the can to loosen it. Wrap the package in aluminum foil and store in freezer.

Use within 3–4 months. Thaw in refrigerator overnight.

OYSTERS

Oysters are edible throughout the whole year. But it is only during the winter months from about October to May that they are at their best. The old saying that oysters should be eaten only in months with an "R" is very close to the truth, if only coincidentally. During the warm summer months, the oysters are spawning. Their food value is at a minimum, and to most people oysters in this condition are unpalatable. By October most of them are prime once again.

The oyster is a highly nutritive source of food. These shellfish contain large amounts of phosphorus, calcium, iodine, and iron, all essential to a balanced diet.

Oysters are indeed a satisfying food with a long history of nourishing the human race. To the ancient Greeks the oysters were the perfect prelude to a meal. Records show that the Japanese, Chinese, and Romans were farming them before the Christian era.

Three species of commercial importance are the eastern oyster of the Atlantic, the Japanese (Pacific) oyster, and the Olympia oyster of the Pacific coast. The exotic European oyster through plantings has become established in the Canadian Maritimes, New England, and the state of Washington.

Today the natural, though declining, abundance of oysters along the east coast is concentrated around Chesapeake Bay. A highly developed and well-managed oyster farming industry, operating in Louisiana on 450,000 acres of natural oyster beds on the Gulf of Mexico, accounts for the majority of oyster production on the continent. The Pacific or Japanese oyster was imported on the Pacific coast where it has flourished, although the Pacific oyster as a fishery is small in the overall picture. The small Olympia, native of the west coast, occurs mainly in Puget Sound.

The eastern and Olympia oysters are generally marketed in the shell. The Pacifics grow much larger but they do not command the price that the other two do; they tend to have brittle shells and are marketed shucked as fresh-frozen or canned oyster meat.

A few tips for gathering your own oysters:

Pick your oysters at the lowest possible tidal point; this is where you will find the prime ones. Pick them as far from human habitation as possible. Locate your oyster bed and make sure you are not on a registered oyster lease. These are posted with signs. As mentioned earlier, check local regulations.

RAW OYSTERS ON THE HALF SHELL

6 to 8 oysters per person

Before opening oysters, scrub the shells clean under cold running water, using a stiff brush. Don't let them stand in water. To open, hold the oyster firmly with flat side of shell up. Insert a strong, blunt oyster knife between the edges of the shell opposite the hinges, and with a twisting motion pry the shells apart. Open, cut the muscle from the top shell, remove it, and discard the top shell. Cut the lower part of the same muscle from the deep half of the shell and leave the oyster in it, along with the juice.

Carefully arrange the oysters on individual plates imbedded in crushed ice, with a small glass of Cocktail Sauce for Seafood in the middle. Garnish with parsley and have lemon juice, fresh-ground black pepper, Tabasco sauce, and wine vinegar in which chopped shallots have been steeped available on the side.

FRIED OYSTERS

12 large, fresh oysters   Pepper
2 tablespoons each butter and   1 egg, beaten
    cooking oil   1 cup fine soda-cracker crumbs
½ teaspoon salt

Open and remove oysters from shells, as for oysters on the half shell. Drain on a thick towel to dry them off. In a deep frying pan heat butter and oil. Season oysters with salt and pepper, dip them in egg, and roll them in cracker crumbs, letting them take up as much as they will. Put them into the hot fat and fry quickly until crisp and golden on all sides, turning them once. To turn, use a broad-bladed knife or narrow spatula, and flip each one over. Don't crowd the oysters in the pan—rather fry them in two or more lots. As they are done, set them on thick paper towels to drain and keep in warming oven. Allow 6 or more oysters per person, depending on their size.

This recipe may also be used for clams.

OYSTER STEW

3 cups milk   2 teaspoons salt
2 cups light cream   ⅛ teaspoon white pepper
1½ pints shucked oysters with juice   Pinch nutmeg, freshly grated
⅓ cup butter

Scald the milk and cream in a saucepan or over boiling water. Keep hot.

Examine the oysters for bits of shell. Drain, strain, and reserve the juice. Melt the butter in a saucepan and add oysters and juice. Cook until the edges of the oysters begin to ruffle. Add oysters and liquid to scalded milk; add seasonings. Serve at once in soup dishes. Garnish each with a small sprig of parsley.

CLAMS

Clams of various species are more or less plentiful in all sea coastal waters of the United States and Canada, and the kind you cook and eat is generally the one most easily available.

On the Atlantic coast, the name "quahaug" (or "quahog") pretty well covers the edible hard-shell clams. It includes the small littleneck (age 3–4 years) and the cherrystone (4–6 years), which are growth states of the quahaugs. Razor clams, which grow to 6 inches, are found on both Atlantic and Pacific coasts.

On the Pacific the littleneck, or rock cockle, which is quite small and delicate, is widely distributed along the coast. Butter clams are also abundant, while razors are found on sandy surf-swept beaches of the open northern west coast. Pismos, once abundant on California beaches, are now protected.

The California coast claims the largest of our clams, the geoduck. The geoduck (pronounced "gooey-duck") measures up to 8 inches and has an edible neck or siphon that extends a yard long—so long, in fact, that the clam cannot contain it all within its shell.

Soft-shell clams are the "steamers" of the famous New England clambake. "Soft-shells" occur on both coasts. Their culinary merits as compared with the hard-shell clams are subject to differences of opinion. Each has its devotees.

Clam digging is regulated along many coastal areas. Check with local authorities regarding restrictions, and also regarding the safety of eating local clams. Polluted water does them no good.

	Approx. number shucked clams per cup	*Method of cooking*
Atlantic		
Littleneck (quahaug)	35–45	Half shell, (steam)
Cherrystone (quahaug)	30–40	Steam
Big quahaugs	25–30	Chowder
Razor	15–20	Dice: fritters, chowder
Soft-shell (steamer)	25–30	Steam
Pacific		
Razor	15–20	Dice: fritters, chowder
Butter	30–40	Steam, fry, chowder
Littleneck (rock cockle)	35–45	Half shell, steam
Geoduck	10–15	Grind or dice: chowder
Pismo	10–15	Half shell, steam, fry, chowder

All edible clams make good chowder.

CLAMBAKES—EAST AND WEST   The clambake of the Eastern Seaboard, like that of the Pacific coast, is a legacy from the Indians to the white man. In principle it is similar to the underground ovens of the west coast used for cooking roots, fish, and game meats.

Dig your clams the day before steaming. Put them in a tub or bucket well covered with sea water, and throw in a handful of cornmeal. This treatment helps rid the clams of sand and waste.

STEAMED SOFT-SHELL CLAMS   The live soft-shell clam shows an opening at the lip of the neck; otherwise it should be shut tight.

Pick over the clams and discard any with open or too easily opened shells. Thoroughly scrub the clams with a stiff brush to remove any sand and rinse them well under cold running water. Put into a kettle just big enough to accommodate them comfortably. Some connoisseurs say to let them cook in their own juice; others say to put a half inch of water in the bottom of the kettle. However, clams cooked both with and without water in the pot are delicious.

Cover the kettle with a tight-fitting lid and place over medium heat to steam until the shells open. During cooking, move the clams around with a long-handled wooden spoon or stick to expose all to the steam. Discard any clams whose shells have not opened during the cooking.

Remove the clams, letting the juice drain back into the pot. Heap them on a big heated platter.

Let the pot of broth rest a moment to let residue settle, then pour it off carefully into a hot bowl. Leave a little broth behind in the bottom of the kettle with any residual sand that has settled and discard it.

Melt a large chunk of butter into the hot broth.

Now you may eat the clams in all their immediate succulence. Remove the clam from its shell with an oyster pick or pickle fork, or your fingers. Remove the black cap with beard from the neck. Dip the whole clam in the butter broth and pop it into your mouth.

In the Canadian Maritime provinces, the small quahaugs (littlenecks) are steamed according to the same method. On the west coast littlenecks and butter clams are steamed.

CLAM CHOWDER   Traditionally, clam chowder takes two guises. There is the New England chowder which is made with milk, and the Manhattan which uses tomatoes. Chowder is a corruption of the French *"en chaudière"* – something one could cook in the great black iron hearth kettle.

As the dish has worked its way to fame throughout the continent, liberties have been taken with both methods and utensil. Many excellent recipes for clam chowder list ingredients far beyond the resources, if not the imagination, of its pioneers. That this is all to our good is evident in the West Coast Clam Chowder, Manhattan style.

Others retain their basic native simplicity. The Canadian "down-Easters" claim "you can't beat a right good Maritime dish," and into the pot where the clams have steamed in the traditional manner, without fuss or ceremony they toss a dice of potatoes, onion, and ham along with the shucked clams into the hot juice to cook, and, when the beautiful aroma is more than a mortal can stand, add milk and seasonings, heat and eat. And they suggest, "It won't disagree with a little dark rum."

However you choose to embellish your clam chowder, no flavor must be allowed to superimpose itself on the flavor of the clam. Seasonings must enhance, not overpower.

NEW ENGLAND CLAM CHOWDER

¼ pound salt pork, diced
2 large onions, diced
½ cup finely diced celery (optional)
2 cups milk
2 cups light cream, or extra milk
3 tablespoons flour
1 pint shucked clams with juice

2 medium potatoes, peeled and diced
½ teaspoon thyme (optional)
Salt to taste
½ teaspoon black pepper
2 tablespoons hard butter, chopped
Fresh parsley, chopped

Put pork into a cold, large, heavy stock pot or dutch oven. Heat over medium-high heat and scar the salt pork on all sides until golden. Remove the pork with a slotted spoon and drain on a thick paper towel. To the fat add the onions and celery, and gently sauté until almost soft.

Scald the milk and cream together, heating carefully in a saucepan over low heat, or in a double boiler over boiling water, until a scum forms on surface. While this is happening, stir flour into vegetables, and stir and cook until blended and bubbly. Into this *roux* gradually stir the clam liquor, then the scalded milk and cream. Add the potatoes. Add the seasonings and bring to a boil. Immediately reduce heat, stirring until it settles down, then let it cook very slowly for about half an hour. Stir frequently. Mince the clams and add them to the chowder. Add the diced pork.

Sprinkle the top with chopped butter bits and pour into a large tureen. Sprinkle chopped fresh parsley over the surface and serve with hot biscuits, or oyster crackers.

Makes about 2 quarts.

MANHATTAN CLAM CHOWDER

2 pints shucked quahogs and juice
¼ pound salt pork, finely diced
2 cups onions, diced
2 cups diced celery (optional)
2 tablespoons flour
2 28-ounce cans tomatoes

4 tablespoons tomato paste
½ clove garlic, minced
1 bay leaf
8 cups water
Salt and pepper
4 cups diced raw potatoes

Drain the juice from the clams and reserve. Cut the hard part from the soft part of the clams and chop the hard part finely. Reserve both parts.

Put pork into a cold, large heavy stock pot or dutch oven and heat over medium-high heat. Sear on all sides until golden. Remove and reserve the pork and in the hot fat brown the onions, celery, and the diced clams (hard part). Over this sift the flour and blend in well. Add tomatoes, tomato paste, garlic, and bay leaf. Reduce heat to medium and cook and stir until well blended. Cook for about 5 minutes.

Add clam juice and water. Return to a boil. Add salt and pepper to taste. Add potatoes and cook gently until tender. Add remaining clam meats. Serve with oyster crackers.

This chowder is best made a day before serving. Let cool and stand overnight; slowly reheat.

Makes about 4 quarts.

WEST COAST CLAM CHOWDER

4 slices of bacon, diced	1 teaspoon salt
1 large onion, sliced fine	1 pint clams and liquid
½ cup chopped green pepper	⅛ teaspoon ground thyme
½ cup chopped celery	3 cups canned tomatoes, chopped
½ cup chopped carrots	2 tablespoons chopped parsley
3 cups diced peeled potatoes	Salt and pepper
3 cups water	

Cook bacon over low heat until nearly done. Pour off all fat but 1 tablespoon. Add onion, pepper, and celery. Sauté until golden brown. Add carrots, potatoes, water, and salt.

Shuck clams. Chop hard part of clams and add to soup with clam liquid. Chop soft part of clams and reserve. Simmer covered over low heat for 30 minutes. Add reserved clams, thyme, and tomatoes and simmer for 15 minutes. Sprinkle with parsley and season to taste with salt and pepper.

Makes about 3 quarts.

STUFFED CLAMS

2 dozen large, fresh quahaugs, scrubbed and steamed	⅛ teaspoon freshly ground black pepper
1 egg	Pinch chili powder
½ cup cream	4 unsalted soda crackers
1 tablespoon minced onion	Melted butter
¼ teaspoon salt	Paprika, or chopped pimiento

Drain the steamed clams, reserving the juice. Open and remove the clams. Save the shells.

Put the clams, juice, egg, and cream into blender on medium speed for about 5 seconds. With blender still running, quickly add onion, salt, and seasonings, then add crackers and blend for a few seconds until well mixed.

Oil the clam shells, heap some of the clam mixture into each, drizzle butter generously over top, and sprinkle with paprika or garnish with chopped pimiento. Bake quickly in a hot oven for about 15 minutes.

Mussels

The edible mussel, often called the poor man's oyster, is a blue-black mollusc found along sea coasts at low tide on gravel rocks and seawalls or any surface to which it can anchor. It is most abundant along the New England coast, and Maine provides most of the fresh mussels to the U.S. market.

New England mussels are edible the year round; they are at their peak from fall into early spring. On the west coast mussels are quarantined during the "red tide" season.

Like clams and oysters, mussels must come from clean, unpolluted areas. If gathering your own, choose only places washed by clean, clear seawater. Mussels must be gathered alive, their shells closed tight.

Mussels have an accumulation of slimy vegetable matter on the outer horny covering and they require a bit of cleaning. Scrub each mussel well with a stiff brush under cold running water, and trim off the beard (a thready tuft). Let mussels stand in a bucket of fresh cold water for a few hours to let them rid themselves of sand. Wash again and drain.

MUSSELS STEAMED IN WINE

2 quarts mussels	1 sprig thyme
2 or 3 green onions or shallots, minced	6 tablespoons butter
	Black pepper
2 or 3 sprigs parsley	1 cup white wine
¼ bay leaf	¼ cup coarsely chopped parsley

Scrub and trim the mussels. Put onion, parsley, bay leaf, and thyme into a large kettle. Add the mussels and half the butter. Sprinkle generously with black pepper and pour the wine over them. Cover tightly, bring to a boil over a high heat, reduce heat to medium, and let the mussels steam just until the shells open. Discard any that don't open.

With a slotted spoon remove mussels to 4 warm soup plates, and keep warm.

Taste the broth for saltiness—it may be salty enough. Add the remaining butter and parsley to the broth; let rest a moment to allow butter to melt and any sand to settle in the bottom of the kettle. Ladle broth over the mussels. Serve with toast.

Serves 4.

FRESHWATER CLAMS

Freshwater clams are actually mussels, but through usage are known as "clams." They occur generally in inland fresh waters. In a survey reported in *Ontario Fish and Wildlife Review* to determine why freshwater clams were not more widely recognized as a table delicacy, R. E. Whitfield of the Ontario Ministry of Natural Resources interviewed several people who had tried them. Judgments varied from inedible, to edible, to excellent, to praise as a cure for stomach ulcers (poached in milk). All had one point in common: The first attempt was the last.

Why aren't they used more readily? They grow larger and are more meaty than some of the East Coast oysters, and are certainly larger than their cousins, the unquestionably edible saltwater mussels and clams. The answer, suggests Mr. Whitfield, lies partly in the fact that the freshwater clam is not as flavorful as the saltwater mollusc. Secondly, one might venture to say that clam and oyster eaters are not born but made, especially in inland areas far from the sea.

There is a vast, widely distributed inland resource of freshwater edible clams—virtually unexploited, except by wildlife. Prepared and eaten like salt-water mussels, the freshwater clams are valuable to the wilderness survivor. Like other molluscs they must come from unpolluted waters.

Mussels may be substituted in clam chowder recipes.

Scallops

Scallops are among the most famous of shellfishes, not only for their epicurean merits but for historical interest. At the time of the Crusades, the shell of a European species was the symbol of the holy pilgrimage and it is still called the "pilgrim" shell. *Coquille St. Jacques* is the name of a French scallop, not a particular recipe.

The sea scallop is currently considered the most important commercial fishery of the molluscs on the northwest Atlantic coast. The value of catches has increased dramatically in the past few years, and it is one species that has a good inland market. The shallow-water bay scallop of the Atlantic coast supports an active industry. It is considered the more delectable of the two.

Delicate and perishable, scallops are shucked at sea as soon as caught. The flat shell and all other parts are removed, except the round, firm adductor muscle which is the meat or "eye" attached to the rounded shell. The meat is cut out and iced immediately. Scallops are marketed fresh, or frozen packaged in salt water or breaded and partially fried. Recently, attempts have been under way to pack and market the mature roe—a fine delicacy.

Scallop shells are used for serving scallops and other shellfish

DEEP-FRIED SCALLOPS

2 pounds frozen scallops	¼ teaspoon pepper
Vegetable shortening, or oil	2 tablespoons paprika
1 cup fine, dry bread crumbs, or	2 eggs
cornmeal	2 tablespoons milk
1 teaspoon salt	

Thaw the scallops as directed on package. Rinse them well and set aside to drain on paper or linen towel.

Using a heavy Dutch oven or an electric deep-fryer, slowly heat vegetable shortening or cooking oil. (See Chapter 3, Deep Frying.)

In a plastic or paper bag combine bread crumbs or cornmeal seasoned with salt, pepper, and paprika. Close the bag and shake well to mix.

In a bowl, slightly beat eggs, add milk, and beat to mix. Dip the scallops one at a time in the egg, then drop them into the bag of crumbs and gently shake until well coated with the crumbs. Gently shake off loose excess crumbs, arrange a few in the frying basket, and plunge it into the hot fat. Fry only as many scallops at a time as can float on the fat without crowding. Keep the fat at a constant temperature and turn the scallops as they rise to the surface. Cook about 3 minutes.

Lift the basket with scallops, letting excess fat drip into the pot, and remove scallops to a hot platter or cookie sheet lined with paper toweling; keep in a warming oven.

Serve hot with hot tartar sauce and lemon wedges.

BAKED SCALLOPS

1 pound scallops, frozen or fresh	Pinch of fennel, or tarragon leaves
1 egg	Pinch of freshly ground black pepper
1 tablespoon water	Lemon juice
½ cup fine, dry bread crumbs	Melted butter
¼ teaspoon salt	

If frozen, thaw scallops, wash, rinse, and let drain on a thick towel for a few minutes. Pat dry. Put egg and water into a bowl and beat lightly with a fork. Combine crumbs and seasonings. Grease individual scallop shells or a baking dish.

Dip each scallop in the egg and roll it in seasoned bread crumbs (or shake in a bag) until evenly coated. Arrange in shells or baking dish. Drizzle melted butter with a few drops of lemon juice over top of scallops. Bake in a preheated, very hot oven at 450°F until golden brown—about 20 minutes. Serve with hot tartar sauce in a side dish.

Variation: Substitute 1 teaspoon mild curry as seasoning. Serve with Curry Sauce.

Abalone

Abalone, a beautiful snail-like mollusc, is a delicacy. It occurs from the Queen Charlotte Islands south to Baja California and is fished and processed commercially. The edible part is the muscular foot—the whole underpart of the shell. It is pounded to break down fibers before cooking; otherwise it is quite tough. Abalone is sold both canned and fresh at seaside markets.

The simplest way to prepare abalone is to pound it with a wooden mallet, cut it in strips, roll it in lightly seasoned bread crumbs, and fry it in butter. It should never be overcooked; overcooking toughens it.

ABALONE CHOWDER

2 tablespoons butter	1 tablespoon flour
2 tablespoons chopped onion	1 pound abalone, pounded, sliced,
1 tablespoon chopped celery	and minced
1 tablespoon fresh chopped parsley	4 cups hot veal or chicken stock
1 teaspoon finely chopped green pepper	Small pinch cayenne
	Salt and pepper
1 teaspoon finely chopped pimiento pepper	1 cup raw diced potato
	½ cup heavy cream

In a deep saucepan melt the butter. Add all the vegetables and cook slowly until soft. Stir in flour and cook and stir until bubbly. Add the abalone and stir in the hot stock. Cook and stir gently until slightly thickened. Add the cayenne, and salt and pepper to taste. Cover and gently simmer for an hour. Add potatoes and cook until barely soft—about 15 minutes. Just before serving, blend in cream.

If using canned abalone for the chowder, drain the juice into the pan with the stock. As the canned abalone is already cooked, it should be cooked no more. Chop it and add when the potatoes are soft, letting it just heat through.

Conch

The conch, a marine snail, most commonly used in the U.S. is the "left-handed" whelk, also known as *scungilli*. It occurs along the east coast of the United States and the Gulf of Mexico, and is found over mud and sandy-mud bottoms. The commercial supply comes chiefly from New England on down to Chesapeake Bay.

The meat of the conch has excellent flavor but like abalone it is tough and needs tenderizing treatment. It is pounded or ground and made into fritters or chowder. Conch chowder is made like abalone chowder.

To prepare conch, cover the live mollusc with cold water, bring to a boil, and simmer for about 15 minutes. Drain and remove the meat from the shell. Rinse meat and drain on a towel.

CONCH FRITTERS

1 dozen conchs
3 eggs, separated
½ cup minced onion
1 large tomato, peeled, seeded and
    chopped
2 tablespoons minced parsley

1 clove garlic, minced fine
1 teaspoon salt
½ teaspoon black pepper
1 cup fine cracker crumbs
1 tablespoon cream

Prepare the conchs and put meats through the food chopper. Beat egg yolks slightly. Combine conch meat, egg yolks, onion, tomato, parsley, garlic, salt and pepper, and crumbs. Blend thoroughly. If too stiff to drop from a spoon, blend in the cream.

Beat egg whites until stiff and fold into the conch mixture.

Heat a well-greased heavy frying pan or griddle to sizzling. Drop the mixture, a tablespoonful at a time, into the hot pan. Cook until evenly browned on one side, turn and brown the other side.

Should provide enough fritters for 4 to 6 people when served with a salad.

Periwinkles

Periwinkles are small, black, snail-like molluscs found fastened in clusters to rocks and breakwaters and on the stony beaches of the coastal waters.

The live winkle when disturbed hides in its convoluted shell with the lid shut down firmly, and this is how it should be to be edible.

To cook, wash the winkles well and steam over boiling water in a covered pot for about 10 minutes, or until the little black cap can be lifted.

Place the hot periwinkles in a hot dish in the fold of a warm, white linen napkin. Provide a darning needle or nut pick and a dish of hot melted butter, salt, and pepper.

To eat, remove the cap and "winkle" out the sweet little morsel of meat. Dip it in butter and eat.

Squid and Octopus

Squids and octopus are molluscs, relatives of the clam. For practical purposes they are alike in both their shape and treatment, and in relatively comparable sizes, they are similar in texture and flavor.

Squids come as short as an inch and as long as the 60-foot monster of Jules Verne fame. All sizes are edible but the big ones are tough; the most desirable is a small squid 10 to 12 inches long. Squid supports an important fishery on both west and east coasts, and has inspired one of Newfoundland's more famous folk songs, A. R. Scammel's "Squid Jiggin' Ground."

The average octopus catch off the west coast is about 2 feet in length.

Both molluscs are popular food fishes on the west coast. Important in Oriental and Mediterranean cooking, both are to be found in inland markets serving an ethnic trade. Canned and smoked, they are available in gourmet specialty shops.

The nutritive value of squid and octopus is comparable with fish in general and, according to some authorities, may even surpass it.

The autumn catch is preferred, as the flesh is firmer and doesn't deteriorate as quickly as in other seasons. As with other fish and shellfish, careful attention to the dressing of these molluscs is essential.

Fresh squid and octopus are handicapped by an appearance and characteristic odor not enticing to everyone. The dressing overcomes the first, and an aromatic court bouillon with onions and/or tomatoes overcomes the second.

Squid and octopus must not be overcooked. Like clams, oysters, and other shellfish, overcooking hardens or roughens the flesh.

As with other molluscs, squid and octopus should be taken alive from the water and kept alive until ready to cook or freeze, or they should be dressed out immediately, washed, and frozen like clams and oysters.

DRESSING SQUID AND OCTOPUS

The squid has a large head on a cigar-shaped body ending in two winglike tail pieces. Eight to ten arms protrude from the head, of which two are tentacles. The body and tentacles are eaten.

The fleshy, muscular body, or visceral sac, is enclosed in a membrane or mantle and is lined with a translucent shell.

When the head is removed, the viscera come out, including the squid's built-in defensive device, a sac of black fluid or ink. Cut off the tail pieces, peel off the skin, pull out the shell, and the fleshy body or sac remains. Cut the tentacles from the head and set aside. These are also edible.

Wash the body, turn it inside out, and scrub well and wash inside and out in several waters. Drain well on towels.

The octopus, squatter and more bulbous in shape than the squid, is dressed similarly. The body lining is soft rather than shell-like, but it comes out the same way. Thus dressed and washed, both are ready to be stuffed or cut up for various preparations. They are fried, baked, poached, stewed, and smoked.

Squid and octopus are marketed both fresh and canned.

STUFFED SQUID OR OCTOPUS

4 squid, 10 to 12 inches long, or 1 small octopus under 2 feet	⅓ cup olive, or other cooking oil
½ pound veal	Salt and pepper
¼ pound veal liver	Pinch ground cinnamon
½ cup lobster tomalley, if handy	4 cloves garlic, crushed
2 large onions	1 tablespoon tomato paste
3 or 4 sprigs parsley	1 scant teaspoon pimiento, diced
2 eggs	½ teaspoon crushed rosemary
1 tablespoon crushed mint leaves	1 teaspoon flour
2 thick slices stale bread, soaked in milk and squeezed dry, or 1 cup cooked white rice	½ cup hot water
	½ cup white wine

Dress, wash, and drain the squid or octopus as directed. Cut off tentacles, cut in pieces, and cook in salted water until tender. Drain. Put through coarse food chopper with veal, liver, tomalley, 1 onion, and parsley. Mix well with eggs, mint leaves, bread, and 1 teaspoon of the oil. Season with salt, pepper, and cinnamon. Fill the squids about two-thirds full to allow for swelling, and sew up the opening.

Mince the other onion and sauté with the garlic in remaining oil. Stir in tomato paste, pimiento, rosemary, and flour. Check the seasonings. Pour in ½ cup hot water and ½ cup white wine (or 1 cup water) and bring to a boil. Arrange the squids in the sauce. Prick with a needle in a few places to ensure thorough cooking. Lower heat to a simmer, cover, and cook gently for about 1 hour. Spoon sauce over the fish from time to time.

When done, move carefully to a deep serving platter and pour the sauce around it.

BEIGNETS OF SQUID OR OCTOPUS

1 pound squid or octopus   3 or 4 cloves garlic, crushed
1 onion, sliced   1 bay leaf
Lemon Batter (see Batters)   2 egg whites, beaten stiff
2 tablespoons olive oil   Cooking oil
1 teaspoon tomato paste

Dress the squid, or octopus, washing it well in several waters and drain. Cut the body into strips and the tentacles into cross-sections about 1 inch thick.

Barely cover with lightly salted water, adding a sliced onion, cover and simmer gently for about 40 minutes. Remove the squid and reserve the stock. Meanwhile prepare the batter and set aside.

In a saucepan combine oil, tomato paste, crushed garlic, and bay leaf; add the squid or octopus stock, adding water to make 1½ cups. Add the squid or octopus. Bring to a bubble, reduce heat and simmer for 20 to 25 minutes. Drain the squid.

Cut the squid or octopus into thimble-size pieces and incorporate into the batter. Fold in the egg whites.

Deep-fry in hot oil, dropping the fish mixture from a spoon into the boiling fat, until light and golden. Don't crowd the fritters in the pot. Fry a few at a time, putting them on absorbent paper in a warm oven until all are done.

Makes 18 to 24 beignets, depending on the size.

Beignets may be made from canned squid. Omit the initial simmering, and use the liquid from the can for the stock if desired.

❧ 7 ❧

Curing Fish

ON SMOKED SALMON

Next to milk, nature's most perfect food. Made with a magic formula which includes judicious portions of the Puritan work ethic and God's gift from the sea, blended by hand with tender, loving care. Step one: Interrupt one portion rich, energy-laden coho salmon early on her way to the hills to spawn. Before the *coup de grâce,* ask her forgiveness and dedicate her to a larger service. Step two: Split and ice to firm the flesh and cleanse. Step three: Cut into hand-size portions. Step four: Brine with salt and sugar, then apply generous portions of alder wood for heat and smoke.

Lucy Crow's smoked salmon,
Courtesy of Kuskokwim Kronicle, *Bethel, Alaska*

The curing of fish by sun, salt, and smoke is an ancient and primitive means of providing against lean days ahead. Effective methods have survived with the peoples who developed them, or, more likely, the peoples survived who developed the effective cures.

The cures have remained virtually unchanged, while picking up embellishment as they followed the course of cookery through the ages. It's interesting to note that early Roman recipes for pickled fish are almost identical with those in general use today. Herring, cod, and mackerel are salted and smoked on the Atlantic coast, and salmon on the Pacific, much as they were in the days of the clipper trade—the only innovations being in handling and packing facilities to process maximum yield with minimum labor. An important innovation, of course, has been the incorporation of modern refrigeration.

As a preservative measure one would think the painstaking old cures would be made obsolete by modern and efficient freezing methods, but the billions of pounds of fish and meat processed on the North American continent, plus that of Europe and the Orient, would indicate that man is not ready to give up fare of such character entirely in favor of the deep freeze.

However, modern refrigeration has improved the quality of cured fish by permitting lighter salting and smoking, yielding a generally more palatable, if more perishable, product and eliminating the necessity of hard drying as a preservative.

Drying

Whether the drying of fish to a parchmentlike texture (hard-drying) had its origin in the tropical sun or the Arctic frost can't be settled here, but it's a good candidate for the oldest method of curing. Drying of fish is preservation by dehydration. Done with or without salting, it not only preserved the fish but relieved it of about 80 percent of its burden on a traveler—as well as its palatability. If one is to believe historical comment, its outstanding quality was its defiance of digestive contentment. Hard-dried fish, which requires lengthy, exacting preparation, appears to have been relegated ceremonial status. (See Chapter 8, Finland.) The process has given way to more sophisticated commercial methods involving the use of salt.

Potting

In between, and within household scale, is "potting." Basically, potting involves the semidehydration of fish by dry-heat cooking, and pounding it with a mixture of fats, sugar, and spices into an elegant little product not far removed from the Indians' pemmican.

The Cree Indians make a fish pemmican by pounding dried fish to a powder and mixing in lard, goose, or bear fat to a thick paste. Berries and brown sugar may be added. The mixture is formed into little cakes which may be coated in fat. The potted lobster and shrimp in Chapter 6 are refinements of the method.

MAKING POTTED FISH

Skin 1 pound of fish fillets. Salt well on both sides. Put on a plate, cover, and let stand overnight. Rinse the fish in cold water and pat dry. Place the fish in a fold of oiled aluminum foil and bake in a slow oven until the flesh flakes. Shred, removing all bones. Starting with ½ cup of fish, break it down in blender, adding butter or margarine until the mixture is moistened and velvety smooth. Add more fish and more butter until all the fish has been used. Blend in 2 tablespoons brown sugar, then season lightly with salt, white pepper, a scant ¼ teaspoon ground mace, allspice, *or* cloves, and a good pinch of cayenne. Don't judge the spices by taste—they develop during storage.

Pack firmly ½ inch from top in small, clean earthenware bowls or glasses, packing and smoothing the paste against the sides of the bowl so that there are no air pockets. Fill the bowl to the top with clear rendered beef fat. If the fat checks or cracks when cold, fill the spaces with more fat. Cover with aluminum foil and store in a clean, dry, cold place. Use after 1 week to 10 days. Once opened, use the entire pot of fish. Do not re-store. Salted fish may be potted as above; omit salting.

Potted fish livers, tongues, sounds. Potted fish livers make a delectable spread. Prepare as above. Take care not to overcook, and use spices to taste but with discretion. Tongues and sounds may be potted separately, or all three mixed.

Salt Curing

Salt curing as a preservative is excellent for the extremely fatty fishes, such as mackerel and herring, that don't take to lengthy freezing. The salted, fatty fish is also a more palatable product than the lean fish, as the oils provide

a moist texture. Lean fish with fragile flesh like the flounders tend to become too dry and to break up.

Salting is a drying process. The purpose of a salt cure is to draw fluids from the flesh, leaving salt in the flesh, and thus to inhibit spoilage. If enough salt is used, the fish may dry out enough to keep in a cold, dry place for a year.

Improved refrigeration has made possible a lighter salting and less drying, and a more flavorsome, palatable product.

On an industrial scale the salting of fish is a highly skilled operation, involving the preparation of various grades and with various degrees of curing required for the different trades. Yet the process is basically simple and can be easily scaled to any household with a surplus catch of fish to preserve.

Two basic methods are used: dry salting and brining. Each usually involves two stages.

DRESSING FISH FOR SALTING AND SMOKING

Fish to be cured should be freshly caught and cleaned. (See Chapter 2.)

Small fish up to 6 to 8 ounces are dressed for salting and smoking in the round and gibbed. Larger fish, according to size, are dressed, or head-dressed and plank (flat) split or kipper split (i.e., split down back) and cleaned and boned, or filleted, steaked, or cut into chunks.

Big fish may be boned. Salting is excellent for bony fish, as the process softens the bones. Fish may or may not be scaled, but the skin is left on wherever possible, as it helps hold the fish together.

The dressed fish are well washed until they glisten to remove all traces of blood (except in the Scotch Cure—see Smoking) and wiped dry.

DRY SALTING

In dry salting, the cleaned and washed fish are packed in dry salt, which draws fluids from the fish, forming a brine or pickle. Salt remains in the flesh, inhibiting spoilage. When no more pickle is formed, the pickle is drained off and the fish scraped clean and repacked in a new brine.

The recipe for Swedish Salted Trout given later in this chapter is dry-salt-cured and is eaten without cooking. For lengthy storage, the fish is preserved in brine after curing.

BRINING

The brine method involves putting the dressed and washed fish into a strong brine for an initial salting to draw fluids; the fish are then scraped clean, and repacked in a new brine for storage.

It's in the repack that the words "brining" and "pickling" part company. Pickling at one time meant simply to preserve in brine. For that matter so did "marinating," as the word implies. The progress westward of the spice trade opened up a whole new prospect for curing fish and meats, and pickled fish has little relation to the salt cures in practice now. Marinades (given with individual recipes) are far removed from sea water.

For salting recipes in the Atlantic tradition, we defer to the seaside experts. The two recipes below are from a collection of old family mackerel-salting recipes gathered from area residents by the Cape May County Department of Public Affairs, and appear here by courtesy of that body. The recipes may be applied to fish generally.

That the salting ritual is an individual affair in the Cape May area is evident in the collection. No two are quite alike.

Of the two Cape May recipes, one follows the dry-salting by a double brining and is heavily salted. The other dry-salts lightly and only once. The one says that it is impossible to use too much salt; the other says don't be heavy on the salt—it might burn the fish. Both speak from experience!

However, all agree with fish salters across the land that earthen, plastic, or wooden receptacles be used; that salt should be noniodized; that no metal contact the brine or fish; and that instructions be closely followed. It is essential, above all, that only *freshly caught* fish be so cured, and it is recommended that novices to the art start off on a small scale.

There can be no hard-and-fast rules for salting to cover all situations. Expertise comes of experience. Generally speaking, heavier salting is required for spring and summer catches where storage conditions depend on the prospective weather. (The heavy salt can also be a matter of taste.) The autumn catch, where a cold winter lies ahead, may be lightly salted. With refrigerated storage, salting may be done at any time. Storage should be in a well-ventilated, clean, dark place, not more than 50–60°. The required storage temperature depends on the strength of the brine. It must not be allowed to freeze.

SALTED MACKEREL
Cape May No. 1

Gut the fish and cut off all fins, tails, and heads. Scrape to remove as much blood as possible from around the backbone and split the fish lengthwise, but do not cut in half. It is necessary to wash the fish in fresh water at this stage.

Thoroughly clean a large crock or tight wooden bucket; do not use metal of any kind. Spread out a generous handful of granulated table salt on the bottom of the container and lay in a layer of mackerel with the skin side down. Spread another handful of salt, and another layer of mackerel. Repeat, keeping the skin side down except for the top layer. The last layer should go in *skin side up.* Top off with a layer of salt. *It is impossible to use too much salt* and foolish to economize, as salt in bulk can be bought for about two cents a pound. Weight down the fish with a heavy stone or crockery plate and leave standing in a cool place for about a week or 10 days.

At the end of this period remove the fish one at a time and clean out the last traces of blood. Remove with the fingers or knife the black membrane that covers the body cavity and rinse the fish thoroughly.

Rinse out the container and build up the layers of fish as before but omit the salt. Make up a solution of salt and water strong enough to float a raw egg and cover the fish with the liquid. Weight down and let stand for another week or 10 days.

Now remove the fish, rinse, and go over them with a final cleaning. Rinse the container and pack the fish back in the same way. Make up a brine solution in cold water so strong that no more salt will dissolve (concentrated), and pour over the fish. Weight them down again. The pickling is now finished and the fish will keep indefinitely.

Clair A. Artz,
Cressona, Pa.

SALTED MACKEREL
Cape May No. 2

Fillet the fresh-caught mackerels. Wash thoroughly, making sure no blood remains on the fillets.

Use a clean porcelain or stone crock about eighteen inches deep and twelve inches wide. Place a layer of mackerel on the bottom of the container and sprinkle a little bit of kosher salt on it. Continue repeating this arrangement until all the mackerel is in the container. *Don't be too heavy on the salt*—it might burn the fish.

Put a strong porcelain or clean wooden plate on top of the final layer of salted mackerel and have it weighted down with a heavy, clean stone—or take a gallon jug filled with water, if no other weight is available.

Cover the container with clean muslin or cheesecloth and let it set for 2 to 3 weeks. This causes a brine to rise, due to being weighted down. In this way the mackerel is completely covered with the brine solution and the fish takes on the salted taste.

After soaking the mackerel in fresh water overnight, bake or sauté in a pan for a very delectable meal. Or, you might try covering the fillets with crumbs and frying.

Joe Bisch,
Philadelphia, Pa.

SWEDISH SALTED TROUT OR SALMON
(a 300-year-old family recipe)

1 4- to 5-pound lake trout or salmon	½ cup sugar
2 large bunches fresh dill	2 tablespoons white peppercorns,
½ cup coarse salt	crushed

Clean and scale the fish. Remove the head and tail. Cut the fish in half lengthwise removing the backbone and the small bones as well.

Place half of the fish, skin side down, in a large glass casserole, or use a wooden box big enough to accommodate the fish. Line the box with plastic to prevent leakage of juices and line the plastic with disposable aluminum foil.

Wash the dill and shake dry. Chop the dill into small pieces and sprinkle on top of the fish. In a bowl, combine the salt, sugar and crushed peppercorns. Sprinkle this mixture over the fish.

Place the other half of the fish on top of the herbs and spices, skin side up. Cover with aluminum foil and set a heavy platter slightly larger than the fish on top of them. Weight them with 3 or 4 heavy tins of food, or cut a piece of board so that it just fits inside the box, then place it on top of the fish and weight it down with five or six bricks.

Store in a cool place or in a refrigerator for at least 3 days. Turn the fish every 6 hours the first day, then every 12 hours, replacing the cover and the weights every time. When the fish is ready, transfer to a cutting board and separate the halves. With a table knife, scrape away the dill and the seasoning and pat dry with a paper towel or damp cloth. Place one half of the fish, skin side down, on the carving board and start slicing the fish halves thinly on an angle diagonal to the tail without cutting through the skin, and serve. This is a traditional Swedish supper dish.

Keep the rest of the fish in a large earthenware crock filled with salt-sugar brine marinade and fresh chopped dill. Often additional brine has to be made by boiling one gallon of water and adding enough salt to make the brine strong enough to float an egg. Add a few bunches of finely chopped dill and cool. Fish prepared in this way keeps for a year.

Berndt Berglund, Managing Director
National Wilderness Survival, Inc., Campbellford, Ontario

GREAT LAKES CURE

Freshwater fishes are commonly salted to deal with difficult-to-bone fishes like shad, pike, pickerel, perch, and suckers.

Clean, scale, and head-dress or fillet the fresh fish, depending on size, and wipe dry. Use a clean plastic or wooden bucket, or a crock of size to accommodate the number of fish.

Cover the bottom of the crock with a layer of pickling (noniodized) salt. Add a layer of fillets, flesh down, on the salt. Repeat layers of salt and fish, finishing with a good layer of salt over the top. Cover the fish with a plate weighted with a clean glass or a plastic gallon jug filled with water. Leave for a week, until the fish are under brine and no more forms. Remove the fish and discard brine.

Prepare a new brine of cooled boiled water, enough to fill half the crock, adding salt until it will float a raw egg.

Scrape or fillet each fish clean of drawn blood, wipe with a cloth, and return to the crock. Add a few peppercorns, cracked. Pour the fresh brine over the fish. Cover again with weighted plate. The fish must be well under the brine. If necessary, make more brine. Cover with clean muslin.

Leave in a well-ventilated, cold, dark place and use after 2 weeks. The fish should keep in this manner through the winter.

Harry Souci,
Sault Ste. Marie, Ont.

COOKING SALTED FISH

Salted fish are freshened before cooking. Scrape or scale the skin. Rinse under cold running water. Cover with fresh cold water and let stand overnight. Rinse, drain and pat the fish dry between towels. The freshened fish are then cooked like similar cuts of fresh fish—pan-fried, poached, baked, or made into fish soups or chowders. Salt fish is excellent *en casserole*. (See Cod au Gratin in Chapter 4.) Reduce or omit salt from recipes for fresh fish; a matter of taste.

Keep in mind when cooking salt-cured fish that it is practically cooked already and requires very little cooking. Salt fish, freshened or right out of the brine, well drained and dried of surface moisture, is delicious when quickly heat-smoked.

SALT FISH FRITTERS

2 cups salt fish, diced	Black pepper
4 cups diced raw potatoes	Fat for deep-frying
2 eggs, well beaten	2 cups Sauce Espagnole or Tomato
3 tablespoons butter or margarine, softened	Sauce

Rinse the fish well in cold-running water. Put into saucepan with potatoes, barely cover with boiling water, and cook until potatoes are tender. Drain well. Return the mixture to pan and shake over low heat to dry off remaining moisture. Transfer to a mixing bowl and mash finely. Add eggs, butter, and pepper to taste. Beat with fork or in blender until light and fluffy.

Deep-fry in hot fat. (See Chapter 3, Deep-Frying.) Drop a tablespoon at a time into the fat and fry until golden, about 2 minutes. Don't crowd the fritters in the fat. Drain on paper towels and serve very hot with heated Sauce Espagnole or Tomato Sauce.

SALT FISH HASH

1 cup salt fish	2 cups cooked potatoes, diced
2 tablespoons butter	Salt and pepper to taste
1 large onion, minced	Parsley

Soak the fish overnight to freshen, changing water once or twice depending on saltiness desired. Drain and shred the fish.

Heat butter in large skillet and sauté the onion until translucent. Add the fish, cover, and cook gently for about 5 minutes. Add the potatoes, season to taste, cover and cook until lightly browned on the bottom. Turn the hash, add about a tablespoon boiling water and a little minced parsley, and cover and cook until lightly brown. Turn with a spatula a few times rather than stir.

Serve with vegetables and a white or cream sauce.

SOLOMON GUNDY

4 salt herring	2 tablespoons brown sugar
2 large onions	Black pepper
Vinegar	

Wash herring thoroughly. Remove skin, cut away fillets, and cut them in chunks. Soak in cold water overnight to freshen. Drain, rinse, and drain again. Put fish and onions in layers in a deep bowl. Heat enough vinegar to cover, adding sugar and pepper. Pour over the herring. Cool and refrigerate a few hours before serving.

Pickling

That the basic methods of pickling fish in use today have survived the fall of Rome should be testimony to their excellence. Apicius, famous gourmand of fourth- or fifth-century Rome, is believed to have written the first cookbook of the Western world, and his *Roman Cookery** gives recipes for preserving fish that are practically identical with those in use today. In simple terms, they direct the cook to fry the fish quickly, immediately remove it from the pan, pour hot, spiced vinegar over it, and store.

While in the days before the Dark Ages spices of the East were valued, and priced, like precious jewels and bartered accordingly, it was at the end of the thirteenth century that the spice trade opened up to more widespread,

---

* A recent translation of the Apicius work by an English team, Flower and Rosenbaum, with updated adaptations, has been published by George C. Harrap & Co., Ltd., London and Toronto.

if still luxury, usage. Fish and meat pickling in Western Europe took on a degree of sophistication unknown to North America until the settlers arrived with their spices and formulas.

Practically all firm or coarse-fleshed fish pickle well—the fatty ones better than the very lean. Those of fragile texture, like the flounders, should be avoided. Usually small fish are kipper-cut or filleted; medium-size fish are filleted, skin left on or skinless, and cut to desired size. Larger fish may be steak-cut and tied.

PICKLED FISH
Basic Recipe No. 1

Cut small fillets of fish in half; cut bigger ones into bite-size pieces or serving portions. Then cook by one of two methods:

Dust with flour seasoned with salt and pepper and lightly pan-fry in cooking oil until barely colored;

Or salt lightly, and arrange on a greased pie plate; lay a piece of aluminum foil over the top and bake in a hot oven only until fish barely flakes to a fork.

Arrange the pieces of fish in the bottom of a deep bowl. Heat spiced vinegar (see following recipes) to boiling and pour over fish. Add oil from frying pan or freshly heated oil to cover the entire surface of the pickle. Let cool. Check the oil and add more if necessary to cover. Cover and refrigerate up to a week; should keep two weeks *if* undisturbed.

AROMATIC SPICED VINEGAR

1½ cups white or cider vinegar	2 green peppers, diced
½ cup water	1 garlic clove, crushed (optional)
1 large onion, diced	½ cup mixed pickling spices
1 large carrot, sliced	2 or 3 tiny chili peppers (optional)

Combine everything in a saucepan, bring to a boil, reduce heat and simmer over low heat for 15 minutes. Strain into hot, clean bottle and let cool. Cap tightly and store.

SPICED SWEET VINEGAR

1½ cups white or cider vinegar   ½ cup water
½ cup pickling spices, tied in   ¼ cup brown sugar
    cheesecloth

Combine everything in a saucepan; stir until sugar is dissolved. Bring to a boil; cook for a minute or two. Turn heat to low and simmer for 15 minutes, removing spice bag when spiced to taste. Strain into hot, clean bottle; let cool. Cap tightly and store.

SPICED WINE VINEGAR

3 onions, sliced thin   1 tablespoon peppercorns, cracked
1 carrot, sliced thin   4 cloves
2 cups white wine vinegar   2 cardamom seeds, cracked
1 cup water   ½ teaspoon mustard seed
1½ tablespoons salt   1 teaspoon celery seed
4 bay leaves

Combine everything in a saucepan, bring to a boil and simmer for 15 minutes. Strain through fine sieve or cheesecloth into hot, clean bottle. Cool, cap tightly, and store.

PICKLED FISH
Basic Recipe No. 2

8 to 10 pounds of whole fish, under   2 cups white vinegar
    2 pounds each: pan-dressed   2 tablespoons mixed pickling spices,
    trout, salmon, pickerel, pike,   tied in cheesecloth
    walleye, eel, lamprey, perch,   1 teaspoon peppercorns
    herring, shad, etc.   1 bay leaf
Coarse pickling salt   1 carrot, scraped and sliced very thin
6 small onions, sliced thin   2 tablespoons sugar
6 cups water

Cross-slice the scaled fish, leaving skin on and bones in. (The pickling process softens the bones.) Wash the pieces in clear, cold water, rub with coarse pickling salt, and refrigerate for an hour or two. Drain well.

Cook the onion in the water for about 15 minutes. Add remaining ingredients. Bring to a boil and cook gently for about 5 minutes. Add the salted fish, reduce to a low simmer, and boil very gently for about 20 minutes, until fish is barely cooked. Let cool in stock. Remove the fish to a clean crock or earthen bowl. Reheat the stock. Adjust the seasoning with salt, sugar, or vinegar. Remove and discard the bag of spices. Pour the stock with its contents over the fish, cover closely, and let cool, then refrigerate for 2 or 3 days before serving.

The pickled fish may be packed in small, hot, sterilized glass jars, hot stock and vegetables added to cover, and sealed and stored in refrigerator for about a month. It improves from day to day.

MEDITERRANEAN PICKLED FISH (Sharp)

6 herring, shad, rainbow or brook trout, or small fish of about 1 pound, kipper-dressed or filleted	2 teaspoons salt
	3 tablespoons brown sugar
	1 tablespoon peppercorns
	Hot vinegar
6 small onions, thinly sliced	

Prepare a brine of 1 quart cold boiled water and enough salt to float a raw egg. Wash and dry the fish and brine it for about 2 hours. Remove the fish, drain, and pat dry. Remove skin and any bones. Cut in cross-strips ½ inch wide. Arrange in a deep bowl or individual glasses, about two-thirds full.

Spread onion slices over the fish. Sprinkle salt and sugar over the onion, add the peppercorns, and add the hot vinegar to cover. Cool, weight lightly with a clean plate, then cover and refrigerate. The fish will be ready in about 6 hours and, covered and refrigerated, will keep for a week.

Pickled fish may be used as a cold entrée, an hors d'oeuvre, or mixed with mayonnaise in a sandwich spread. Strips of pickled fish, usually herring, rolled around a cucumber pickle or onion and secured with a toothpick, are called rollmops, a German preparation.

FISHES EN ESCABÈCHE

A special pickling method, *en escabèche* is suitable for steaks, fillets, or small, freshly caught pan fish, of a kind or mixed.

Panfish en escabèche. Clean and scale fish, wash, and dry between towels.

Season lightly with salt and pepper, dust with flour, and fry quickly in cooking oil, or better, olive oil. The oil should be about ¼ inch deep in the frying pan, and the fish fried to just a light color.

Arrange the fish in the bottom of a deep bowl, and follow one of two methods:

1. Prepare Spiced Wine Vinegar, or Aromatic Spiced Vinegar, including the garlic and chili peppers. Add ½ cup pitted ripe or green olives.

Heat the oil in which the fish have been fried and stir in the hot, spiced vinegar. Pour over the fish until covered by the mixture.

2. Heat the oil in which the fish have fried to just short of smoking. Add 1 large diced onion, 1 sliced carrot, 1 diced green pepper, 1 sliver of garlic and sauté for 2 or 3 minutes. Add a few bay leaves, a blade of mace, 1 tablespoon peppercorns, 1 teaspoon each of whole allspice and mustard seed, and 2 or 3 small, whole chili peppers, along with ½ cup pitted ripe or green olives. Add the 1½ cups vinegar and ½ cup water, bring to a boil, and cook for about 10 minutes. Immediately pour over the fish. This is not strained.

Let cool, weight lightly with a clean plate, and cover and refrigerate for at least 24 hours before using. Should keep up to a week in refrigerator, improving daily.

STEAKED FISH EN ESCABÈCHE

4 to 5 pounds or more fish, pan-dressed or filleted, skin on; preferably the red-fleshed fatty salmons and trouts	1 cup cooking oil, preferably olive oil
	1 cup wine vinegar
3 teaspoons salt	2 medium-size onions, sliced thin
½ teaspoon ground black pepper	1 teaspoon peppercorns
Flour	2–3 bay leaves
	1 tablespoon pimiento, sliced thin

Cut pan-dressed fish into thick steaks; cut fillets into serving-portion size.

Mix salt and pepper and rub into the pieces of fish on both sides. Dust with flour seasoned with remaining salt and pepper. Heat the oil in a large skillet and quickly fry fish on both sides, two or three pieces at a time, until just colored. As fish is done, arrange it closely in a layer in the bottom of a deep bowl, in such a way that the vinegar will cover the fish.

Add the remaining ingredients to the hot oil and simmer for about 5 minutes. Pour the hot mixture over the fish. If it does not cover the fish, heat more vinegar and add until it does. Weight lightly with a plate. Cover. Let cool and refrigerate at least 24 hours before using. This will keep a week. Serve as a cold entrée or as an hors d'oeuvre.

SPICED TROUT, SALMON, OR CHAR

The pink or red flesh of the larger trouts is very attractive when pickled. Pink-fleshed catfish is also.

Steak or fillet a 4- or 5-pound salmon and cut into serving portions. Tie loosely in cheesecloth. Cover with water and simmer gently until the flesh barely flakes to a fork.

Remove the package of fish and put it on a thick, clean towel on a platter. Reserve the stock. Open the cheesecloth and spread the fish to drain. When cold, move to a clean platter, cover with a towel, and refrigerate overnight.

Using the reserved stock instead of water, make Spiced Sweet Vinegar, doubling the recipe. Boil as directed, cool, and refrigerate overnight.

Next day place the fish in a clean, deep, earthen bowl. Pour the vinegar over the fish; it must be completely covered. If necessary, prepare more spiced vinegar. (Cooled boiled water may be substituted for fish stock.)

Pour a bit of mild cooking oil over the surface until fully coated. Weight gently with a plate. Cover with a clean cloth and a plate or lid. Store in a ventilated, cold, clean, dry, dark place. Use after a week to 10 days. Under these conditions, the fish should keep for several weeks.

WINE-MARINATED TROUT
(small rainbow or speckled [brook] trout, kokanee, or pink-fleshed catfish)

1 medium carrot, thinly sliced	1 bay leaf
1 medium onion, thinly sliced	Pickling salt
1 teaspoon peppercorns	5 or 6 small trout, freshly caught
Few heads of fresh dill, or ½	and filleted, skin on or off
teaspoon dill seed	White wine

In the bottom of a deep earthen bowl arrange a layer of 2 or 3 carrot slices and onion rings, add a few peppercorns, a bit of dill, and a fragment of bay leaf, and sprinkle salt over all. Add a layer of fish fillets. Repeat until all fish is in the bowl, ending with a layer of vegetables and salt. Pour wine over fish until covered. Lay a clean plate on top for light pressure, cover bowl, and refrigerate undisturbed for 1 to 2 weeks.

Smoking

The universality of the practice of smoking foods leads to the speculation that its benefits were accidentally discovered either as man learned to control fire to cook his meat (as any novice to campfire cookery might testify), or when he found that smoke kept the insects off his meat as he hung it in the sun to dry it (cold smoking), and as the smoke got hotter, it began to cook and smelled good enough to eat on the spot (heat smoking). Or maybe the smoke came first—the smudge burst into flame, the meat fell in and cooked without benefit of sun and smoke, and cooking by direct heat was under way.

Where salting, or brining, came into the process is also obscure. It seems likely that it predated smoking in coastal lands. However the combination came about, it has been a fortunate one for fish lovers.

Salt and smoke impart the delectable flavor and texture that boosted the coarse, unmarketable Winnipeg goldeye to epicurean fame and fortune (see Chapter 4, Goldeye) and transformed the lake sturgeon of North America into a gourmet viand of worldwide demand. (See Lake Sturgeon.)

For strangely enough, it is often the coarser, fatter fishes, low on the flavor scale, that when heat-smoked become fare of distinction on any table. The coarse grain of the flesh takes up the moisture-drawing salt and permits the aromatic smoke to permeate and gently cook the meats.

As the salt-smoke cure is a drying process, the oily or fatty fishes retain a more palatable texture than do the lean fishes. For this reason the oilier sea herring are preferred to lake herring by inland commercial smokehouses.

Oversize fat trouts, salmons, and chars are famous smokers. The lake whitefish, cisco, sea lamprey, eel, carp, ling, shad, and the catfish with their pink flesh are all excellent smokers. Suckers and drums are as well. The saltwater bluefish, butterfish, dolphin, and drumfish, from pan size to too big for conventional kitchen methods, are smokehouse candidates.

Most lean fishes respond well to a flavorsome salt-smoke treatment, but those of fragile flesh like the flounders are too delicate and tend to disintegrate.

HEAT SMOKING AND COLD SMOKING

There are two types of smoking, heat smoking and cold smoking, and both require a precure of salt for best results.

Cold smoking is a preservative process whereby the salted flesh is exposed to an extended period of smoke drying in a smokehouse at a temperature of around 90°. The smokehouse may vary in scale from a backyard barrel to the high-rise barnlike structures seen along the northwest Atlantic coast, where salted herring are kippered to the degree of smoky succulence dear to the tastes of Scandinavians, Scotsmen, and Atlantic maritimers.

Cold smoking, to be successful on any scale, requires the know-how that comes of experience, and patient attention to the project which can go on for many weeks. The weather—humidity, winds, heat, and cold—are all factors affecting the smoking.

Heat smoking, which is done at 110°–120°F, partially cooks the fish for immediate consumption. Fast, simple, and fabulously successful, it is the method generally preferred by the home smoker and the one that will be discussed here.

SMOKEHOUSES

Through the ages smoking has been done by whatever means served the purpose. The smokehouse might be anything from a crude canopy of brush or a hollow log (see Chapter 1), to a discarded refrigerator, a metal drum, or a whiskey barrel, to a sophisticated barn-size smokehouse constructed for the purpose. Foods may be smoked in the chimney or in an outdoor fireplace. It all depends on the situation and scale of operation. Sophisticated small-scale heat-smoking appliances, some operated electrically, are available.

The smoke barrel and refrigerator smoker are illustrated here. Both are efficient; the barrel is more of an asset to the landscape than a discarded fridge.

The refrigerator smokehouse is a simple arrangement similar in principle to the primitive tepee smokehouse. Briquets are fired in a barbecue outside the smokehouse. Two or three burning briquets placed in a frying pan are sprinkled with sawdust and smoke is generated. The pan is placed on the floor of the smokehouse.

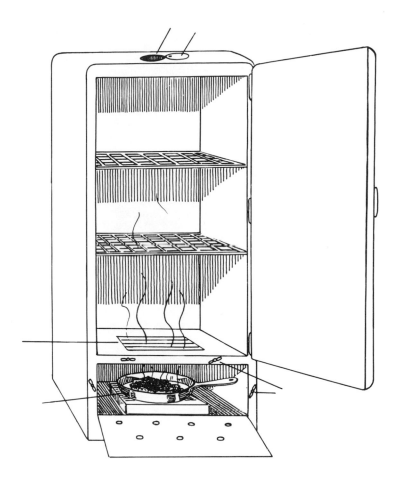

The refrigerator shown here has a motor housing or storage space under the floor, serving as firebox. In another model the box may be the space between the floor and the first shelf.

Abandoned or idle, an empty refrigerator poses a hazard to children. The latch must be removed (the door may be propped closed), and unobstructed ventilation must be provided which is essential to the operation of the smokehouse in any case.

The interior is stripped of all but lining and shelving. Baffling is cut into the floor, and an exhaust vent and cover into the roof. The door, which may be an original part of the refrigerator, is held in place by wingnuts. Ventilation is provided by holes cut in the firebox door.

Note: Smoke is frequently generated in the refrigerator-smoker by charring a pan of sawdust on an electric hot plate. This must be done with caution. The refrigerator and hot plate must have adequate provision for grounding.

The metal oil drum is converted to a smokehouse in essentially the same manner as the whiskey barrel. The metal oil drum should be well burned out to eliminate traces of its past contents.

THE SMOKE BARREL

A century ago the smoke barrel was a not-uncommon backyard fixture beside the forge and the woodpile on the pioneer homestead. The combination of fire, chips, sawdust, and fish and meats provided an efficient production line to meet the family needs.

In its simplest form, a barrel was up-ended and the meat suspended inside. Small scrap iron, heated red hot at the forge, was placed on a long-handled pan, liberally covered with hardwood chips and sawdust, and introduced into the barrel at ground level. By alternating two such pans, a good smoke could be kept up for days if necessary.

The forge and the woodpile are gone, but the smoke barrel is no more beyond the enterprising family than their homemade barbecue.

The smoke barrel illustrated here consists of a firebox to generate the smoke by way of a pipe system through a 42-gallon (Imperial-measure) whiskey barrel in which the meats are to be smoked.

THE BARREL   Not just any barrel will do. A distiller's recent discard is the choice. The mellow old charred oaken cask that has served to age brandy, rum, gin, or whiskey over the years is an epicurean prize to a smoker. Smoke readily picks up the aromatic fumes from the liquor soaked up over the years

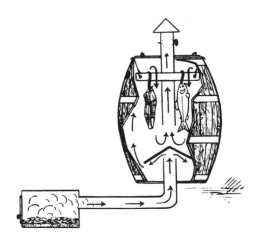

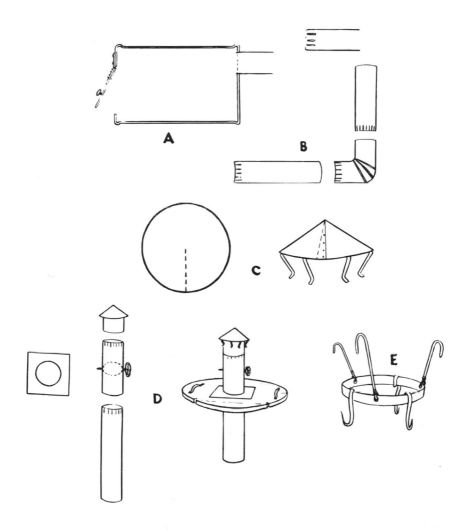

Smoke-supply system for barrel smokehouse

   A   *5-gallon drum for firebox.*
   B   *Smoke feed to barrel. Pipe is standard 3-inch flue.*
   C   *The smoke baffle is made from sheet-metal disc.*
   D   *The top assembly—all standard components for stove flues—fits through the*
        top of the barrel.
   E   *Support ring and hooks should be of heavy iron.*

by the charred oak to lend a delicate quality and bouquet to the foods in the barrel.

If you can't get a distiller's discard, and they are getting scarce, another strong, large oak barrel of similar or larger size, in good condition, will do the job admirably. There are certain qualifications, however. The barrel may be old, but it should not be dried out with its staves shrunken from years of disuse; this condition can present a formidable if not impossible caulking job. A used barrel should have contained only inoffensive products such as wine, vinegar, cider, sugar, salt, molasses, or the like. *Do not use* a barrel that has stored turpentine, tar, creosote, fuel or lubricating oils, or other resinous, bituminous, or petroleum products.

The used barrel requires some work. The ends must be taken out, the hoops painted, the barrel generally cleaned up, and the outside varnished. The best end is reserved for a barrel cover, and a hole cut in the center for an exhaust pipe. If the cover is not workable, a new cover may be cut from plywood or anything that fits the need.

The barrel should be smoketight. Caulk the seams where necessary with string caulking, such as is used on small boats, or with clay. Plug the spigot hole with a bung. A thermometer may be inserted through the bung if an eye on heat control is desired. (It may not be possible to get a smoketight fit around the cover. To prevent smoke escaping during use, wet burlap or canvas may be packed around the edge of the cover, or the seam packed with wet clay or mud filler.)

Two coats of a good spar varnish will finish the outside of the barrel.

THE SMOKE SYSTEM   The smoke system comprises a clean 5-gallon can or drum for the firebox, an old oven broiler rack, standard 3-inch stovepipe fittings (see diagram), and a large baffle. The 5-gallon can was retrieved from a neighbor's garbage and broiler racks were found for pennies each in a secondhand store. Pipe fittings may be bought at a builder's supply or cut to order at a tinsmith's. The large baffle, if not available ready-made, can be cut from a round of tin. The door may be hinged on the firebox if necessary, but any arrangement will suffice that will cover the opening and also allow for draft control.

The tin work is not exacting and there should be no problem doing it yourself.

The smoking process places no strain or pressure to speak of on the smoke system, which merely directs smoke into the barrel and lets it out the top. Built into an incline, the underground feed pipe arrangement precludes damage to pipes and smoke leakage from this source.

The support for the fish or meat, however, must be strong and secure. The arrangement shown here is an iron ring suspended from the top of the barrel by means of three long steel tent pegs. Bent to hook over the edge of the barrel, the pegs are stapled down securely to the outer edge of the barrel. Heavy "S" hooks or meat hooks, bought at a hardware store, are hooked over the ring to support the meats.

The smoke may be generated right in the firebox, but for this relatively small operation, and especially for fish, which cooks quickly, it is preferable to fire charcoal briquets in a barbecue. The briquets are easy to handle and refueling can be done without heat interruption, allowing control over the smudge, smoke, and heat in the barrel. Above all, it cuts the risk of fire in the smokehouse. Briquets hold intense heat, and only three to five in the firebox, covered with sawdust, will provide a good, steady, hot smoke. Expertize comes with experience and until your judgment becomes well honed to the job, it's interesting and helpful to keep a thermometer in the smoke barrel. It can be inserted through the bung plug in the barrel.

FUELS, FIRE, AND SMOKE   The best fuels for smoke-curing as a rule are hardwoods. The smoke is made by firing green hardwood or charcoal to the glowing red stage, and covering the coals with sawdust, preferably from maple, hickory, oak, apple, or other hard fruitwoods. Most of these may be bought from a lumberyard; some builders' supply houses carry sawdust for smoking. While these are considered best, the rule is not hard and fast. Successful smoking has been done over poplar and aspen—even over peat moss in the North. The roots of berry bushes are used in the West. In some parts of the North the distinctive flavor of pine smoke is considered flavorsome. Seaweed and chipped driftwood lend their own flavors to smoking on the coasts

TIMING OF SMOKING

Timing in the smokehouse varies with the size and density of the fish, and even with the length of time in the brine and its strength. Taste-testing will ultimately settle the desired degree of doneness. The temperature in the smokehouse may vary until you become expert at its control. Humidity also affects the smoking process.

Properly controlled heat-smoked fish is done when it takes on a gold-tinged shiny glaze, and gives off an irresistible aroma. A few trial runs should put the chef at ease with his smoker.

Generally, fast-cooking small fishes like smelts are ready to eat after about ½ hour of smoking at 110°–120°; meaty fillets may take 2 hours. Thick, bound sections, and whole fish of 5 or 6 pounds, can smoke for the better part of an evening.

STORAGE OF SMOKED FISH

Heat smoking is a cooking process; it is not a preservative. Opinions vary as to the storage qualities of heat-smoked fish. Some experienced smokers recommend weeks of refrigeration and lengthy freezer storage. This may be satisfactory as far as spoilage is concerned, but experts with 50 years experience at the famous Booth smokehouses in Winnipeg say that to enjoy heat-smoked fish at their peak of succulence, they should be eaten as soon as possible after smoking. They may be refrigerated up to a couple of days and eaten cold or reheated, but should not be freezer-stored, as smoked fish loses much of its unique delicate quality in the freezer.

They say it is better to freeze the freshly dressed fish until ready to smoke, as fish that have been frozen take up the salt and smoke-cures more readily than fresh fish flesh and give a superior product.

PREPARING FISH FOR SMOKING

Clean fish, wash well until glistening, and wipe dry.

All of the market cuts are suitable for smoking. (See Chapter 2.) Care should be taken in cutting out gills from whole fish so as not to cut through throat or backbone if the fish is to hang in the smokehouse.

Dressed, scaled fish up to 3 or 4 pounds handle well in the smoker. Fillets and kipper-split fish should have skin on, as the skin helps hold the flesh together. The racks in the refrigerator smoker offer the handiest arrangement for fillets, but fillets and kippers may be safely hung in a barrel smoker by lacing butcher twine through the fillets and leaving loops by which to hang them, as was done in the chimneys of rural Scottish hearths. A convenient method is to put the fillets in wire toasters or hinged grills and hang them in the smoker. Thick steaks or cross-cuts are tied by running butcher twine through the thick, solid part, drawing the flesh together, and tying securely, leaving loops from which to hang the fish.

BASIC CURES FOR SMOKING

1. DRY SALT

Proportions

1 cup coarse pickling salt   1 teaspoon coarsely ground black
½ cup brown or raw sugar   pepper

Spices and herbs, singly or in combination, may be added to taste to lend variety or to develop a specialty of the house: cayenne (in pinches) or chili powder, ground cloves, curry, cardamom, sesame, caraway and cumin seeds, dill and fennel weeds, tarragon, and extensive savory seasonings of the mint family. Use fresh herbs wherever possible.

Spread a layer of plain salt over the bottom of a bowl or crock. Combine salt, sugar, and seasonings and rub well into all exposed surfaces of the fish. Tuck fresh herbs in cavities, between layers of fish, and sandwich between flesh sides of fillets.

Overnight in the cure is sufficient for small fish and fillets, and longer for bigger fish, generally following a rule-of-thumb of 12 hours per pound of whole fish, or two days for a four-pound fish. This applies as well to the brine which follows.

2. BRINE

1 gallon water, boiled and cooled, or   ¼ cup brown or raw sugar
    demineralized   1 tablespoon cracked peppercorns
Coarse pickling salt   1 bay leaf

Dissolve enough salt in water to float an egg. Dissolve sugar in a small amount of brine and stir back into brine.

Add herbs and spices as desired to the brine. (See Dry Salt Cure above.) Tuck fresh herbs into cavities of fish and in between layers. Dark molasses is an interesting variation of sugar.

Note: Fish preserved in salt (see Salt Curing) may be smoked. Already cured, they require only a quick flavor-aid treatment in the smokehouse.

BEER AND MOLASSES SMOKER

4 cups water
1 cup coarse pickling salt
1 12-ounce bottle beer or ale
½ cup dark molasses

1 teaspoon peppercorns, cracked
½ teaspoon whole cloves
Pinch cayenne, or chili powder

Make brine of water and ½ cup of salt.

Combine beer, molasses, remaining salt, pepper, cloves, and cayenne or chili powder and mix well. Smear the mixture over all surfaces of the fish. Put in a deep earthen bowl or crock and refrigerate for an hour or more, depending on the size of the fish—about an hour per inch of thickness.

Stir remaining beer-molasses mixture into the brine and pour over the fish. Let stand 3 or 4 hours for small fish (to 1 pound) to overnight for thick cuts. Drain as directed and heat-smoke.

Good for drums, sheepshead, suckers, catfish, and fat, coarse-fleshed fish. Good also for carp.

SCOTCH CURE

Scotch-cured salmon is a traditional favorite in the land of its origin. "These fish," says Sir Walter Scott in *Sir Guy Mannering,* "dried in the turf smoke of their cabins, or shealings, formed a savory addition to a mess of potatoes."

Scotch-cured fish have a distinct, characteristic flavor, favored by many a gastronome at home and abroad. This peculiar flavor is due to the residual blood left in the fish. The fish are cleaned and the gills cut out, but they are *not* washed, before dry-salting, and they are left in the initial brine. They are then hung to drip-dry in a shady, breezy place and then smoked.

Herring thus processed have long been popular in North America; the method was adopted by the Alaska fisheries 50-odd years ago.

SCOTCH-KIPPERED SALMON

4- to 6-pound salmon

Salt cure in proportions:
1 cup coarse pickling salt
1 cup dark brown or raw sugar

1 ounce saltpeter
1 teaspoon peppercorns, cracked

While any fatty fish of good size may be Scotch-kippered, the colorful flesh of the salmon-trout family lends itself to a spectacular result. The fish must be fresh from the water.

Scrape or scale the fish. Split through back to clean. (See Chapter 2, Kipper Cut.) Cut off the head and tail, but *do not wash the fish*. Remove the bones.

Rub well all over with coarse salt and let drain overnight. Soak up the moisture with a towel, but don't wipe. Lay the fish skin down on a large earthen platter or on a plastic-lined baking sheet.

Rub the cure mixture into the raw flesh, then smear it on until the flesh is well covered with the cure. Prepare more cure if necessary. Fold the fish, flesh and cure inside, and cover it with a weighted board. Leave undisturbed for 2 days in a cold, clean, dark place.

Hang the fish in a dry, cool, shaded place, spreading it with sticks to permit even drainage, until a filmy skin, or pellicle forms. Heat-smoke for about 4 to 6 hours, depending on the thickness.

When Scotch-curing smaller and leaner fish in this manner, omit the initial salting.

❧ 8 ❧

Traditional and Festive
Dishes from Other Lands

A pursuit as elementary and enduring in civilization as fishing was bound to inspire myth and legend and it is not surprising that the fish through the ages has held a place of honor on Old World festive boards.

The feast may be a remnant observance of pagan solstitial rites (such as New Year's) and fish offered in symbolic deference to a provident sea; it may be modern Christmas and Easter festivities harking back to the days when the fish, usually in the form of a dolphin, became the symbol of Christianity. (The Greek word for fish, *ichthus,* comprises the initial letters of the words "Iesous Christos, Theou Uios, Soter" or Jesus Christ, Son of God, Saviour.) It may be as personal as a birthday or general as a national event. And of course in less festive terms the fish has been the answer to menu problems on days of fast and abstinence from meat.

Bohemia

Sea foods comprise a short chapter in Bohemian cookery books, says Bert Jarsch. His native land has no sea. Bohemians depend on fish markets and on local streams and lakes to provide carp and pike for pre-Christmas and lenten meatless days.

PIKE WITH ANCHOVIES
(Hecht mit Sardellen)

1 3-pound pike   ¼ cup butter
1 dozen anchovy fillets

Wash, scale, and clean the pike, leaving head and tail on as preferred. Score the fish with diagonal slits and insert anchovy fillets. Melt the butter in a baking dish, place the pike in the butter and bake in a moderate oven until the flesh flakes, basting constantly with the butter.

Serve with hot anchovy sauce: Mash 2 or 3 anchovies to a paste. Melt the remaining butter, blend into the anchovies and pour over the fish. Serve with parsley, potatoes, and a green salad.

Bert Jarsch,
Chef, Club Edelweiss,
Toronto, Ontario

England

EEL PIE ISLAND EEL PIE
(Tiny Bennett's version)

For many years people used to flock to Eel Pie Island on the River Thames at Richmond, England, to enjoy this dish, which gave the name to the island. The eating place there was most popular about 110 years ago, and while it is no longer possible to enjoy this rich dish there today, it is still as popular among gourmets as with the monks of Olde Englande who first cooked it.

2 eels of 1½ to 2 pounds, *or* 3 sea lampreys from Lake Ontario	2 glasses dry sherry
2 shallots, *or* 3 green onions	3 hardcooked eggs, cooled and sliced
1 lemon	Butter
Fresh parsley	Flour
Nutmeg, pepper and salt	¾ pound puff pastry

Skin and clean the eels, then rip out the dorsal and ventral fin bones up against the way they lie, and cut the eels into two-inch chunks. Country folk in England used to dry the eel skins and use them wetted as bandages for sprains.

Sauté the shallots or green onions in two tablespoons of butter for five minutes.

Add a few sprigs of chopped fresh parsley, salt, pepper and a few grinds of whole nutmeg, plus the two glasses of dry sherry.

Allow to blend for a moment and drop in the chunks of eel. Cover with a court bouillon made by simmering the heads of the eels in water to which 2 ounces of dry vermouth has been added, for 15 minutes. Strain before pouring over the eels.

Bring to the boil, turn down the heat, simmer for two minutes and then remove the portions of eel and keep warm.

Chop and mash 2 ounces of sweet butter into 2 ounces of plain flour, add to the pot, stir gently and allow to incorporate at a simmer point. When smooth, add the strained juice of the lemon, stir again, and pour the sauce over the pieces of eel set in a deep pie dish.

Cover the top with slices of hardcooked eggs, set a pastry support, or a china egg cup in the center of the dish, and roof it over with puff pastry. Decorate the top of the pastry in traditional style and bake in a hot oven 425°F for one hour, brushing the top of the pie crust with beaten egg and water for a glaze. Cover the crust with foil if it shows signs of becoming too dark.

Some like it hot, some cold, but the best way is to eat it hot, and then snack on what's left the next day, when it will have turned to jelly.

Tiny Bennett,
Bolton, Ontario

Note: Tiny Bennett, who considers the Lake Ontario lampreys to be even superior to eels for this festive dish, is a native of England. He is Outdoor Editor of the *Toronto Sun* and author of *Art of Angling.*

Finland

The parchment-like sheets of dried cod that appear in the fall leaning like so many kites against the walls of the fish markets are for the Finnish and Scandinavian Christmas trade. Whatever various fish dishes are on the Christmas board of these northern countries, a traditional preparation of dried cod is common to all.

In the old country the cod is dried outdoors by the housewives. Mrs. Kay Salomaa, chairman of Finnish Arts and Crafts in Canada, recalls the cod drying on the clothesline as a harbinger of the festive season.

The dried cod, several weeks before Christmas, is put into a solution of lye—about 1 tablespoon to a gallon of water—and soaked until two weeks before Christmas. It is then soaked in fresh cold water until the final day, the fish rinsed and the water changed daily to leach out the lye, and only then is it cooked—ever so gently—in water until it flakes.

The cod is then flaked into a hot white cream sauce and seasoned with only fresh ground pepper. It is put on the table in a huge tureen, accompanied by peeled boiled potatoes.

France

LA BOURRIDE

This dish, whose origin is in the deepest antiquity, belongs in the top rank of Provençal specialties. In the country, it is served as a wedding night soup, made with perch alone.

It is a subtle form of bouillabaisse, made with white fish only—mullet, ocean perch, and pollock are all suitable. For a perfect bourride you should use only ocean perch.

4 ½ pounds white-fleshed fish	2 bay leaves
1 ¼ cups boiling water	3 strips orange peel
1 ½ cups dry white wine	½ teaspoon thyme
1 leek, cleaned and minced	Salt and pepper to taste
1 medium onion, peeled and chopped	2-4 cloves garlic
	1 tablespoon olive oil
1 carrot, peeled and chopped	6 egg yolks
2 thick branches fresh fennel, or 1 teaspoon fennel seeds	10–12 slices stale bread

Cut the fish into serving portions. In a large saucepan place the water, wine, leek, onion, carrot, fennel, bay leaves, orange peel, thyme, salt, and pepper. Bring to a fast rolling boil and boil 10 minutes. Remove from the source of heat, add the fish, bring back to boil, and simmer over medium heat for 12 minutes. Then remove the fish with a perforated spoon and strain the bouillon through a fine sieve. Keep fish warm.

Fry the garlic in the olive oil—be careful, as it takes only a few seconds to brown. Beat the egg yolks, add the fried garlic, and place in a soup tureen or in a saucepan. Carefully pour in the strained bouillon, stirring constantly with a wooden spoon or a whisk until the whole is smoothly blended. Place over very low heat and keep stirring until very hot and creamy, but do not let it boil.

Place a slice of bread in each plate, pour a spoonful of sauce on top, and then a portion of fish. Serve to taste with a garlic-flavored mayonnaise.

*Madame Jehane Benoit,
Sutton, Quebec*

Germany

BLUE CARP

Blue carp is indispensable to a northern German's New Year's eve, for on its scales depend the family fortunes, so the story goes, for the coming year. If the carp comes to the table with its coinlike scales firmly anchored, prosperity lies ahead.

Cooking blue carp and keeping the scales in place means close attention to its preparation.

Use a carp of about 2½ pounds. Of first importance is that it be freshly killed and quickly prepared for cooking. It should be killed by a sharp blow to the head. It is immediately eviscerated, but not scaled. The cleaning must be carefully done as the natural sticky protective secretion that covers the fish must not be disturbed or the carp will not cook *au bleu.* Thus the fish is not washed.

Before proceeding, have ready (1) a boiling mixture of one pint water and one pint vinegar; (2) a large oblong earthen or glass baking dish, or an unscarred enamelled roasting pan with a platter in it or the bottom covered with sliced raw potatoes to support the fish; (3) oven heated to 375°.

Rub the cavity of the carp with salt, taking care that no salt gets onto the outside of the fish. Place the fish carefully and quickly in the pan, spreading the cavity so the back is up. Pour over it the boiling vinegar-water and bake for about 40 minutes. The dorsal fin is movable when the fish is done.

Five minutes before removing, pour melted butter over the fish. Lift the carp carefully, let it drain a moment and arrange it on a white-napkin-covered platter, garnish with parsley and serve at once. Serve melted butter on the side.

Alex Eberspaecher,
Thornhill, Ontario

Holland

In Holland there is no fish dish with specific symbolic meaning, says Mrs. Van der Ree—"We simply cook elegantly and eat well." On a special occasion the following recipe is used for freshwater walleye or lake whitefish fillets as well as sole.

DUTCH SOLE WITH BANANAS

4 thick fillets of sole	2 ounces cognac
Seasoned flour	½ cup slivered almonds
Clarified butter	Lemon juice
2–3 firm, yellow bananas	

Wipe the fillets with a damp cloth and dust with seasoned flour. Melt the butter to about ½-inch depth in the pan. Cook the fish quickly in the butter, turning once, until golden on both sides. Reserving the butter, lift the fillets carefully to a heated oblong fish baking dish, preferably copper or glass for appearance, lay a piece of aluminum foil over the top, and keep warm in oven.

Peel and split the bananas in halves, then quarter each piece. Dust lightly with flour. In the hot butter in which the fish cooked, brown the bananas until golden, turning them gently. Arrange the bananas over the fish in the warming oven.

Warm the cognac by pouring it into a small pitcher and letting it rest a minute or two in a bowl of hot water. Brown the almonds in the remaining hot butter and sprinkle them over the fish, now out of the oven. Sprinkle lightly with lemon juice. Pour the warm cognac over the fish, ignite, and bring flaming to the table.

Betty Van der Ree,
Toronto, Ontario

OYSTERS AND CHAMPAGNE

Simple, elegant hors d'oeuvres are in order when Dutch families assemble for a festive occasion, says Anastasia van Breda, and such is the tone of party fare in her Toronto home.

A favorite is oysters on the half shell, arranged on a large wooden platter and served with champagne. Others are fish croquettes and a lobster cocktail.

DUTCH LOBSTER COCKTAIL
(for New Year's Eve and special occasions)

1 cup (6-ounce can) lobster meat	1 tablespoon brandy or sherry
1 cup mayonnaise	Paprika
2 tablespoons tomato catsup	1 hard boiled egg

Chop yolk and white of egg separately.

Combine mayonnaise and catsup, blend in lobster, then brandy or sherry. Refrigerate until needed. Serve in cocktail glasses in a nest of lettuce or cress. Garnish with bits of egg and a light flick of paprika.

Serves 4. Multiply according to needs.

CROQUETTES OF FISH

The fish may be cooked fish, shellfish, or a mixture.

2 cups fish meats	Bread crumbs
1 cup heavy Binding Cream Sauce	Oil for deep-frying
1 tablespoon rum or sherry	

Mix everything until well blended. Spread over a pie plate and chill in refrigerator until firm. Form into little balls and roll them in fine bread crumbs. Arrange in a deep-fry basket and deep-fry. (See Chapter 3, Deep-Frying.)

Anastasia van Breda,
Toronto, Ontario

Ireland

PRAWN PEARS

In Ireland prawns come large and small. If using large prawns, chop rather coarsely.

4 ounces cooked prawns, shelled and deveined	2 tablespoons mayonnaise
	A little lemon juice
3 fresh pears	Lettuce leaves
3 tablespoons whipped cream	Paprika

Cut each pear in half lengthwise. Using a grapefruit knife, remove center flesh of pear. Discard pips and chop flesh coarsely. Sprinkle pear-shells and flesh with lemon juice. Arrange pear shells on salad plates with a few leaves of lettuce. Mix whipped cream and mayonnaise with pear flesh and prawns. Season if required. Spoon this mixture into each pear cavity and sprinkle with a little paprika.

Serves 6.

Jean Power,
Mississauga, Ontario

Japan

KAMA–BOKO
(a Japanese New Year's dish, eaten with rice cakes)

2 cups cooked lake whitefish
1 raw egg
About 2 dozen green peas, fresh or
    frozen

1 strip green pepper, minced
1 strip pimiento, minced
Batter

Shred the cooked fish with the fingers, removing all trace of bones. Mix well with the raw egg, incorporating the peas, green pepper and pimiento (which are for color only) to a cohesive, sticky consistency. Form into small flat patties.

Make a thick, puffy batter:
2 eggs
Salt

½ teaspoon baking powder
Flour

Separate the eggs. Beat whites stiff, adding a pinch of salt. Beat yolks until light and lemon color. Blend the whites into the yolks. Mix in baking powder. Add flour by the spoonful, mixing each addition, until batter is on the thick side.

Press each fish patty in and out of batter and deep fry in a suitable kettle or in a tempura pan.

Mrs. Kuki Kono,
Toronto, Ontario

Norway

Norway is famous for its cultivation of rainbow trout and methods of their cookery as well. Norwegian chef Arne Tjerno finds North American rainbows equally suitable for his Rakórret, which, like Oka cheese, is beautiful food once you get it into your mouth. It smells to high heaven, he says, and "if it ever catches on, here is the recipe."

RAKORRET

Take fresh caught rainbow trout, split and clean them, leaving heads and tails on. In a large wooden bucket, approximately 3 to 4 gallon size, spread a layer of coarse salt 2 inches deep. Spread the trout over the salt, skin up, in a layer one fish deep. Barely cover with salt. Continue until you run out of fish and the bucket is full. Set outside to dry in the sun. This is a fall weather method, and the temperature not likely over 70° (or the equivalent of Norwegian fall weather). Usually 30 to 40 rainbow trout are prepared for the Christmas season.

After three or four weeks the fish are ready. Take out of the tub as needed, trim the fish and lift out the bones. Serve on *lefse* (a thin, soft oat cake), rolling the trout up inside with prepared hot mustard.

Arne Tjerno,
Toronto, Ontario

Philippines

In the Philippines, the milkfish is the festive fish. In North America, the Filipinos stock their freezers with freshwater game fish, and use lake whitefish or walleye for the Christmas bangus.

The bangus (pronounced *bamoos*) is a whole fish, boned and stuffed with its own meat.

BANGUS

1 3- to 4-pound lake whitefish, dressed
Vegetable oil
1 clove garlic, minced
1 large onion, diced

1 teaspoon sesame seeds
Salt and pepper to taste
1 cup chopped tomatoes

Bone the whole dressed fish. Cut away the flesh from the sides of the fish—always careful not to cut through the skin. Reserve the skin, head and tail attached.

Cover the bottom of a large frying pan with vegetable oil, and heat. Add minced garlic, onion and sesame seeds, season with salt and pepper and sauté until onion is translucent. Add tomatoes.

Chop the fish coarsely and add to the mixture. Cover tightly and simmer slowly until the fish is almost flaky, but not quite. Remove from heat and stuff the fish skin with the mixture. Sew it up, easing it into a semblance of its original shape. Put into a baking dish, preferably oven-to-table, garnish with sliced tomatoes and bake in a moderately hot oven (375° to 400°F) until golden brown. Garnish with fresh greens and serve.

Mrs. Tonie G. Zapanza,
Toronto, Ontario

Poland

Any number of fish dishes are on the traditional Polish Christmas eve buffet. Anna Ejbich used carp and ling fillets for her favorite aspic; she now likes to use Canadian pike, walleye or whitefish.

RYBA W GALARECIE
(Fish in Aspic)

1½ pounds fish fillets or a 2- to
  3-pound fish
2 carrots
2 sticks celery
1 parsley root or a parsnip tip
1 onion, quartered

1 bay leaf
3 peppercorns
Salt
6 cups water
2 tablespoons white wine or 1
  tablespoon vinegar

Combine all ingredients, except the fish, for the court bouillon and boil over medium heat for ½ hour; let cool. Put the fish in a deep saucepan. Strain and add the court bouillon. Cook over low heat for about 15 minutes or until the flesh flakes to a fork. Let cool in the stock and carefully lift the fish and arrange on a shallow platter. Reduce the stock by half its volume.

Make the aspic: Soak 1½ tablespoons gelatin in ½ cup of the stock for 5 minutes. Add 2½ cups of the hot stock, stir to dissolve, then stir in vinegar or white wine. Chill until slightly thickened. Pour half of this aspic over the fish. Chill until set. Pour the remainder over the fish, chill. Garnish with thin slices of hard boiled egg, tomatoes and cucumber, and sprigs of fresh parsley.

Serve with mayonnaise or Sour Cream Mustard Sauce (blend 1 teaspoon hot prepared mustard into 1 cup sour cream).

Mrs. Anna Ejbich,
Toronto, Ontario

Spain

The paella, to North Americans synonomous with the cookery of Spain, had its colorful beginning in that country when the Moors arrived with rice and saffron. It is believed to be a descendant, along with other widespread related rice dishes, of the ancient Persian *pilaf.*

Traditionally made of chicken and fresh shellfish, the paella may also be made of all fish. A dish of color above all, the firm pink or red flesh of the trouts and salmons is desirable, although any firm-fleshed fish may be used, or a mixture.

PAELLA VALENCIANA

Paella Valenciana is one of the most famous of paellas.

1 pound spring chicken	2 small lobsters
1 carrot	2 cups long-grained rice
1 onion, cut up	2 cloves garlic, crushed
½ cup olive oil	½ teaspoon saffron
½ cup chopped onion	½ cup lima beans
1 tomato, skinned and coarsely chopped	½ cup green peas
¼ pound fillet of pork, cut into small pieces	5 cups bouillon (plus Accent or chicken bouillon concentrate)
2 squid, cut into pieces	16 fresh mussels
1 sweet red pepper	Salt
8 shrimp, or scampis	Pepper, freshly ground

Wash the chicken and cut into serving pieces; cover with water, add 1 carrot and 1 onion, and boil until cooked. Reserve the bouillon to cook the rice.

In a frying pan, heat the oil and the chopped onion. Before onion browns, add the tomato. Cook for a few seconds, then add the pork, chicken, squid, red pepper, and the shrimp still in their shells. Split the lobsters down the middle, remove the meat, and add to the above ingredients. Cook for 5 minutes. Add the rice, garlic, and saffron,* and fry for 3 minutes. Add the lima beans, peas, and the 5 cups of bouillon reserved from the chicken. (You

---

* Dry saffron on a piece of paper in a warm oven for a few minutes. Pound. Steep in a little bouillon.

may add a touch of Accent or chicken bouillon concentrate to give more flavor.) Bring to a boil and let cook on top of the stove slowly for 25 minutes.

Five minutes before the rice is cooked, add the well-washed mussels. This will give a delicious flavor to the rice.

Be sure that you use good, large, round-grained rice. The grains of rice should not stick to one another. This is important in a Paella Valenciana.

Variation: Paella Marinera: If you use only fish and seafood, and no meat, the dish is then called Paella Marinera. Use snails in their shells, periwinkles, octopus, small clams, salmon, whiting, etc.

Serves 4.

Tony Roldan,
Executive Chef, Westbury Hotel,
Toronto, Ontario

LENGUADOS RELLENOS A LA CUBANA
(Shrimp-Stuffed Fillet of Sole)

½ cup chopped onion
6 tablespoons olive oil
8–10 small shrimp, cooked, shelled,
    and minced
½ cup fine bread crumbs
1 egg, beaten

6 fillets of sole
1 lemon, thinly sliced
1 cup white wine
¼ teaspoon salt
Dash pepper

Cook onion slowly in olive oil until tender; add shrimp, bread crumbs, and egg. Divide mixture into six parts; place in center of fillets, roll up, and secure with small toothpicks.

Cut 6 large squares of aluminum foil; brush inside of each with olive oil and place a rolled fillet in center of each square. Lay a lemon slice on each fillet, spoon wine over each, and fold foil to seal. Bake at 350°F for 30 minutes. Remove foil, and garnish with lemon slices and parsley.

Serves 6.

Gloria Montero,
Centro Para Gentes de Habla Hispana,
Toronto, Ontario

Sweden

GLASSBLOWER HERRING

Much speculation has been made on the origin of the name of this Swedish dish—whether the salty fish was eaten to offset the effects of the intense heat generated by glassblowing, or whether the name comes from the preparation itself, its bluish sheen resembling that of freshly blown glass.

¾ cup white vinegar
½ cup water
½ cup sugar
2 1- to 1½-pound salted herring
2 small onions, preferably red, peeled
    and thinly sliced

2 teaspoons whole yellow mustard
    seed
2 teaspoons whole black peppercorns
2 large bay leaves

Bring the vinegar, water, and sugar to a boil in a 1- to 1½-quart enameled or stainless steel saucepan, stirring constantly until the sugar is completely dissolved. Remove the pan from the heat and let the pickling liquid cool to room temperature.

Meanwhile, scrape and wash the herring in cold running water and cut them into ½-inch pieces. Arrange a thin layer of onions in a 1-quart glass jar with a tightly fitting cover. Top with a few slices of herring and scatter a few mustard seeds and peppercorns on top. Repeat until all the ingredients have been used.

Pour the cool pickling liquid into the jar, close the jar securely, and refrigerate for 2 or 3 days.

Berndt Berglund,
Managing Director, National Wilderness Survival, Inc.,
Campbellford, Ontario

DILL-FLAVORED CRAYFISH

The first day of the crayfish season in Sweden is looked upon as a national holiday, and celebrated with community crayfish parties.

3 quarts cold water
½ cup coarse salt
3 bunches fresh dill

20 live fresh water crayfish
1 bunch fresh dill for garnish

In a large enameled kettle, combine the water, salt, and 3 bunches of dill tied together. Bring to a boil over high heat and boil briskly, uncovered, for 15 minutes. Wash the crayfish carefully under running cold water, then drop them a few at a time into the boiling water. Wait until the water is at a rolling boil again, then add a few more. When all of the crayfish are in the kettle, cover tightly and boil for about 10 minutes.

Line a large bowl with the last of the bunches of dill, using only the crowns. Remove the kettle from the heat, and with a slotted spoon transfer the crayfish from the kettle to the bowl, placing them on top of the dill.

Strain the stock through a fine sieve over the crayfish, and let them rest in the juice in a cold place until they reach room temperature. Cover the bowl and refrigerate for at least 12 hours. About 3 hours before the crayfish are to be served, take the bowl out of the refrigerator and let the crayfish come to room temperature. Drain and pile them high on a platter. Garnish with sprigs of fresh dill.

Berndt Berglund,
Managing Director, National Wilderness Survival, Inc.,
Campbellford, Ontario

Ukraine

JELLIED FISH MOLD

In the Ukraine, this jellied fish mold is used on a typical meatless Christmas Eve table.

1 2-pound piece of halibut or sturgeon	A few peppercorns
½ teaspoon salt	¼ teaspoon allspice
1 bay leaf	1 envelope unflavored gelatin
1 onion, sliced	2 ounces white wine

If using sturgeon, parboil to remove oil, skim, and drain.

Tie the fish in cheesecloth, put into a deep saucepan, cover with cold water, and add salt, bay leaf, onion, peppercorns, and allspice. Bring to a boil and simmer gently until the flesh flakes to a fork. Skim the stock. Remove the fish to a platter and let cool.

Reduce the stock to about 2 cups. Make an aspic: Dissolve gelatin in cold water and stir into the hot stock. Bring to a boil, stirring constantly until well mixed. Strain through a cloth. Stir in white wine.

Coat the inside of a fish mold with the aspic. Let remainder cool until thick but not set. Shred the cooked fish, mix it into the aspic, and pack it into the mold. Refrigerate until set.

Turn out on a plate and garnish with olives, thinly sliced unpeeled cucumbers, and slices of hard-boiled egg. Serve with Beetroot and Horseradish Sauce, or sour cream with diced cooked beets and fresh grated horseradish mixed in (prepare in advance).

Mrs. Bohdanna Dzura,
Toronto, Ontario

INDEX